Winning
A writers' helper and commonplace book to stimulate imagination

Malcolm E Brown has over 90 publications. They span a remarkable range. He is a columnist and award-winning article writer. Publications include scientific papers, short stories and a novel. Acclaim for articles, his main output, includes "exceptionally elegant" and "He paints a superb picture."

He can do so because he is something of a polymath. A retired pharmacist, MRPharmS and BA, he also has master and doctorate degrees in natural and social scientific research. That is extremely unusual.

He has worked as an industrial production manager and in senior positions in the British National Health Service (NHS). As Director of Pharmacy and Civil Emergency Planning at a district general hospital, he liaised with blue light services.

Later, as a consultant, he trained the "entire" UK sales force of a major international company on selling medicines to the NHS. He certified batches of medicines as an EU Qualified Person (QP): a "quasi-governmental" role. Several licences, for human, animal and investigational medicinal products, named him. He audited and advised in several countries. The keynote speaker at an international multidisciplinary conference at *The Hague*, his brief was to stimulate thinking "outside the box."

He delights in his reputation as a quirky commentator and interpreter of worlds. He is widely travelled and an experienced mentor.

Winning Words

A writers' helper
and commonplace book
to stimulate imagination

Malcolm E Brown

Watermint Publications

Published by Watermint Publications
Lyndhurst, Beccles, Suffolk,
UK, NR34 0ES

Copyright © Malcolm E. Brown 2014

Printed in USA by *CreateSpace* 4900 Lacross Road, Charleston, SC 29406

The moral right of the author has been asserted

This book is designed to provide information on aiding writing and the imagination of writers. This book is not a complete and exhaustive presentation of the subjects. While every effort has been made to make the information presented as complete and accurate as possible, it may contain errors omissions or information that was accurate as of its publication but subsequently has become outdated by marketplace or industrial or scientific changes or conditions, new laws or regulations or other circumstances. No liability or responsibility to any person or entity with respect to any loss or damage alleged to have been caused, directly or indirectly, by the information, ideas, opinions or other content in this book is accepted. This book does not provide professional information (for example, financial, legal, medical or pharmaceutical). You should seek independent professional advice from a person who is registered and / or knowledgeable in the applicable area before acting upon any opinion, advice, or information contained in this book.

A record of this publication is available from the British Library

ISBN 978-0-9928059-0-6

Contents

Acknowledgements ix
Foreword xi

Part 1 Tactics

1   All writing 2
     Writing addiction.. 2
     Your wonderful brain...19
     Keeping fit 22
     Write in the best environment............................27
     Steps to overcome writers' block 28

3   Finding the time 35
     The problem 35
     The solution...35
     Next steps 37

4   Non-fiction article 41
     Why write non-fiction 41
     Subjects for non-fiction...................................... 42
     General advice.. 43

5   Non-fiction book...46
     Subject... 46
     Length 47
     General advice...47
     Advice on biography 51
     Advice on biography 51
     Advice on auto-biography................................... 52

6	Fiction short story	56
	Manipulation of emotions	58
	Step by step action	59
7	Fiction book	65
	Lengths	65
	Genre	66
	Tactics	67
8	Poetry	73
	The magic of poetry	73
	Favourite poems	75
	Characteristics of poetry	76
	Categories of poem	79
	Tips on writing poetry	83
9	Research for writers	86
	Primary data	87
	Secondary data	88
	Tertiary data	88
	Keeping records	88
	Tips on where to find information	89
10	Introduction to the data bank of provocation	92
	Personal commonplace book	92
	Sociological Journal	96
	Accepted journalistic maxims	96
	Google big data zeitgeist	97
	What the databank is	98
	What the data bank is not	99
	Surprises	100

Specific headings 100

How to use Part 2 of this book 105

Part 2

Data bank of provocation / commonplace book

Academe	108
Aged	115
Appearance	116
Art	130
Astronomy	134
Behaviour	138
Biology	154
Chemistry	169
Children	174
Class and Status	177
Class and status (non-human)	202
Communication	203
Cooking	204
Courage	206
Decay and despair	207
Drugs of addiction	218
Food and drink	221
Gardening	236
Generations	240
God	247
Goodbyes	256
Health	260
Jargon	270
Joy	271
Location inside	274
Location outside	283
Love other	294
Love people	296

Macabre	301
Mathematics	308
Medicines	310
Mistranslations	315
Money	317
Museums	326
Music	329
Nationalities	332
New beginnings	339
New horizons	341
Occupations	343
Physics	366
Politics	369
Power	374
Psychology	375
Reading	376
Relationships	377
Sensuousness	379
Sex	381
Smell	394
Sociology	400
Technology	405
Travel	416
Unexpected	425
Viewpoint	434
War	444
Writing	452
Further Reading	459
Index	461

Acknowledgements

To my family, especially my wife, Susan, for help, support and tolerance, I owe much. I am also indebted to many writers more eloquent than I and to the Beccles Creative Writing Group. I am grateful to academic supervisors and others who have helped me to think. They include Prof Paul Bellaby, Prof Geoff Booth, Dr Howard Caygill, Dr Shirley Ellis, Mr Jon Gubbay, Prof Bruce Hauptli, Dr Steve Hubbard and Dr Peter Linley. Mr Dave Balcombe, Mr Brendan Caffrey, Mr Richard Palmer, Mr Alan Weyman and Mr Paul Woolley, have helped and encouraged me. I thank them. I apologise if I have failed to acknowledge any author for a direct published quotation or artist for image. If you notice any, please inform me. Omission will be gratefully acknowledged in the next edition. Any errors remain my own.

Over decades, I have been privileged to meet many people; they seeded the data bank of provocation. I cannot acknowledge those individuals by name for reasons including anonymity. I thank them all. They humble me.

Images substantially enhance this book. I thank all those who kindly gave permission to reproduce images:

p21: Brochan Inaglory. Two silhouette profile or a white vase CC BY-SA 3.0; 104: Netalloy. Spiders web (public domain [pd]);109:Egore 991.University hat. CC BY-SA 3.0; 128: Nemo. High heels. pd CC0; 132:svk-ab. Glasses with eyes pd; 161: Greg Emmerich. Vector DNA CC BY-SA 3.0 (modified to monochrome; [mtm]); 135,6-,342, 405: NASA pd CC0 1.0 Un; 166:Nickyhannaway. Buck – A Fine Example of A German Shepherd. CC BY-SA 3.0 universal; 167: Toby Hudson. *Latrodectus hasseltii* mtm CC BY-SA 3.0.; 170: *Clker.com*.

Pipette ;175: Florence Scovel Shinn. Unitarians...as caption. Pd.; 188: Werber Briggette. Black & white pencil drawing DigitalArt Work pd CC0; 196: Peekaoopink. Longleat House (pd) (mtm); 203: F.Boyle. As caption. The Illustrated London News 1864. mtm pd; 205:As image c 1900; 216:Van den Venne. Dodo 1626 pd; 217: Chadwick H.D. Post-and-Grant Avenue 220:cocaine As image 1885 pd; 223:Child_of_Light.Banana bunch Line Art (pd); 1906;245: Ribberlin: Franz Xaver Winterhalter Family of Queen Victoria 1846. pd.; 248 pd: Pearson Scott Foresman. Line art drawing of a skull and crossbones (pd); 252: H.S. Gorham (text). *Proceedings ... Zoological Society London* (vol. 1883 [author died >70 years ago], plate XVIII) (pd); 255:Oren Jack Turner. Albert Einstein (pd); 270: Sage Ross.Pile of round acyclovir tablets;272:j4p4d.Kid and Cake. Pd; 294:Alcohol. Public pd CC0;295: t_sapto_adji. Silvery car. Pd;296:Open lips. Heart Love Valentine 3d Red. CC0 1.0 Universal (mtm)PublicDomainPictures; 300: Nemo.Marriage proposal. Public Domain CC0; 308:Dicklyon.Fibonacci spiral with square sizes up to 34 pd; 298:David BCC BY-SA 3.0.; 309: enbennick.Möbius strip CC BY-SA 3.0 (mtm);314:Pierre Jean François Turpin. 1833 Ilium verumoo pd;316:Fulwellmillfront1. Fulwell Windmill. mtm CC BY-SA 3.0.; 318: gringer (untitled but interpreted as "piggy bank") (mtm) (pd); 320:Annuities advance notice pd mtm;328:Sheperd and Radclyffe. Hunterian museum 1853 mtm pd; 331: Cyberscooty. Music notes pd; 338: Alvin Lee. 1945 blank world map; 344:St Bede 8th c. pd; 368:Prying open crate.M.Doodnow 1919. pd;373: Klem. Yin and yang. Pd;376:OpenIcons.Reading pd; 374:elpedro. Fist. Pd; 375: Nemo Brain pd; 376: Reading CC0 pd 378: IMAGE-WS. Bears Pd; 384:Gustavb.Gender symbols side by side pd; 393:Popular Science Monthly. Sacramento salmon 1902. pd; 400;Max & Marianne Weber 1894. pd; 407:Tomasz G. Sien icki. Self-locking machines CC BY-SA 3.0; 416: Nemo. Eiffel Tower Paris Silhouette Historical. CC0 1.0 Universal; 430:Gaurav Pandit. Cute cat. Creative Commons Attribution 3.0 Unported; 432:Enrico Mazzanti (first illustrator 1883). Pinocchio. pd; 442:Didacus Valades 1579. Great chain of being. pd; 453: Cassandra Austen 1873 pd; 453, 45 *et al* : Presquesage. Writing quill and inkwell (pd); 457:Andrew Dunn. Booba-Kiki. CC B Y-SA 3.0; 458 : Grin. Best Seller Stamp. pd.

Foreword

This book has two main parts. The first is shorter. It is an outline about how to write; it covers much of writing. Its main thrust offers *practical help: tactics*

Its aim is to be useful to a wide range of people. The writer of natural genius requires no help; the rest of us do. This book outlines what worked for me. That may help you.

It offers tips on how to find ideas. It details how to use the second part of the book in your quests; one is overcoming writers' block. It offers help on finding the time to write and keep healthier. This book is for you if you are striving to achieve your first publication – whether fiction or non-fiction - to achieve that proud title *"writer."* It also offers help ranging from non fiction articles and books, short stories, novellas and novels to poetry.

The second, far longer, part is a sort of goad or provocation to the writer's imagination. It is a data bank of ideas. It bursts with stimulation. Sources are:

1. the author's commonplace books that span 40 years,
2. the author's "sociological journal" spanning 18 years,
3. journalistic maxims such as the "3Ls": "lust, loathing and lucre" and
4. the latest *Google* global *zeitgeist* of most popular search areas. A gargantuan data set informed that.

This book's *data bank of provocation* divides alphabetically into the most useful categorisations for modern writers; 55 headings emerged. They range from predictable areas such as appearance, art, behaviour, class, God, location, love, macabre, relationships, sex and war to, perhaps, less expected ones. Examples are astronomy, biology, chemistry, drugs, physics, mathematics and technology. It is an unashamedly quirky compilation extracted with modern eyes, for today's technologically-driven world.

This data bank – a modern-day cabinet of curiosities - is also *fresh*. Dip into it for an enjoyable browse or ideas, or to kick-start you into starting (or restarting) your own commonplace book. Do you wish that you had written a row of your own commonplace books? If not, feel free to capitalise upon this book's databank. Some of the "hard labour" is completed for you. Mine the second part of this book for your golden inspiration. Who knows?

> You may produce the successor to a certain young wizard of J.K. Rowling.

Part One

Tactics

1 All writing

Writing addiction

Reading, the master skill, is a joy. You read whenever you can. But ever and again you have thought: I could do that: I could write. That realisation has grown. Maybe it is a new year's resolution. Maybe you want to see your name in print – to become a published author. That desire is so intense that it hurts. Maybe you see writing as a way to earn some bread. Maybe you just itch to write; only writing will sooth that itch. It has become intolerable. You must write and write *now*.

> However, before you go any further, stop for a "*sanity check.*"

- Ask, brutally, IS THERE A MARKET FOR MY WORK?

    It is impossible to overemphasise the importance of this question. If the candid answer, the one that you know in your bones, is "No", a mainstream publisher is extremely unlikely to publish you.

Do you still wish to continue? If *YES*, read on.

- You are unlikely to earn a fortune.
- As many newspapers contract, even some professional journalists struggle to find work.
- "Writing makes no noise, except groans ... and it is done alone." *(Ursula K. LeGuin)*
- Editors will inflict numerous rejections upon you.
- Your skin must be thick enough to sustain that assault and
- the resulting emotional baggage.

All writing

Do you still wish to continue? If *YES*, read on.

- Also continue if you feel that those warnings "overegg the custard." Writing can also be a lot of fun.

Perhaps you lack the time to do a writing course let alone study for an MA in creative writing, with its emotional challenge and public admission that you want to be a writer. You may lack the £6,000 or so for the fee. Perhaps you lack the time to delve into libraries full of advice, to read weighty books. Then, this book in your hands may help. It gives you an edge over other competitors who wish to write and be published.

This chapter:

- offers an overview of the steps that worked for me and
- unveils my secret weapon.

First step: research your market and readership

> First and foremost, research what your key market and readership want. It bears restating, if you are serious about publication, that you must always bear in mind that commercial orientation.

It is impossible to over-emphasise the importance of this stage.

Start by scrutinising the latest edition of the *Writers' & Artists' Yearbook* (London: Bloomsbury Publishing).

Decide where you will market your writing. Examine samples of accepted work, for example, articles in a magazine. Write like it. Match, for example, sentence, paragraph and total length, number of words and style of titles, readability of English and viewpoint. Write for the sort of people who are likely to buy your writing.

- Be mindful that what editors crave is another book along the lines of the one that is currently selling in barrow loads.

That might seem boring and mechanical, stopping you getting on with the actual writing. But you will only be published if you choose to write what the publisher wants. Strive to develop a canny awareness of what your editor or publisher wants.

Second step: start your *own* personal writer's commonplace book

What you need next is something different, an unusual turn of phrase, association, emotional experience and so on. You need a data-bank that bursts with thoughts and phrases, to stimulate you. It will offer grist to your creative mill. It will sprinkle sparkle onto your writing, whether fiction or non-fiction. For example, adding two or three nuggets to a 1,000-word non-fiction article may help the editor notice and accept your piece.

- Your data bank is your "commonplace book" and it is *your secret weapon*. Far more about it will follow. Presently, I will just emphasise one point.

- For YOU, your commonplace book is better than *mine*.

Note within your "commonplace book" any striking turns of phrase that you have heard (including from the radio, television, newspapers, books including dictionaries of quotations, museum and art galley captions, web and even dreams), interactions with people with emotional intensity, triumphs, accidents, notable events in your life, conversations, anything. Expert writers include journalists and politicians (or their speechwriters). Their phrases or sound bites occasionally "hit the spot." Repeat their *bon mots* soon and your readers would notice and condemn: it is old hat, a mere copy, just a crib. But here's the thing:

- *Wait a few decades and it becomes again fresh, just waiting for you to trawl and incorporate into just the right part of your creation.*

All writing

This is where the miscellany, cabinet of curiosities, cocktail, *smörgåsbord* - the veritable cornucopia - in **your** decades-long commonplace book fits. It will turbo charge your writing.

This is not theft. But you must be careful. The Berne Convention lays down minimum copyright requirements. It exists in written work as soon as created and for 50 years after the author's death. However, this is a minimum; individual countries may offer more protection. In the UK, for example, copyright lapses 70 years after the death of the author. You may require permission and acknowledgement with longer passages. Before that, any very few words are not subject to copyright if for criticism or review. Borrowing them is fair if the quotation is attributed and it is short. As a "ballpark" illustration, "short" means not more than 300 words from a book, 50 from an article or two lines of poetry that does not repeat the title. See information on copyright in the *Writers' & Artists' Yearbook*. Copyright on lyrics may exceed 70 years; quotation is astonishingly expensive.

However, we *must* all use the same words. For example, decades ago, I noted, "The toastmaster, splendid in scarlet livery, dropped his gavel and intoned his creamble." A "creamble" sounded intriguing, but insufficiently intriguing to check what it meant. I assumed it was some sort of hard-wood sounding board that the gavel hit. But on checking, even Professor *Google* could not find the word "creamble." It did not exist because nobody else had used it. The correct word was "preamble." Only by repeating the same words and phrases, can another person understand us. That is the nature of speaking the same language such as English. Individuals from *William Shakespeare* to *Hilary Mantel* to *Brian Cox* just shuffle up English words. Some words, once fresh, are so apt that they are overused and become hackneyed and stale. An illustration is "nice." Avoid them.

Some English words possess a history from fresh and creative to pedestrian and boring to dated and hackneyed. A spectrum results. Your aim is to feast on the sweetest spot for your generation.

So - start accumulating a "fact file" of observations or clippings ("research") that:

- excite you AND
- you believe would interest your target readership in your selected market.

It might be in your technical area. For example, as a sociologist I keep a "sociological journal" of observations or insights including about class, power relationships and so on.

> ***If you have not yet accumulated forty years of your commonplace book, use my databank in Part 2 of this book.***
>
> ***Quick-reference sections contain the most useful topics for writers.***
>
> ***They capitalise on well-accepted maxims for commercially successful writing and the Google zeitgeist that used GARGANTUAN "big data" to discover the most popular searches.***

Keep paper and pencil, or other means of recording thoughts, such as audio-recorder or smart phone, with you always. An important location is at your bedside. Note down ideas before you forget them.

If your new thought shows signs of having legs and running to yet more novel places and you want to write more, do so. Write furiously, as if possessed, while your inspiration flows. Do this anytime, anywhere, that it is safe to so do. Seize and record those thoughts. *They are your gold.*

All writing
Other focussed preparation

Ratchet up the clarity of your English by studying, for example, *The Complete Plain Words* by *Ernest Gowers*.

Join a local writers' circle, take a writing course or attend a literary festival or some other sort of writing apprenticeship. Free on-line MOOCs (Massive Open Online Courses) exist. Targeted concentrated commercial courses exist with fees of some hundreds or thousands of pounds. So do many local undergraduate creative writing programs; they require fees of several thousand pounds in the UK. However, students benefit from a formal academic credential (typically a BA), extensive peer criticism and networks - and, perhaps, a somewhat bohemian sort of professor. The "gold standard" is probably an MA (or MFA particularly in the USA) in creative writing.

Reading part 1 of this book is one, less expensive, starting point. You may well disagree with some of its contents; *reflecting* on such disagreement boosts learning. Your particular, style, voice, will develop. Style, according to *Jonathan Swift,* is the "proper words in proper places."

Decide what kind of writing e.g. non-fiction, fiction, poetry.

- You need to have *something to say*.

It is your key idea for that market. It may bubble up, for example, from your – or (within this book) my - writer's commonplace book.

Note down your key idea, within a circle, on the centre of a blank sheet of paper. Add the date. It is a milestone. You have decided to lasso your idea and made it concrete, within the material world. There it is, captured, glued into paper. Notions slither. You may forget them or they may morph into something less powerful.

Start thinking about your title. Note ideas on the top of your idea sheet. Aim for the average number of words found in the titles of your target market.

Decide *your* favoured style. Style cannot be deliberate but, if you have a favourite author, read many examples of his/her work. Work out what so pleases you. Copy it shamelessly. You are unlikely to be able to reproduce it exactly. Something else, melded to your particular style, will emerge.

- Be yourself.

The next step is crucial because few people can manipulate, make the most of, ideas in their heads. I cannot. To help the process they must record their thoughts. Seeing them, concrete, helps them think. Retrieve your sheet with the central key idea. Scrutinise your key idea from all angles, finger it, and see how it connects. Around it draw a diagram: a "spidergram" because it is a web or network of related content. My preferences are a 2B pencil, freshly-sharpened, that precisely produces a confident, assertive mark and, for corrections, a soft natural india rubber, the sort that started life oozing from a tree, material that smells. It is my fetish; writers are notorious for their obsession with their writing equipment. Use computer software if you prefer.

Take every point from your spidergram; rearrange them as detailed linear headings of your text (fiction or non-fiction) with a logical flow.

- This list is your writing "skeleton" or "girdle."

I am a list anorak and make lists for everything; possibly connected with experience as a pharmacist: lists keep patients safer.

Do not expand out of your list. It constrains you but enables you to expand efficiently within it.

> Position your *best* point at the *start* (an immediate "hook" for the reader) and your *second best* at the *end*.

All writing

Decide length.

Note target lengths on each section of the skeleton. Calculate and note the cumulative word lengths up to each section. That avoids writing and polishing copy that you must later discard.

First draft

Plan the order of writing the parts. That may differ from the final. Consider writing the key parts, or end, first

Write. Any sentence should be understandable on reading once only. If it is not, redraft. Using one breath only, you should be able to read a sentence aloud. If you cannot, shorten.

Some parts will be easy, almost writing themselves. Other parts require lengthy agony. *Anthony Trollope* wrote about 1,000 words a day; you will probably write less.

Word process on your computer. It is your friend and confidant. It will check word length, spelling, and grammar and speed web access. That may unearth, from the other side of the planet, that golden nugget of information. Your computer will remember your work and file it. Always work on the *latest* version of your file; double-check. Label unambiguously; consider using the date. Even with that precaution,

- your computer can sometimes fail. So remember to back up on a site other than the hard drive (e.g. removable flash drive or in the cloud), if work exceeds 30 minutes. Any more is too painful to lose.

Firm up your title.

Start with your best point within your first 25 words.

Ruthlessly write to the word length specified in each section of your skeleton.

Winning Words

Use computer spelling and grammar checker. However, do not rely on your spelling checker. It is blind to two sorts of error. One is a word that differs from that desired by a letter that is omitted (e.g. not/no), added (e.g. you/your) or substituted (e.g. if/of), but remains a valid word. The other is homophones. They are similar sounding words with different meanings and spellings (e.g. to/too/two).

Use at least three of the five classical senses (sight, sound, touch, smell and taste) and the sixth sense of proprioception (feeling of balance) and interoception (feeling internal to your body such as indigestion, muscle pain). That originates deep within the body where there are few nerves; when they fire, pain results (e.g. in heart) that demands immediate attention. It is easy to cover two senses just by reporting speech and describing visual scenes. Including a third is more difficult – especially in shorter pieces - but repays with extra vividness.

Capitalise upon the strongest verbs. HMS "Endeavour" sounds more vivid than HMS "Try."

Prune out unneeded adjectives/adverbs. Less is more.

- If in doubt, leave it out.

Use specific instead of general nouns e.g. "tuna", not "fish."

Choose mostly short (English) words, fewer of average-length, and only a few, long. That follows "Zipf's Law". That claims that adherence is characteristic of intelligent communication. Astronomers listening for messages from extra terrestrials, apply it. "Zipf's Law" seems to apply to English and dolphin clicks. But be careful. *J.R.R. Tolkien's* imagined (intelligent) "Elvish", Chinese and Vietnamese, for example, do not follow. Tones and manner of speaking (e.g. flippant or solemn) also add meaning.

Punctuate perfectly.

Add from a book of proverbs e.g. about love.

All writing

Add from Brewer's *Dictionary of Phrase and Fable* or similar reference works.

Add pictorial, original analogies.

Use metaphors (see chapter 8: poetry). Ensure that your metaphors are not dated but relate to the life experience of your readers and so are *alive*.

- Add original colour, seasoning, novelty and *fire* from *YOUR writer's commonplace book*. This is your best source.

If you have not spent the last 40 years writing it, please feel free to use mine. Distilled extracts are in Part 2 of this book.

Words are your scalpel. Each word must pull its weight. Place with accuracy in the most fitting part of the sentence and with precision to mean exactly what you intended. For example, if you must use an adjective, ensure that it is the most apt. Use an on-line thesaurus. Avoid "jargon." Avoid ambiguous words.

A convention in English is that "it", "that" s/he or similar words refer back to the last thing, person and so, written about in the previous sentence. Check you have done so or the later sentence may convey a meaning that differs from your intention. It may even be nonsense.

Style (e.g. having a pleasing rhythm) such as:

"... I counted them all out and I counted them all back."
(Brian Hanrahan)

That is an illustration of a "balanced sentence." However, for emphasis, the most important point may be at the start (e.g. "Prison is the best place for her") or at the end (e.g. "The best place for him is prison"). Vary sentence structure.

Winning Words

Consider alliteration e.g. words following start with the same sound or letter. Alliteration is not poets' monopoly. E.g.:

> arrive alive,
> castrate confidence,
> compensation culture,
> Coventry kid,
> criticised commission culture,
> elusive as eels,
> fanatical about pharmacy/film,
> gurgling in the gulley,
> harder to hope,
> plunge into a pothole,
> sensational service, and
> welter of wicker chairs.

Consider onomatopoeia (echo words) such as the "grunt" of a pig or those that mimic anatomical movements of the mouth such as "globe": the mouth is round and so seems the word - or "keen": lips are almost closed and the word feels sharp.

Think about conveying complex notions with homely "concrete" comparisons. For example, if describing numbers of galaxies, avoid astronomical numbers with many zeros such as "trillion"; instead use grains of sand on a beach.

Decide your tone (mood). That may vary from playful to desiccated and academic. In a thesis, every word must convey an unambiguous meaning; each word may be a hostage to criticism.

Style is not too "purple." "Murder your darlings" as *Arthur Quiller-Couch*, a Cambridge professor of English, said in the early 20th century.

Enliven by injecting some direct dialogue between speech marks: "…" even if only a few words. An individual's speech is seldom more than about twelve words. If a dialogue, avoid "ping-pong" back and forth; vary, interrupt and so on to mirror normal conversations. Generally use "said." "Murmured", "shouted", "scalded" etc make the author visible.

All writing

Think about occasionally using earthy language such as *Alan Bennett*'s, "I went out for a pee."

Use the active ("The cat sat on the mat") wherever possible instead of the passive ("The mat was sat on by the cat"). Active is shorter and delivers more punch.

However, consider using the passive occasionally. It has one big advantage. The word with impact is right at the end of the sentence; that boosts its power. The passive is also routine in scientific reporting. One reason is that, in science, anyone should be able to do something and get the same result. The name of the individual is unimportant so is omitted. In arts, humanities and fiction writing, individuals vary; individuals may well have different takes on the same situation. Subjectivity is treasured.

Mix long and short sentences. Amidst longer sentences, an extremely short one carries punch.

Replace "There is/was etc" to shorten; e.g. "There were dishes drying" to "Dishes dried."

Use positive, rather than negative, statements, whenever possible.

Check factual accuracy including names and figures.

Check formatting (e.g. font size of heading, paragraph indentation) is uniform.

If something is problematic or uncertain describe using only one "degree of uncertainty." For example each of these words conveys one "degree of uncertainty": "may", "seem", "reasonable", "suggest", "possibly" or "like." So stating "The cat may sit on the mat" is sufficient while "The cat may possibly sit on the mat" carries unnecessary emphasis.

Avoid plagiarism. That is when you quote from an author at length without acknowledging. It is bad; in academic writing, atrocious. Interestingly, briefly quoting, amalgamating, two or more authors is considered "scholarship." That is good.

Each paragraph must contain a separate idea and match the paragraph length in your chosen market.

Link paragraphs. They must flow logically. Some aspect in the final sentence of one paragraph must connect to something in the first sentence of the next paragraph. Simple tactics include repeating one of the same words or using "Firstly", "Second", "Third" etc.

Check that the readability scores (e.g. Gunning Fog Index or Flesch-Kincaid Grade Level) match your market requirements. Copy and paste your text into a free internet resource. Request analysis. You will receive a score. Some websites highlight particularly clumsy sentences. Concentrate on improving those.

Simplify. Your mum or dad should be able to understand your text.

Check that you have not meandered from your main topic to one that fascinates you but is not pertinent.

Print your hard copy. For many people, mistakes are more obvious on a printed page than on a screen.

Pencil your improvements and corrections, including mere typos.

- There will be a lot.

That is your first copy edit/proofread. Resign yourself to this being the first of many. To maximise your efficiency:

All writing

- Scrutinise while alert.

- Repeat many times; 10 – 20 sounds heroic but is not excessive. Even then, professional proofreaders/copywriters may well spot more errors.

- Do in a different location (e.g. library, greenhouse, parked car) to where written.

- Know the errors that *you* most frequently make and be alert to them. Be aware that you may be blind to certain types of errors.

- Read slowly; an opaque ruler under the line may assist.

- Unless you read s-l-o-w-l-y your brain *will* add missing words - subconsciously.

- Point e.g. with a pencil.

- Read letters/numbers backwards. In package inserts in foreign languages or licence numbers that fail to form intelligible English words, this is common practice in the pharmaceutical industry.

- Check that the numbers of any illustrations such as diagrams match with numbers in the correct text.

Check total word length.

Read aloud. It is surprising what leaps out and bites you on the nose that did not when merely written. Can you make it sound more musical or evocative? Pencil corrections again.

Subsequent drafts

R*evise* (meaning re-*see*) draft 1. Does it just need polishing? Or are you so discontent that only heroic amputation and reconstruction will work? If the latter, I can feel your pain. But, just do it.

Review title. Particularly consider if a few words from your text would better encapsulate the spirit of your text. For example, instead of a less intriguing book title such as "Perfect Punctuation", the writer *Lynn Truss* selected *Eats, Shoots & Leaves*.

Double check word length.

Review all of the previous points.

Check unambiguous.

Consider whether reshuffling the order of paragraphs would improve clarity or power.

Put aside to "mature in the wood" like a fine whisky. The time scale can be shorter but leave at least overnight and preferably for a week. Review with "fresh eyes."

Proof read/edit, reading aloud, again. Scrutinise, especially, for omissions, repetitions and a conclusion not following from a premise.

All writing

Double check: get a trusted person (preferably another writer) to proofread and criticise

If a writer, you could agree a working relationship (that excludes the taxperson). You barter. You copy edit, proofread and criticise for each other. Be especially alert to typos, unclear sentences, wordiness and repetition.

That external view is the only way of benefiting from truly fresh eyes.

Yet *more* rewriting, proof reading and polishing, repeatedly.

General points

Decide on a time table for the various parts.

Record it.

Stick to it.

Capitalise on *your* best time of day. For example, the creative parts, carving the work out of the rock should be at your freshest time. But sometimes read drafts when you are fresh.

- It bears restating that you should expect up to, say, 20 drafts.

During each reading, expect to keep finding errors. You are unlikely to find them all. That is a consequence of statistical probability and being human. Even the published work of accomplished authors (and PhD theses) retains some errors.

- So do not be too hard on yourself.

To understand the reason, consider this. If you discover, say, half of the total errors at each proof reading, then only half of the errors will remain to find at the next proof reading, that is a quarter, after the next proofreading one eighth of the initial total will remain and so on. Errors will *never completely disappear*. Figure 1 illustrates this.

Figure 1 Number of errors remaining over time

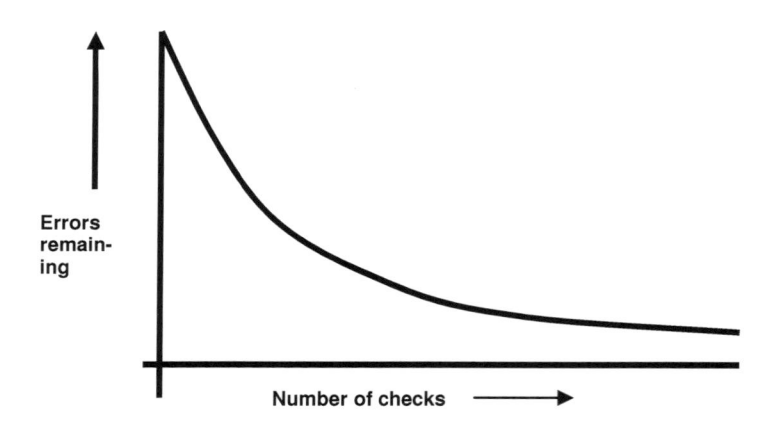

Errors remaining vs *Number of checks* — a decaying curve.

This is akin to the half-life of the radioactive decay of an element. Radiation will never completely disappear.

Expect a lengthy wait before hearing from the editor. If you are lucky enough for the answer to be yes, the editor accepts your copy, (s)he will probably only give you a short deadline for proofreading.

You can live with that. That editor is publishing you: that is the main thing.

2 Stimulation of ideas

Your wonderful brain

> Your brain comprises just 2% of your total body mass yet guzzles about 25% of the nutrients and oxygen that your *whole body* requires.

That is an enormous investment. Rather than developing bigger muscles and so on, humans think, and communicate so that their species as a whole can do things better. It gives us a warm glow to believe that evolutionary development gave us the edge over other species.

Human culture ratchets upwards.

> Writing contributes.
> It stores collective knowledge.
> It lives after individuals die.

But first, the brains of writers must deliver new ideas. They matter. But, put brutally, there probably are no new intellectual ideas; however novel your thought, some ancient Greek scribbler probably got there first. What is new is something discovered by scientific investigation of the material world, such as in Norfolk, UK, when *William Hyde Wollaston* discovered the element palladium in 1802 – and in 1804 another element: rhodium. Afterwards, a discovery in the material world just is, now, just as a work of art, once created, just is.

But the process of creation, or design, is an attempt to change the future. That demands confidence, a kind of religious faith. If writers think, and no ideas come, they may speak of "writers' block." They become anxious. Writers crave new stimulus in the hope that new ideas will follow; the understanding of cognitive psychologists is valuable here.

Limitations of brain and language

The brains of any individual are a container for thought. "Valves" such as eyes or ears let sensations in. "Ladles", such as speech or writing scoop the ideas out. A writer may have all sorts of notions in the container but to communicate them must use, for example, the English language. That has just twenty-six letters in its Graeco-Roman alphabet; other languages offer more such as the thirty of Bulgarian.

Figure 2 Strangulation of communication

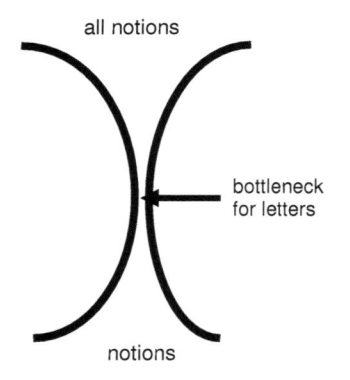

There are an infinite number of notions. The key point is that, to communicate, the writer must squeeze them through a narrow bottleneck of a severely limited number of letters formed into words that Figure 2 illustrates. The reader must then extend those letters to form all possible notions. This impediment is so severe that unambiguous communication seems near to impossible.

Some philosophers believe that our language constitutes the only world that we *can* imagine. The limits of our language are the limits of our world. People's choice of language has resulted

Stimulation of idea

in execution by burning. For example, in 16th century England, *Lollards* believed that the common people should have the opportunity to read the Bible for themselves in their own language: English, rather than replying on translation from the Latin by an expert priest.

However, we know more than we can tell. Our very bones tell us that some things are ineffable: we cannot put them into words. It follows that I cannot offer examples but can illustrate conduits of such communication. They include music and touch.

Anyway, valves admit all sorts of notions: a metaphorical miscellany of leaves and stalks, grass cuttings, carrot peelings, coffee grounds, and so on, into our mental "compost heap."

- They mature into a fine friable sweet-smelling loam. It makes your writer's garden bloom.

Sometimes a new perception just happens from the gourmet compost of this brain "container." One moment there is nothing; the next, something. But eruption seems from the whole gestalt.

Figure 3 A gestalt

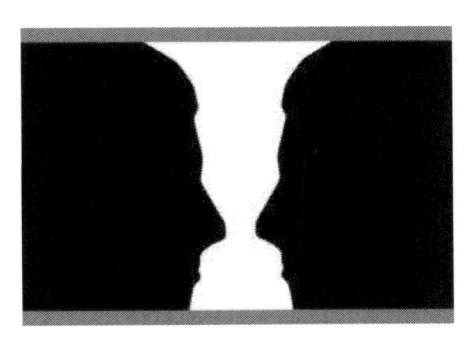

For example, you may perceive the image in Figure 3 to be a vase *or* two faces. As if from nowhere, suddenly, the image snaps into a different meaning. I cannot perceive the two meanings simultaneously. Such images mess with our minds.

A thought may be unbidden, an unconscious process. If you are lucky, it will happen to you. Capture that thought in your common-place book as precisely and accurately as your twenty-six letters will permit. Capture it; *nail it*, before it vanishes as abruptly as it appeared.

I cannot tell the writer of brilliance anything about getting ideas. But less fortunate writers must actively work on their compost heaps. Each need earthworms and microbes as allies and the heavy labour of periodical turning over with a spade. Your heap requires conscious encouragement and tightly focussed strategies to cultivate serendipity. Tips follow, outlining what worked for me.

First, be mindful that becoming ill would compromise your ability to write. So you must *work at* keeping fit.

- You might dispute this. After all, was not *Elizabeth Barrett Browning* confined to a sofa? The *Brontës*, surely, all died of tuberculosis. Famously, *Dylan Thomas* drank like a fish. Quite a few successful writers have been physically handicapped.

All true. However, I argue that, had they been healthier, they may well have achieved *even more*.

Keeping fit

> Look after yourself.

Get into condition for the demanding labour of nurturing that compost heap of ideas. Writing is an "unhealthy" sedentary activity. Writers may spend long hours hunched over keyboards so do need to pay attention to their health. A retired British pharmacist, you would expect me to favour the motto (1844) of the Royal Pharmaceutical Society; it is a translation from *Cicero* "Habenda ratio valetudinis". We must exercise in moderation, take just enough food, and drink to maintain our health and not to overwhelm it. *Cicero*, twenty-two centuries ago, offered that advice to old men but it remains pertinent to writers of any gender and age. It is so important that I now flesh it out.

Stimulation of idea

The brain: the writer's main organ, will only flourish with support from the rest of a healthy body. Witness: you can seldom write sufficiently well to achieve publication while you have influenza.

Find some way to compensate for the sedentary nature of the writer's occupation. Train your body with *exercise*. You need two sorts: aerobic and muscle-strengthening.

> For *aerobic,* for example, every week undertake cardio-vascular workouts of at least 2 ½ hours of moderate-intensity activity such as fast walking. Your heart rate must rise. You must break a sweat.
>
> For *"anaerobic"* muscle-strengthening activities, on two or more days every week, work all major muscle groups (including abdomen, arms, back, chest, hips, legs and shoulders). A regime such as gym, swimming, step aerobics (carrying light weights to increase the calories burned if required) before the television or brisk walk are vital parts of your training to write. Just slow walking, golf (with walking between all holes) or team sports (where you spend most of your time being inactive) are better than nothing.
>
> But:
>
> > choose something you enjoy
>
> because you will need to stick at it for decades.

Eat sensibly. Balance your diet between protein, carbohydrate and fat and include roughage and your five items of fruit and vegetables every day.

Winning Words

- Exercise and diet should result in your body mass index (body mass in kg divided by the square of your height in metres) nestling within the normal range (18.5 to 24.9), unless you suffer from some underlying medical condition.

Notoriously, writers drink alcohol. Maybe the solitude drives them to drink – or the rejection slips. But alcohol is a depressant that blocks thoughts and so blunts your creative edge. Therefore, do *not drink more than the recommended amount of alcohol a* day. This is, every week, not more than 21 units for men and 14 units for women. A unit of alcohol (ethanol) is about 10 mL.

To calculate the number of units, multiply the volume, in mL, of liquid you drink (V) by the percentage of alcohol (a) and divide the number resulting by 10.

$$Units = \frac{Va}{10}$$

So for a standard (120 mL) glass of wine that contains 12% alcohol

$$Units = \frac{120 \times 12\%}{10}$$

= 1.44 or about 1 ½ units.

Alcohol also contains calories. A unit of pure alcohol such as vodka contains about 55; wine also contains sugar contributing extra calories.

Caffeine is another crutch for writers. However, this crutch is probably beneficial, in moderation. It is a stimulant, a legal psychoactive drug. It temporarily wards off drowsiness and restores alertness. Thoughts seem faster and clearer and it becomes easier to concentrate. The normal dose range is up to

Stimulation of idea

about 500 mg a day; more than 1,000 mg may harm you. Overdose produces anxiety, flushing of the face, restlessness, irritability, increased urination and an unusual, rapid heart beat. Thoughts tend to ramble, undesirable for the writer.

Caffeine's half-life, after which only half is available to act in the body, is five hours. After another five hours, only half of a half (i.e. a quarter) remains and so on. (Figure 1's curve illustrates half-life.)

- *So you should not drink coffee for a few hours before sleeping.*

A cup of *espresso* or filter coffee contains about 100 mg, of tea about 50 mg. Drinking chocolate also contains other psychoactive ingredients including theobromine and cannabinoids. The *Cadbury's* flake girl seemed satisfied during the 1960s advertisements.

Do not let biscuits become a habit. Each may contain 50 calories. Ask whether you would enjoy as much, FOUR fat crunchy chilled grapes, totalling 12 calories.

- Fruitcake containing mace and nutmeg will offer a dose of myristicin, another psychoactive agent.

Victorian elderly ladies, cats rubbing against their legs, who enjoyed gossiping over a leisurely afternoon tea and cakes, may have become a little more intoxicated than they realised.

Another crutch is *smoking*. It is cancer-inducing and life shortening. Smokers today in the UK suffer pariah status but some other nationalities view smoking more favourably. Tobacco addiction is difficult to break but, if you value your health and smoke, *stop*.

Your body is about 60% water. Crucially for the writer, adequate *hydration* leaves your head clear; dehydration may lead to headaches and other problems. Men should drink about 3 litres, and women 2 litres, of watery beverages every day.

Winning Words

> You can easily tell whether water intake is sufficient. Your urine should be colourless or light yellow.

If it is dark yellow or brown, water intake is too low. However, it is normal for certain foods such a beetroot, rhubarb, asparagus, and few drugs to colour urine.

Look after your eyes. Writers make particularly heavy demands on their eyes. Write within sufficient light: say at least 500 lux if using a screen, somewhat higher if paper. Daylight, that is far brighter (overcast 15,000; blue sky 20,000; direct sunlight 110,000 lux) is preferable. You need brighter illumination as you get older. If you wear spectacles, keep them clean (e.g. use optical wipes and then a clean cotton handkerchief). Keep those appointments for checkups with the optometrist who will assist you in making the most of your sight and check for early signs of several serious diseases.

Use health services, such as those of medicine, dentistry and pharmacy if you have issues and for regular check-ups. Males, compared with females, seem loathe to use such services. That is despite males, at every life stage, suffering a lower life expectancy than females. If you are a male writer, bear in mind your increased risk and that care is available.

Sleep for 7 – 8 hours a day; adolescents need slightly longer. *Sleep "clears" the brain.*

A regular routine, avoiding non-sleeping activities such as watching the television in the bedroom and avoiding drinking too much liquid, especially containing caffeine during the 2 – 3 hours before bedtime, increase the chance of benefiting from that sleep. Sleeping is a vital part of training as a writer. Remember that transmogrification within the compost heap.

Develop a *defence against rejection by editors.* One definition of insanity is doing the same thing repeatedly but expecting a different result. But that is what little-known writers do. They repeatedly submit to editors, and are rejected ever and again.

Stimulation of idea

The writers know they are sane. But as insurance, develop your psychological strength and stamina. Having friends, valuing your worth in other ways, feeling in control of other parts of your life, humour, stress management and physical activity such as uprooting weeds or other socially-acceptable destruction may help. Annihilate your stress ball or cook scones. But do whatever works for you.

- You know your own body and mind better than any other person can. Seize sufficient confidence to do the things that you know make you well; avoid those things that you know damage your health.

> Exercising, eating, drinking sensibly and generally behaving as the paragon suggested above should result in fighting fitness to write.

Write in the best environment

Work in sufficient fresh air. Your inhaled carbon dioxide may "poison" you in a small musty room lacking ventilation. Instead, inhale plenty of fresh air. You need its oxygen for your brain to burn your food to create those thoughts that buy your bread.

Periodically change your working place. For example, I relish working in the greenhouse. It offers peace and comparative quiet: no telephone, computer or household noise; only the sound of insects buzzing around tomatoes with their fresh smell.

- Clear your head, periodically. Do something that is physically active. For example, take a walk in the fresh air outside.

We cannot all have *Darwin*'s "thinking path" in the countryside. At Down House, Kent, UK a sand-covered path still winds through shady woods and returns toward the house along a sunny, hedge-lined field. While walking along that very path, *Charles Darwin* developed the thoughts that changed the way that we see the world.

Endeavour to walk somewhere with plants If you are in a traffic-polluted city; plants clean up particles from the air by "filtering" through their pores. Plants are also the source of vital oxygen. A large potted plant or three in your writing room is better than nothing. But avoid species to which you know you are allergic.

Work in your writing environment in bursts of say *45 – 60 minutes* only. Between, take breaks (say 10 minutes each) that offer a change of scenery. For example, make yourself a coffee, visit the toilet, do some press-ups, look at your texts (if you must), cut some lawn edges or chat at the water cooler. Sometimes you will feel like continuing your break; sometimes *any* activity (such as scrubbing out the WC bowl) seems more attractive than writing. To avoid delaying your writing, stop writing just before a chunk that you suspect will be easy or particularly enjoyable. Then, you are more likely to look forward to continuing writing.

Suppose that you have followed all those tips and still cannot create anything "new." You then have "writers' block.

Steps to overcome writers' block

These are not exactly drawing by joining up numbers but they might feel mechanistic. But they have worked for me.

Remember the container with valves letting in the raw material that you need to make your "original" sweet-smelling compost ideas. First, you must have new, rich input. Seek it ruthlessly. Drink it in.

- Note it in your commonplace book.

Visit sites that some sort of group values so highly that they have poured in funds and hired experts who have pre-digested the site for your stimulation. Powerful examples are art

Stimulation of idea

galleries and museums, especially those outside your comfort zone. They need not house national treasures.

Even little local or specialist museums may offer something that makes you think, "Wow!" For example, observing, in *Gainsborough's* house in Suffolk, UK, a swordstick that a prudent gentleman carried in more violent (Georgian) times affected me. I peered closely at the actual artefact. It was a fashion statement about the owner's class. I read the plaque. Brow furrowed, I thought how the needle-sharp stick could thrust through the body and stick out the other side. I imagined what it would be like for one to stab you in your guts. Before antibiotics, probably a small thrust meant death within two weeks. I am a writer, not a painter or warrior, and expected little from that museum. But that weapon affected me, engrossing me so that all else disappeared. A collection of household objects might remind you of a younger you.

Visit small and large outdoor sites, preferably with an expert local guide. Again they do not have to be one of the present 1,007 world heritage sites – with the eye-ball bulging impact of, say, Victoria Falls or Uluru. But, if nearby, seize the opportunity:

> *all* new experience is grist to your mill.

Other examples include: web search engines, local radio stations, globally, streamed free on the internet (imagine *that* event happening near you) or public demonstrations such as of kitchen chemistry. Consider blogs, (group) brainstorming, visiting a zoo or safari park, sitting outside before sunrise listening to the dawn chorus, imagining "what if" you reversed a stereotype (e.g. occupational; witness *Bradbury's* firemen in "Fahrenheit 451), or holiday journals.

- They detail the shock of the strange. That is the anthropologists' stock-in-trade: their eyeballs bulge in amazement with different languages, life experience and customs.

Other material includes a specialist magazine, the reactions of children seeing something for the very first time or the throw-away comments of seasoned trade's people

You could write about anything. However, there is too much out there. That intimidates. So limit it; that makes it easier. The suggestion that it is easier to write about a little instead of a lot might rail against your intuition. But writers, like architects, find a tight brief from clients easier than a blank slate. Obviously write what will sell in a particular market. It is splendid if your editor commissions your work and briefs you; if you lack that luxury, scrutinise the topic areas of previously published work.

Rich pickings result from mixing two disparate fields (a and b in Figure 4).

Writers will have thoroughly trampled the turf of each, but their join may have overlaps or gaps that remain unexplored. You discover one following some personal event or interest, "an "accident", as the arrow c in Figure 4 illustrates.

You hit the spot: an overlap, gap or new synthesis never before discovered. You may be the first to enter that particular location. You will know when you have created something spanking new because your emotions will boil, "Gotya!" This tactic harnesses serendipity to your end.

Stimulation of idea

You might just, in Figure 4, have found a *new* perspective on knowledge.

Figure 4

Guided serendipity

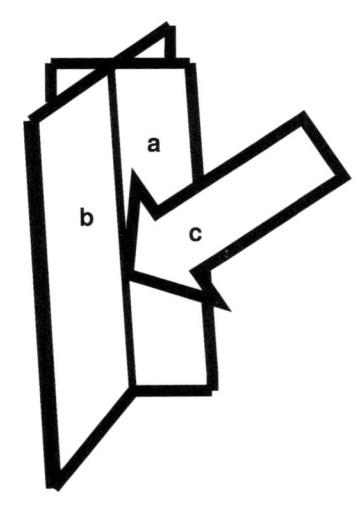

Knowledge used to be divided into stable recognised categories such as law, science, religion and so on. Our culture had so classified and we accepted those classifications. But for decades, boundaries have shifted and knowledge became categorised and perceived in new combinations.

This is the perspective of the sociologist *Michel Foucault* in "The Architecture of Knowledge." Once a new way is accepted, it becomes like hot water poured down the surface of jelly. The water carves out a new channel. Subsequent water will tend to flow that way. Its channel will deepen. Maybe you could start a new channel. Also be aware that your mind may block certain perspectives; *Sigmund Freud* made those blockages famous.

Take whatever you have found and see if it is a fertile notion. If it seems barren, consider its reverse, opposite or reciprocal. For example, filling an "empty" container (that is full of air) such as a bath with water, makes it heavier; water displaces air upwards. *R.J Weber* suggests pondering how you could make it lighter. Answers include pouring hot air or hydrogen *upwards* to fill a balloon; the less dense gas displaces the more dense air downwards. Your mental gymnastics deserve to result in novel perspectives. Editors claim to crave novelty.

Figure 5 illustrating extrapolation and interpolation.

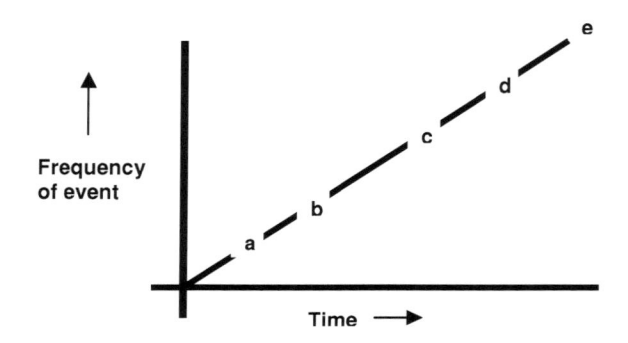

Take what you know and extrapolate (extend) it. In Figure 5, if b and d are known, then a and e are extrapolations. This is suitable for opinion pieces or science fiction; *Arthur C. Clarke*, an engineering graduate, was a master in this area. For example, you know how technology developed from old into present-day. Predict future enhancements. Cultural behaviour has changed rapidly. For example, in the West, respect for authority has declined since the 1960s. Will that trend continue or is a backlash overdue?

Take what you know and *inter*polate it (imagine between known points). This is suitable for historical or romantic fiction; for example, *Tony Parsons* capitalises on time spent in China; that shows. Suppose you know from your research what happened at two dates in the past, as b and d in Figure 5 shows. Imagine a plausible event c in the time between. Perhaps c caused d. Or predict e by *extra*polation. You can usually be more confident about interpolation than extrapolation.

Capitalise on changes in meaning between translations. For example, the book title "*l'Homme révolté*" in French was translated into English as "The Rebel." However, "Indignant Man", offering a more passive nuance, might be more precise.

Stimulation of idea

Famously, "The Grapes of Wrath" in English became in Japanese "The Angry Raisins."

Turbocharge this technique. Translate between several languages so it is akin to a "Chinese Whispers" exercise. Take a sentence in English. Translate that sentence into another language; translate that into another language and so on. Then translate the word, eventually, back into English. Capitalise upon the peculiar quirks of, for example, English, Catalan, Bulgarian, simple Chinese, traditional Chinese, Czech, Danish and Dutch and back to English. Free on-line translation engines will "instantly" perform that cascade for you. The result may astonish and prick you into further thought. You may leap into novel areas: your very own innovation that startles.

Certain words for physical materials are fertile for thinking. Man may manipulate, metamorphose materials into different forms, just as a caterpillar changes into a pupa that develops, abruptly, into a butterfly. *Levi Straus*, anthropologist, felt that food was good to think with.

Figure 6 metamorphoses between states

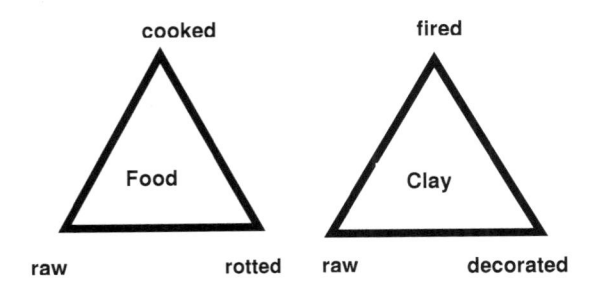

```
        cooked                    fired
         /\                        /\
        /  \                      /  \
       / Food\                   / Clay\
      /_____\                  /_____\
   raw      rotted           raw      decorated
```

Figure 6 triangles stimulate my thoughts about food, clay and other materials or situations; that figure may stimulate your thoughts, too. You may also find it valuable to reflect upon what happens to materials that are to hand such as a pencil making marks on paper as the graphite rubs off. Analyse the *grain* of the flow of your emotions.

Winning Words

Develop your own rituals. For example, on shampooing my hair, I sometimes decide to think about a particular writing blockage. It is surprising how often a thought occurs that dissolves the blockage. I cannot believe that results from mechanical stimulation of the brain, for if so, surely, it would be an accepted technique and creatives would routinely be bald. I speculate it is something about me and my personal experience, rewards and confidence; you may discover your personal activity that stimulates ideas; if so, use it, shamelessly. I also fabricate obsessively, with more flourishes than a barista, the one or two mugs of strong Napoli *espresso* coffee that I permit myself daily. When my favourite round-bottomed-mug is in my hand, my mouth puckering with the intense flavour, I expect my next chunk of writing to be good.

Creating your glittering new notion demanded your sweat. Make the most of your idea. That is what other artists do. For example, the sculptor *Henry Moore*, who capitalised on the style of holes to earn his bread, made not one sculpture but several. So do filmmakers or novelists with sequels. Do not undervalue your notion by selling it as a one-off.

Convert the one-off into a batch or even a continuous process – before someone else does.

Put in that groundwork.
Stack the odds in your favour.
Fresh vibrant ideas *will* bubble up.
As the chemist and microbiologist
Louis Pasteur, encouraged,
"Fortune favours the prepared mind."

3 Finding the time

The problem

Proverbially, if you want a job done, ask a busy (wo)man. Some people seem to have time and energy to do so much with their lives while others do not. You need to be one of the first group. The reason is that writing does not just happen. You have to put in the hours. Advice, such as within this book, can help, but ultimately, it is down to you to fix your pants onto your seat and write and, as you write, learn to write better.

- You may fear that you have not the time. You have the time. If you feel that you lack time, you must make it. This chapter explains how.

The solution

> *Motivation* is your essential starting point.
> You must want to write with a passion.

Confirm that by performing a type of SWOT (<u>s</u>trengths, <u>w</u>eaknesses, <u>o</u>pportunities and <u>t</u>hreats) analysis. Imagine that you have put in the labour and succeeded. You have become a published writer.

- *Allow yourself to dwell on that glorious moment.*

In the strengths box of Figure 7 you might list feeling good about yourself, increased income and so on. In the opportunities box perhaps you list public acclamation, increased chance of achieving your second publication, travel etc. Give each one a (positive) mark. Add the strengths and opportunities together in their total box.

Figure 7 illustrating SWOT analysis matrix

	Beneficial	**Harmful**
Internal	Strengths	Weaknesses ... ...
External	Opportunities	Threats ... ...
	Total ...	Total ...

In the weaknesses box list your personal fears and costs such as stress. In the threats, perhaps list risk of adverse review and your guilt following resentment from a significant other that you are unavailable while writing. Guilt gnaws. Add the weaknesses and threats together in their total box.

Subtract the harmful total from the beneficial total. Note the score. It is a positive or negative number.

Finding the time

Populate another figure. There, you imagine that you have not attempted to write but done something (or nothing) else with the time released. Compare the two scores. If writing produces a higher number, logically, you should act on it.

Obviously, this is inaccurate because you awarded each item equal weight. After calculating your result, ponder whether it reflects your gut feelings. If it does not, ask why. At least all this will force you to thoroughly think through your desire for publication. The question,

> "If I died tomorrow, would I be satisfied with my life?"

may also help to focus your mind. But also bear in mind that even graduating with a glittering MA in creative writing does not guarantee publication.

By the end of this exercise, you will have thought through your desire to write and what it costs. That included ferreting in the unpleasant corners that you had not before confronted. You will have based your decision on a cool-headed systematic assessment. Hopefully that will reinforce your desire to write. Let us assume that you are adequately motivated.

Next steps

- Decide when you will start. Someday means never. Mark the day on your calendar.
- Inscribe a big bold red circle.
- Start.

Brace yourself against the magnitude of the task. One fear about deciding to write seriously for publication is that the task of constructing your *magnum opus* is too *enormous*.

Winning words

One author of many scientific papers took against my using the word "enormous," saying, "It always reminds me of an elephant." One elephant yarn is:

> "How do you eat an elephant?"
> "In small pieces."

So, split your writing into *bite-sized* chucks, each small enough to tackle. List each bit within *a plan*. Plans not only allow you to divide your labour into manageable tasks but also to know where you are going. If you are uncertain where you are going, you may meander and be inefficient. You will squander your resources. Firm up your plan.

> **Focus like a laser.**

Specifically, construct a schedule for the various parts such as research, initial draft, second draft, and so on to submission and publication.

As you pass each stage, tick it off. Each tick is a hurdle jumped. Each time you tick, enjoy that boost of satisfaction.

Your biological clock dictates how much sleep you require between waking periods. Determine accurately. You might need less than assumed. Get up after that period. Set your alarm clock for less sleep. Do not waste time sleeping. *Florence Nightingale* and *Margaret Thatcher*, alpha female achievers, got by on four hours a night. (See Chapter 2, Tactics to stimulate ideas, for the normal range.)

Know whether your biological clock makes you a "morning" or "evening" person. For example, I am most clear-headed at about 5 am.

Decide where you are writing. It does not have to be at your desk or kitchen table, although a quiet undisturbed space is preferable. Avoid writing on or in your bed. You need to associate bed with sound sleep and not alertness. You *need*

Finding the time

your scheduled sleeping time. Travelling by train or bus, especially if seated, plus time in any waiting room, creates chunks of time. If you retain a lunchtime or tea breaks, do you need all of them? Could you reduce them? Do you watch the news/serial/sport that you do not like all that much? Perhaps you have slithered into a mindless habit. Spend time writing instead. Avoid starting to watch, or listening to, any new serial. They obliterate time.

Put differently, simplify your life. If something is no longer delivering "bangs for your buck", stop it. Write instead. Each of these re-allocations may only deliver a small chunk of time for writing. But they add up.

If this lists depresses you and you retort, "I would not have any pleasure left," keep some. Your writing and anticipation of success: *deferred gratification*, are your pleasure.

> There is pain. Sorry – but, "no pain, no gain."

Make writing, while writing, your top priority.

- Do not break off after 30 minutes to "just do a bit of ironing."

If living with others, they must understand the strength of your need, its importance to you. Of course, they also have needs and you will need to compromise. Negotiation is the way forward: give and take.

Write at maximum efficiency.

- Divide into chunks of say not more than one hour.

Body efficiency plummets after that period. Working for hours on end is ineffective abuse of your body. Many psychological studies show that breaks increase the amount of work done. So,

Winning words

take breaks between chunks. Try to arrange that, when you return to writing, it is to an "easy" part of your work.

Set your alarm clock for one hour. Then, timing is one thing less to worry about. When your alarm rings, stop, make yourself some strong coffee (unless within a few hours of sleeping; then drink *de*caffeinated), exercise in the open air, wash your face and so on. You know your body best.

> As only *you* know best, encourage its maximum performance.

After you achieve each milestone, allow yourself a little treat. Enjoy it.

- Tell others what you are attempting. Generally, they will be supportive and make allowances for you. Also, making your aspiration public makes it more difficult to say the sad sentence: "I quit."

Discuss your work with other writers. Look for somewhere, e.g. a Writers' Circle, where peers criticise each other's work. Members can carry onward together, astonishingly fortified, as on a wave or the V – shape of a flock of geese, flying overhead, having a good gossip on their journey. That V – shape is not a co-incidence: less air resistance results. The journey becomes easier. Make all these changes into a new *habit* as quickly as possible so that your new way continues of its own accord. A habit, once acquired, does not need emotionally, or physically, draining justification. It becomes just what you do.

> Tick off your final hurdle; publication.
> You have made it!
> Reward yourself and any partners in negotiation.
>
> If you can, deliver to them more than they expect.

Non fiction

4 Non-fiction article

Perhaps non-fiction feels less glamorous than the oceanic feeling of having your free-roaming creative fiction, your very own work of art, published.

Why write non-fiction?

- If there is a market for your topic, it is worthwhile and useful.

- Your article could make a difference, even if only in a small and humble way such a leading a novice through the stages of replacing a cracked tile or saving labour in cooking.

- If you succeed in selling your piece to a particular market (that you have first meticulously researched) it could be part of your portfolio to earn your bread.

- If published as a book, another edition, in some future year, may require comparatively little labour from you and boost sales - and your income. (However, if your book "dates" very quickly, you might have to do quite a lot to update it.)

- About *five times more* non-fiction than fiction is published. That may mean it is easier to place the book in the market. However, there must be a gap in that market (that your research has identified). You need to plug that gap quickly before other authors – your competitors – do.

Winning Words

Subjects for non-fiction

What do you write about? Famously, you should write about what you know. Examples are your occupation, your location, hobby or other passion. Anniversaries and seasonal also sell. However, submit long before required e.g. summer for Christmas.

Sometimes, areas between topics are fruitful, ripe for delving; people have seldom written about that space. For example, I have written about the area betwixt and between pharmacy, medicines, healers and culture and, similarly, betwixt and between astronomy and anthropology. You know that you have tapped into a need when an editor starts e-mailing you, asking for your particular take, in say 2,000 words, on a topical matter by the next Wednesday. Maybe another editor will commission you to write a regular column.

> *The databank in part 2 of this book bursts with ideas about topics*

The *Writers' &Artists' Year Book* lists specialist magazines. Examples include gardening, New Age and pets.

Do not forget filler articles (for gaps between larger pieces) in all manner of magazines and journals including company in-house newsletters and supermarket freebies. Typical length is about 50 words. Although each piece is small, fees add up. Letters to the editor may be up to about 400 words. Although often unpaid, they add to your CV. Clearly every word must be succinct, the writing effort required to word-smith each sentence akin to that of a poem, the result a minor jewel. D-I-Y, health and other tips, humour and nostalgia sell well. Bear in mind that you can capitalise upon the whole of your life experience – and commonplace books. Check out well-thumbed magazines in waiting rooms for markets that convert your "dead" time into cash.

Non fiction

You might know someone locally who is under-recognised, expert in his or her field and possesses much under-recognised knowledge. That individual may be loath to self-publicise, not interested in writing or too busy doing his or her own high quality, courageous or honourable thing.

Someone too busy to meet you in the flesh may spare time for a telephone interview. Interview and report. At least that person is likely to read your piece.

General advice

- Your editor is crucial to you.

Match the layout of your target market. For example, organise some text into a "strap line" and/or "sidebar(s)" if that is the normal pattern. If the first word of text starts with a letter or word in capital(s), copy that house-style. If the publication prints subheadings with a particular colour, also copy. If an article ends with a succinct biographical description of the author, in italics, offer it. Match the typeface, if possible. The editor may smile wryly at your "amateur" efforts and have to re-typeset. But you will have shown that you know their existing convention. You might even make it easier for the editor who may therefore regard your work more favourably.

- You need to be opinionated and not reticent.

This may mean, sometimes, being bold if your topic is controversial. Only undertake if you are comfortable with the risk of being criticised. Some individuals hold an opinion but, for whatever reason, say nothing while others communicate. Those who are silent may be circling like piranha fish to nip those venturing opinion.

- State the gist of your article at the beginning.

Winning Words

If any briefing from the editor received, include. It may suggest a particular take on the topic. Be grateful if you then have to write less. If you must write more because the editor's steer is from a completely different angle, also be grateful. Put yourself into the editor's shoes; a commissioned writer who omitted proffered advice would disappoint you.

The substance of your piece follows in some sort of systematic order. Illustrations include chronological such as considering components in their order of assembly. If all else fails, fall back onto the six questions of *Rudyard Kipling* (1902):

> "I keep six honest serving men
> (They taught me all I know);
> Their names are *What* and *Why* and *When*
> And *How* and *Where* and *Who*."
>
> (my *italics*)

If you appear to have more points than your word limit permits, include only those most exciting for readers.

If practicable, ask recognised experts for their opinions. Report accurately.

Let your style show in your presentation and perspectives on topics. Over time, editors may recognise this and even commission your work. To celebrate, eat a cream cake.

After a theoretical statement, a practical example illuminates.

Non fiction

Illustrations are worth many words. Note how you can understand from Figure 4 about the two fields, accident and "Gotya" event more easily with the diagram, than by just reading many words. A combination, with text explaining it is required. For some topics such as DIY manuals, illustrations linked to text seem almost essential.

If something is important, "signpost" it, such as: "It is crucial that ...."

- End by telling readers what you have told them. Check that you have said what you will write about, written about it and reminded that you have done so.

Cultivate the habit of adding *nuggets from your commonplace book*, say, two within each thousand words.

> *Those nuggets are just as important for non-fiction as fiction – if not more so.*
>
> *They are* your secret weapon.
>
> Editors may say,
> "We like yours because it is different,"
> and return for more.

5 Non-fiction book

Subject

Textbooks are "true." They condense the best knowledge and belief; as their word label ("non-fiction") succinctly, accurately and precisely states, such writing is non (not) fiction. An exemplar, today, is a scientific textbook. It offers current perception of "the truth" but is expected to become obsolete and superseded by later versions of "the truth." It contrasts with a novel. That contains open falsehoods or tales where the novelist – in connivance with the reader - capitalises on literary wiles to suspend disbelief.

> Metaphorically, fiction readers roll over, legs in the air, to have tummies tickled. Non-fiction readers are guard dogs that growl at any falsehood.

As with fiction, writing non-fiction about what you know is easiest. An example is a personal devotional work, subject that you teach or travel account such as *Robyn Davidson*'s 1,700 mile trek, solo, across the Australian outback. You may make something; writing a user manual (that typically is now only available on line) offers advice at your fingertips.

The subject is timely, responding to current world events such as conflict and/or timeless (such as child-rearing practices). To appeal to a mass market, your non-fiction must be interesting enough for a wide audience to purchase. For example, biological waste disposal by activated sludge fascinates me. On passing a sewage works, whenever possible, I stop, stare, sniff and savour. However, a text book concentrating on sewage sites is a minority taste. But it does have a market; although a comparatively small one, it commands a premium price and its author benefits from revenue from copying in public libraries.

- Again, ask is there a market? That is crucial.

Ask why your non-fiction is better than or different from that already on the market. What is the unique selling proposition of your offering? Ask whether you are a professional in the field, considered an expert on the subject, undertaken extensive research on it or have collaborated with an expert.

Length

This is typically, about 100,000 words. The Bible is about 775,000 words. *Martindale: The Complete Drug Reference* (2011), a standard, single-volume, work about medicines for health professionals, is probably of the order of over 7,000,000 words. Many larger tomes have many authors.

General advice

The title should be descriptive, invite inquiry, shock, soothe or in some way attract attention. An illustration is "... for Dummies." It is ingenious. It pokes gentle fun at experts. It recognises that the reader wants to know and be caught and is actually quite sharp. In another place or time, that tone and use of English might lack those nuances, jar, and damage sales.

Outline the benefits for the reader. Consider dividing into a specific small number of steps to achieve some aim; a title specifying a small number of steps suggests that the task is easy.

The writing should avoid jargon: scientific or technical terminology unfamiliar to the lay person. Omit slang that tends to date the work.

- Claiming to be "fact" it *must* contain what others have published and/or what you, the author, have discovered. Otherwise critics may demand evidence.

Winning Words

Write to a readability score that its readers expect. Non-fiction records from antiquity mainly comprise mundane receipts, taxation returns, legal decrees and so on. They sound heavy going. Today's legal textbooks (for a self-selecting legal group) are dense, and even impenetrable, for a lay person and this may apply to many specialist publications with specific target readers. But, if it is what specialists expect, they will buy. They welcome dense text: it repels lay readers. They continue to lack knowledge. That protects professionals' fees, cynics might suspect.

If you wish to write or interpret an unfamiliar field, to dive into it avoiding a painful belly flop, delve progressively deeper using these sources:

>dictionary (its brevity should not embarrass you: its *function* is to provide a distilled overview)
>encyclopaedia
>web search engine such as *Google*
>*LinkedIn*, or similar social media, contacts and interviews

Suppose that, despite your best efforts, you conclude that the topic includes a substantial area where your knowledge is inadequate. Then, write with a co-author, expert in that area. Mutual respect is required rather like within a marriage. Use the tracking facility (making changes visible and allowing acceptance or rejection of any proposed change) in *Word* or similar. Hopefully, the result will not show joins between your writing styles.

Non fiction book

A typical structure is:

> - About the author
> - Title
> - Foreword
> - Contents
> - List of tables
> - List of figures
> - Acknowledgements
> - Chapters and subchapters (paginated)
> - Endnotes chapter by chapter (expected in learned tomes; destroy market in other books);
> - Appendix
> - Index

Presentation should be attractive, appealing and professional-looking for its intended market. Construct it to be akin to their normal offerings; something too different may be viewed askance and rejected. Markets include your occupational field or hobbies such as travel.

Consider numbering tables and figures to include the chapter number. For example, the first figure in Chapter 1 becomes 1.1., the second 1.2., the second figure in Chapter 4 becomes 4.2. and so on. Including many illustrations is a complex task. This tactic simplifies it.

Short of co-authorship, a small input from outside your topic area may enhance more than a similar size input from within.

For example, if you are a scientist offered any co-operation or collaboration with an English graduate or similar, jump at the opportunity. To be meticulous about the microscopic detail of laboratory work, for example, yet casual about the English of communication is madness. If you are an artist or humanities scholar, show your draft to an approachable scientist. That person's eyes may glaze over. A common reaction is "Where are the diagrams?" They may well clarify the meaning of your text.

Another reaction is "Where are the numbers?" They may increase credibility.

- Periodically, ask yourself how to describe your book in one, two or three sentences to a lay person.

Insert your answer prominently e.g. in your introduction.

If the market expects references, provide them. Reference meticulously. If available and pertinent include at least one from the 19th century or before. That telegraphs the depth and scope of your scholarship. Similarly, if available, include one or two references to your own work.

Users will take it for granted that an index is included. Indexing requires delving into the *meaning* of your book's contents; your brain must be in gear, unless you hire an indexer. The index must be helpful to its anticipated users. It is not a list of the commonest words. Its headings should include people's names, places and events, and notions useful to the reader. Illustrations of components include:

activities,
artefacts,
beliefs (e.g. religious),
conditions such as illness,
dates,
events,
institutions (e.g. parliament),
life-forms,
materials,
methods,
phenomena (e.g. tornadoes),
products,
properties such as conductivity,
shapes (e.g. mathematical),
structures and
subject areas (e.g. astronomy).

Non fiction book

There must be a compromise between it being adequately inclusive and impracticably long.

Theses

You might think that an academic thesis is an ideal candidate for a book. It seldom is. Readers outside academe loathe regurgitated academic style.

The first thing to appreciate about writing an academic thesis is that it is like no other. Academic writing is formal and indigestible; it uses long words compared with most non-academic writing. Theses and dissertations must also be unambiguous. They must conform to strict university requirements. Theses are seldom published in original form. However, occasionally, in specialist areas, publication does occur. Almost all successful theses are already in the public domain so are, in that sense, "published."

Advice on biography

Decide whom you want to write about. Examples include: ancestors, friends, heroes, idols, your parents, grandparents, great-grandparents, occupational antecedents, other relatives or any other special person or celebrities. The latter may be difficult to access but the most potentially profitable.

Collect as much information as you possibly can while (s)he lives, from birth date to the most relevant facts of life through letters, journals, newspaper clippings, pictures, and conversations such as with older family members. It is valuable to take notes or record conversations as in the chapter on research.

As always, plan before starting to write. Decide which part of the person's life you would like to highlight. Attempt to place the life in context.

Winning Words

The Mass Observation Archive is useful there. It specialises in material about everyday life in Britain. Source material includes the Mass Observation social research organisation (1937 to early 1950s), including "diaries" that ordinary people kept and newer material since 1981. The archive, parts being searchable on line, is in the care of the University of Sussex.

- As in non-fiction articles, ask, "W*hat*, *Why*, *When*, *How*, *Where* and *Who?*"

Other questions abound. What makes this person so special and interesting? At root, how can (s)he be described? Which were the events that marked or changed his or her life? Which is the most important? How was (s)he an influence to family, profession or society?

When writing about somebody else, describe his or her appearance, (e.g. "he is tall, very tall"), habits, features and way of talking. Record carefully the names of any quoted informants interviewed about the subject of your biography.

Edit the biography; read it aloud to feel its rhythm and the sound. That will also help you notice if you are repeating information.

Advice on auto-biography

Which of your selves should it be? Work, home, internal, hobbies? Will you write about your variety or project the (self-censored) image of what you would prefer as your public *persona*?

What (abstract) theme sums up your life and your book's central message?

- Research your own life. Your tale is unique.

Avoid starting with the time and place of your birth. Ask instead why you were born where you were, and how your family's experience led to your birth. Give full weight to your family background. Consider starting your story some

Non fiction book

generations back. You are not *Alex Haley* writing the novel, *Roots: The Saga of an American Family*, but can learn from such emotional story telling.

Cover an overview of your personality, your likes and dislikes, and the special events that shaped your life.

Your region or culture is so familiar to you that it seldom interests you. But it may well seem very different, and therefore interesting, to others.

What do you know about your grandparents? Your great-grandparents? Have you ever asked what your grandparents did for a living, or how they came to settle in a certain part of the world? For example, maybe your grandfather was of good socialist stock, a hewer of coal – but when his pit closed, work ceased. He got on his bicycle and found work and "digs" (lodgings) a hundred miles away. Did he fight in a war or have a reserved occupation? Older family members may well love to talk to you about olden times. To them, their distant past may be exquisitely detailed and crystal-clear, while remembering where they put their slippers, five minutes before eludes them. Family members are more easily accessible – and tolerant - than non-related informants. Bear in mind that any informant will not always be there.

What is interesting about the region where you were born? Does it farm fish, mussels, oil seed rape or tulips, for example?

How does your family history relate to the history of that region? Did your family migrate to that region for some reason that affected many people such as a major geopolitical disturbance? Does your neighbourhood suffer extreme weather such as drought, hurricane, sea-fret or smog?

- Highlight the parts of your childhood that had most emotional impact on you or probably would most interest others.

At school, did you gulp down free milk from one third pint bottles? Did cream once float on the top? Other examples are what sort of buildings are familiar to you such as beach hut, dock, grain silo, opera house or petroleum refinery, storage

Winning Words

space (just possible to crouch within) under the stairs, tatty cinema or tornado refuge?

Country folk may be agog at the trappings of cities. They include an underground, walking to school, riding in a taxi, browsing a multi-level department store or internationally-renowned museum, cheering on a grand pageant, jostling through crowds, anonymous individuals avoiding eye contact, or seeing – with their own eyes - a prominent personage. Most people, globally, now live in cities.

Many people who grew up in the suburbs or inner city have never eaten food picked straight from a garden (e.g. a lettuce or strawberry), fed chickens or wrung their necks to kill them, watched a headless chicken wander around in circles (for a surprisingly long time), bottled jam in Kilner jars, scalded and frozen twenty kilograms of carrots or had time to greet a passerby. They have never attended a county fair or small town festival.

Try to have outsider's eyes. There will always be something about your childhood that will seem unique to others. Reflect upon how strikingly different were the customs and homes of other nationalities, met in their countries. Strive to step outside your life and speak to the readers as if they knew nothing about your region and culture.

That embraces customs that come from your family's values and beliefs, holidays you observe, foods you eat and names (pikelet *v.s.* crumpet) clothes you wear (e.g. slippers to mud-caked Wellingtons for some country folk; high heeled, shiny boots for city folk). Men of all classes around 1910 sported hats on perambulating along seafronts of holiday resorts. Inside, all students in chemistry laboratories wore little hats, but no safety goggles. Posters printed plain black with just the stark white words, "NO REPLACEMENTS. WEAR SAFETY GOGGLES," lay ahead. The games you play, the special phrases you use, the language you speak and the rituals you practise will excite.

Non fiction book

How were you graded at school? Did you take the British "Eleven plus" or "SATS."? What did the brightest, less bright and so on, study at university? For example, in the 1960s in Britain, the most able pupils at some grammar schools were expected to, at university, study classics, the less able, sciences and, below that, technologies such as engineering. Today, schools and society's expectations have changed.

How did your family celebrate or observe certain days (e.g. birthdays), events (such as harvests), and months (December and so on) or special moments? Did you ever have table decorations? Describe them. Why were they so formed? What was the most special gift you ever received? What was the event or occasion surrounding that gift?

Is there a certain food that you identify with a certain day of the year such as chicken at Christmas if you were lucky? Are there clothes that you wear only during a special event? (E.g. dinner jacket, bow tie, cricket whites, christening robe.)

Have you ever driven, or ridden on, an ambulance, bullet train, cable car, camel, cruise liner, elephant, funicular railway, hearse, horse, hot air balloon, limousine, mountain bike, river-crossing pontoon on a chain, sailing boat, speed boat, *Segway*, wheelbarrow or tractor? Have you ever walked on a beach, mudflats, mountain path, rope river-crossing, volcano, the Great Wall of China or in a cave?

How was your experience of one of these topics related to your family culture, e.g. gathering samphire as a seasonal vegetable?

Combine the best bits of your life story and craft into an engaging book.

6 Fiction short story

Why do humans value fiction so highly?

Writers of fiction, short or long, possess a very particular talent or knack. They possess the wonderful ability to engross people. Fiction comprises imaginary events, untruths or downright lies. Perceiving a fiction writer, professional liar of excellence, in the context of *Darwin*ian evolution is illuminating and thought-provoking.

Presumably, an individual social animal, that could communicate, living in a group, found it advantageous for survival to sometimes hide information from others. For example, suppose individual A alone knows the location of food. Individual A does not show individual B where the food is. So only individual A, having the knowledge, could eat that food while B could not: self-interested behaviour by A. Chimpanzees can show that. Arguably, that has similarities to lying.

However, an individual needs the group and has to get on with other members. An illustration is dolphins swimming together to herd, and then eat, fish, more efficiently. Much buzzing, tangled, social interaction seethes within groups. To remain a part of the herd, individuals must keep their wits about them; otherwise they might be shunned or excluded. That could be fatal. That may occur in elephants. To help them "rub along" with others, to smooth over interrelationships and fortify vital social cohesion and empathy, the animal equivalent of "little white lies" are told. Humans do this all the time. We are the champion liars of all creatures. It demands much brain power. Remember that, the next time you delete, and fume over, a plausible e-mail and zip attachment that is a noxious phishing fraud attempting to extract your bank details.

We became so good at lying and lie so well, that simple lying now bores us. During our quest for novelty, we have added yet

Fiction short story

another layer of complexity. The group plays a game. It gives the storyteller permission to lie. We like to hear those lies. We remain aware that they are untrue. Despite that, we choose to lower our defences; we indulge in a mind-game of pretending that the lies are true. We clamour to listen. We immerse ourselves in it – and enjoy it.

We can speculate that, during pre-history, say 100,000 years ago, a family group chased away the sabre-tooth tiger. They huddled by the open fire in the cave.

> The storyteller spoke and the others listened. The telling and hearing of a tale took them to another world, made them happy and improved their social cohesion. As stories were told and heard, little by little, we learned to become more human.

Early fiction includes *the Epic of Gilgamesh*, from Mesopotamia, about the 18th century BC. We had progressed, by the 10th century AD, to *A Thousand and One Nights* and the Icelandic sagas. *Chaucer* arrived in the 14th century, *Shakespeare* in the 17th, and the novels of *Dickens* and the *Brontë* sisters by the 19th. Since then, the volume of fiction has exploded; every offering quests novelty. Fiction short stories are less complex than modern novels containing sophisticated nuanced accounts of tangled layers of human interactions.

> All fiction still speaks to us about what it is like to be human. It allows us to live (imagine) situations not yet encountered. In our chair, as if in a simulator, we practise having feelings. We try out the emotions.

If we have met a situation in fiction, such as the serious illness of a close family member, it may help us to cope, were that misfortune to occur in our own "real" lives.

Winning Words

Fiction, compared with non-fiction, is more subjective, the creation of a unique mind. It differs from the output of anyone else. However certain basic rules apply.

Manipulation of emotions

At root, in some fashion, the writer must manipulate the reader's emotions. Emotions include horror, joy, sadness, love, hate and humour. The reader should experience the delighted shock of recognition.

> "Yes, it is like that for me, too!"

The reader has evidence that another person (the writer) has the same feelings. That gives the reader permission to have them. It satisfies a basic psychosocial need.

To achieve that, a novel – the "wine" of fiction may take 100,000 words. A poem – the distilled "spirit" – whooshes to towering emotion in a few dozen words. It is a sprint. Witness that soldiers in First World War trenches produced peerless poems but few novels; death might befall before the second chapter.

The added power of music, that words cannot describe, turbo-boost words in a minstrel's ballad or 21st century pop song. The singer capitalises upon a contorted anguished face squeezing out a soulful halting voice; that matches melancholy accompanying music. That performance has mere seconds to hit the spot. In *Paul Simon's* "That's where I belong," sound is said to metamorphose into song in some unspecified place during a brilliant surge.

Chapter 7 provides more advice on novels; Chapter 8 on poems.

- a short short story is under 1,000 words; a short story 1,000 – 7,500 words.

Fiction short story

Step by step action

> Your aim is to "suspend disbelief."
> The reader could be *there*:
> within *your* constructed world.

Your commonplace book, or if unavailable part 2 of this book, will goad your imagination. Details required vary with genre. For example, in historical fiction, intricate embellishments add plausibility. Suppose your setting is healthcare: see sections on health, medicines and drugs. If science fiction, elements of science and/or technology are required. Trawl sections on astronomy, biology, chemistry, physics, mathematics and technology. I chose content likely to be accessible and understandable to non-scientists. Scientists may consider it over traditional and simplistic. If I upset scientists and artists in equal measure it is probably just about right.

- Decide upon a theme, the abstract subject, often just one word such as courage or self-discovery.

It should be important to you, perhaps even an obsession. Even naming it may upset you. Many well-selling themes are sombre and involve suffering.

- The story needs a start, a middle and an end.

For a short story plan, draft for each character and scene the:

- type of character e.g. big/powerful or quietly spoken;
- motive such as winning at a flower show, reducing dust in house; situation such as an accident in a factory;
- complication such as salt spray misting spectacles and
- solution such as a willow hanging to the ground and so hiding something.

Construct a plot plan for the story with rigid lengths for each situation. Refine before starting to draft. For example, for a thriller, within each scene:

Winning Words

> The key character has a problem.
>
> (S)he overcomes it.
>
> A more difficult problem presents.
>
> (S)he overcomes it.
>
> The next problem presents and is overcome, and the next, and so on. Each problem is more challenging than the previous one.
>
> Eventually a problem occurs that is so challenging that the reader cannot imagine how the key character will overcome it. This is the emotional climax.
>
> You, the author, note how to overcome. It is astonishing. Your key character shows your solution in action.
>
> A happy conclusion follows.

Trail approaching crises subtly so that not, entirely, unexpected. For example, the heroine, who must contort to escape from a car filling with water, exercises in the gym.

Decide the time span. It might be within an hour, week, year - or billion years.

You need a location or changing locations. Constructing closing and opening locations in a full circle may add pleasing symmetry. Your commonplace book is, again, valuable there.

Locations have layers within layers like an onion skin. Novels (and part 2 of this book) concentrate on an embarrassingly limited part of that range. They are almost all limited to

Fiction short story

"human" scale, emphasised in *italics* below. Just consider where that fits into 21st century scales. They offer "new" horizons. They include:

- universe-wide,
- galaxy and solar system wide,
- global,
- *human (sagas, romances, chick-lit etc. describing bodily features and human artefacts such as furniture and cutlery)*,
- miniature (hair strands, pond-water creatures, fabric such as lice living upon),
- macroscopic (e.g. tissues, cellulose fibres in wood),
- microscopic (cells e.g. crystals or gut bacteria),
- nanoscopic (e.g. DNA, nanotubes, certain car polishes),
- atomic (atoms interacting to become molecules) or
- subatomic (boson etc).

Four common types of conflict pit the protagonist against at least one of:

- another (human, magician, God),
- society (economics, politics etc),
- nature (time, climate, creatures, aliens) or
- self (conscious dilemmas or hidden**)**

Polti details 36 dramatic situations, claiming they cover all possibilities; he analysed many stories, including from antiquity, in the 19th c. Although dated, one may spur you.

Winning Words

Avoid the "godlike" "Dear Reader" view (ghost etc.): telling the reader what is going on. It reveals the author and destroys the illusion of fact, like bursting a balloon. The characters should reveal the story, slowly. Third person is the most usual; one advantage is varying viewpoints and knowledge between characters. First person can be intimate and powerful but limits perceptions by others.

Maximise any emotion, pain etc. For example the lion does not merely bite the key character's neck; you detail the lion's weight, heavy panting, cold eyes, yellow teeth dripping red with your blood, agony from your wounds, foul breath etc.

Short sentences increase tension. So does one character interrupting another mid-sentence.

Show. Do not tell. For example, show:

> "Damn! I'm *useless* at DIY."
> His blood spurted onto the printout of plans with *HM Home Office* on the top. He stared at the saw cut in his hand.
> His teenage daughter was staring at her mobile.
> "Dad! It's Chicago. They've nuked it!"

Do not tell:

> "The British government, eventually, mailed plans of inner refuge fallout shelters to all households. Competency at DIY varied; injuries started early. The internet provided the first public information. World War Three started after the nuke in Chicago."

Your reader must care about at least one of your characters and what befalls him/her. If your reader does not care, you have failed.

Attitude between protagonists may change over the story such as from contempt to indifference to admiration - or in reverse order.

Fiction short story

- Name characters carefully; do not just choose at random.

    Avoid names of close family connections or friends; using them really would be "playing in the traffic."

    Avoid names such as "Adolf" that fast-track the reader into historical connections.

    Bounce the names off another person, preferably a writer. Check that a similar sort of tale has not used that name.

    Make it easy for *you* (rather than a professional actor/actress) to pronounce; you may be reading from your book in a public meeting.

    Make the protagonists sound very different from each other so avoid, for example, "Jon" and "Tom."

    Take account of ethnicity and religion. An extreme illustration is that a Jehovah's Witness is more credible as a "John" than a "Mohamed".

    Take notice of movie and TV credits.

    Whether strong when "D..." such as "Dick" works well (Dick Steel sounds tough) or shy when "F" or "Ph..." such as "Phyllis" works too.

Create fictional characters by jumbling together characteristics of two or, preferably, more people that you know. Those people may read the fiction and attempt to discover characters who could be them.

Changes in Figure 8, where the sections in the fiction are initially ordered 1, 2, 3 etc., illustrate possible re-ordering. If the most exciting or intriguing part (4, grey-shaded) is in the chronological middle of the first draft of the story, consider transferring that to the start of the second draft. Follow the arrow. After the old middle, tell the tale from the first draft as an extended flashback. Refer fleetingly to the new beginning when you arrive at the new midpoint (3). Continue in chronological order, going forwards.

Figure 8: Moving "hook" to start

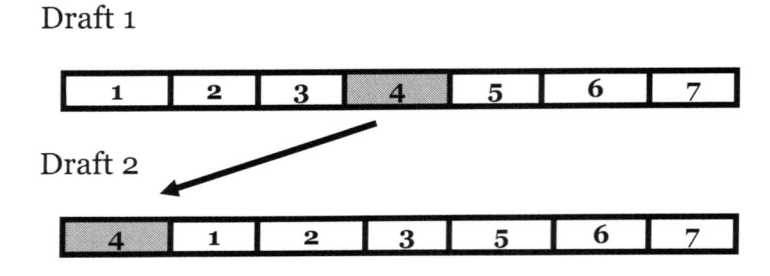

Draft 1

| 1 | 2 | 3 | 4 | 5 | 6 | 7 |

Draft 2

| 4 | 1 | 2 | 3 | 5 | 6 | 7 |

Embellish with telling details sucked from the main artery of life such as from your commonplace book. If you have not yet written it, use part 2 of this book. This will add fire and an impression of credibility.

> If you choose apt quotations, you may achieve an impression of *verisimilitude*. Your reader will think: the author could not have made *that* up. It must be true. In a fashion, it is.
>
> Put differently, your tale becomes *alive*.

7 Fiction book

- This includes the big one, your great work, your *magnum opus*: the book that you know is within you.

Should it stay there or be let out?

It is probably a novel, the premier form of literature in English. It is a wonderful but terrifying project. Your creation will comprise one volume of narrative prose fiction offering, in a continuous plot, characters and action representing real life. Perhaps you have thought about writing that novel, on and off, for a long time. Does just thinking about it make your heart flutter? It is decision time. Are you going to write it or not? Yes or No?

Again, first, consider whether there is a market. If you decide there is, or that you must write that book anyway because the urge so consumes you, next reflect on the number of words required and how long they will take to write, rewrite and polish.

Lengths

Your tale must be longer than a short story. A novelette is about 7,500–20,000 words; a novella about 20,000 to 60,000. A novel is around 70,000 (children's/young adult) – 110,000 (science fiction), typically 100,000, words. Some novels are longer; first-time novelists seldom tackle them.

Can you cope with your selected length? Full-time established novelists generally yelp with despair if expected to complete a novel in less than one year.

- The adventure of writing a novel is a marathon enterprise - consuming a significant part of your life.

If your answer is yes: you can cope, next consider the genre.

Genre

Figure 9 Examples of genres, titles and authors

Genre	Book Title	Author
Adventure	Life of Pi	*Yann Martel*
Autobiographical	To Sir with Love	*E.R. Braithwaite*
Chick lit	Bridget Jones's Diary	*Helen Fielding*
Crime	Let it Bleed	*Ian Rankin*
Detective	The Lady in the Lake	*Raymond Chandler*
Dystopian	1984	*George Orwell*
Epic	War and Peace	*Leo Tolstoy*
Erotic	Fifty Shades of Grey	*E.L. James*
Fantasy	Gulliver's Travels	*Jonathan Swift*
Feminist	The Women's Room	*Marilyn French*
Gothic	Great Expectations	*Charles Dickens*
Historical	Wolfe Hall	*Hilary Mantel*
Horror	Frankenstein	*Mary Shelley*
Medical	One Flew over the Cuckoo's Nest	*Ken Kesey*
Mystery	And then There Were None	*Agatha Christie*
Romance	The French Lieutenant's Woman	*John Fowles*
Science Fiction	A Fall of Moondust	*Arthur C. Clarke*
Space Opera	The Skylark of Space	*E. E. "Doc" Smith.*
Steampunk	The Land Leviathan	*Michael Moorcock*
Teen./young adult	Swallows and Amazons	*Arthur Ransome*
Thriller	The Tenth Man	*Graham Greene*
Utopian	Island	*Aldous Huxley*
Western	Lonesome Dove	*Larry McMurtry*

Fiction book

Figure 9 contains information about some popular types, an example and its author. Some categories are blurred or a novel may embrace two or more genres. Some listed are subgenres (e.g. Steampunk and Space Opera are both Science Fiction).

Tactics

It is fabled that some distinguished novelists just open their exercise book and write, beginning to end, and, behold: the novel. This chapter will not help those of towering talent. However, for the rest of us, it is reassuring to appreciate that we can learn the craft of novel-writing. This chapter offers some pointers.

<u>Plan</u>

Decide upon your genre. Check that it is selling at present. For example historical novels of the loves and losses of women in Tudor times are presently popular, perhaps following some successful television series, but were virtually unsaleable a decade ago. "Misery memoirs" may have peaked and virtually vanished. This seems analogous to the fashion industry. *Crime, mystery, science fiction, and thriller* are amongst today's best-sellers.

Read widely in that genre. If a UK citizen, you do not have to buy those books but merely to borrow them, or reserve as many as you would like from your local public library. They will obtain them for you. *Project Gutenberg* provides free electronic access to numerous splendid works. The result is crucial background education, convenient and free.

Research as in the research chapter (9). You need sufficient to "prove real": to suspend disbelief. Writing about what you know makes that easier; material and credibility bubble out. For example, if you are in any occupation you have insider knowledge. If in the police, compared with outside, detective novels should be easier to write. If you are a health worker, rather than a patient, medical novels should be easier. If an information technologist, a *digitatus*, proud to be a "techie", rather than a computer Luddite, science fiction involving computers should flow more easily from your fingertips. If your novel is fantasy, familiarity with (strange) creatures and magic is prudent; if science fiction, some authoritative element of science and/or technology.

We know most about ourselves; upon that, each of us is *the* world authority. However, do not make it autobiographical. Dangers include characters recognising themselves, perceived unfavourably, and suing you, limitations in scope and squandering of much fecund material early in a career. But this is a counsel of perfection: famously, first novels tend to have autobiographical content. In one sense all fictional and non-fictional writing is auto-biographical in that we receive sensory perceptions using our bodies, perceive in our brains and communicate messages using our bodies again. All experience must be so channelled and is therefore biased.

Trawl your research to select fertile content. It must have legs; it must go far.

A novel is a major exercise. It is like a short story but with many short story plots fused together, gradually becoming more intense. It requires heavyweight planning. It is so large that it even benefits from a "plan of the plan" in one sentence. Select some sort of "blueprint."

- One example is, "My God," said the Duchess, "I'm pregnant. Who did it?"

In other words, include religion, class, sex and mystery. Construct your plan as a storyboard. Successive scenes form successive chapters. The first often starts with conflict or is, in some fashion, startling. Decide the number of each chapter and its word count. Interweave characters between chapters. Plan aided by cards or a timeline in *Microsoft Excel* template: http://writ.rs/exceltimeline. Introduce main characters in the first third. Craft a shapely path, not "lob-sided" with excessive emphasis on one aspect. Note that the end will be harder to imagine than the beginning.

- Decide the point of view for each chapter. Within each, tell from one particular viewpoint, especially from that of the "key character" (hero or heroine).

Fiction book

Only allow each character to know what (s)he at that time could know. For example, the character "feels" something but can only "suspect" the mindset of another. Other chapters may be from other viewpoints (the protagonists). Perceptions of the situation will change from character to character. If you struggle with this, the word "X ... *felt* that," emphasises that you are in the head of X: a particular individual, and not, say, his or her protagonist.

As you tell twin or multiple tales from different viewpoints, the reader enjoys the delicious pleasure of knowing what a protagonist does not. For example, a bomb ticks under the table ... .

Decide how dense (complex) you wish your plot, or other novelty such as location, to be. Broadly, the more dense, the "shallower" the characters. Perhaps it must be so; otherwise the novelty would be too great to digest. Stories set in the least familiar, and so most emotionally challenging, stretches of the universe may well sport "cardboard characters": good, bad, predictable and/or unchanging; witness the space opera subgenre of science fiction. Stories entangling exquisitely defined characters happen in "cardboard scenery" (such as off-the-shelf grand houses, vicarages); 19th century romantic dramas such as *Jane Eyre* might be so criticised.

Ratchet up tension by "enclosing" in some fashion such as a time scale or limited location (e.g. under moon dust/ocean trapped together in a vehicle, with the oxygen running out). Include unexpected, but, with hindsight, adequately foreseeable, twists and turns. For example, the nature of the Wizard of Oz, and an unlikely, humble player discovering it.

Write a potted biography (including family background, occupation, temperament, politics and religion or lack) to launch each character. Spice up each with an extra helping of personality. Expect each to develop. There should be some sort of development and interaction between your characters and plot. Your characters, whether constructed to be unreservedly adored or viscerally hated or something in between, or mingled, should be different at the end to at the beginning. To expose the physical appearance of a third person narrator,

Winning Words

describe an aspect of another character (e.g. curly hair) and mention that it is like the narrator's. Avoid mirrors and shop-windows unless as a last resort.

Construct your schedule for the dates of completing each chapter. Calculate the average number of words that you must complete daily.

Write that on a poster. Display prominently by your writing station.

<u>Write</u>

Now, at last, start to write. Do your best to *actively* keep fit.

Methodically follow your plot plan.

- If, during your writing, a character bursts from your plot plan and seems to adopt his or her own life, that is wonderful.

Discard the "mechanistic" scaffolding of your plan and tell what the "escaped" character has decided to do. Even more characters may escape and cavort inside your head. Welcome their freedom too.

Remember that today's style is not to tell too much about your characters. Your readers want to develop their take or your characters and their take will differ from yours.

Build some sort of "bridge" between chapters e.g. being at the same place or using the same name, phrase or clause (e.g. "The mist surrounded A. The mist surrounded B . . ..")

"Prove real" by detail, e.g. from commonplace book. For the 100,000 words of your novel, expect to be harvesting, preferably, your commonplace book, or if unavailable, part 2 of this book, a lot.

If more ideas such as for another plot erupt, but you cannot include them, note down on an "unused ideas" pile next to your writing station. That will catch, and not waste, your nuggets; then, you can relax. They may seed your next novel. Tomes,

Fiction book

such as those of *J.R.R. Tolkien*, require entire worlds possessing histories, internal logic, languages and physical "laws" and maps. You would require many nuggets.

Continue writing. Progressively tick off those chapters. If you do not complete sufficient words one day, write more the next and the reverse. As you become more and more engrossed in your project, hopefully you will develop your own momentum.

- Do not edit in detail as progress, just get words down until there are sufficient.

Expect a bumpy ride including despair. Why did you take on such a gargantuan task? *Were you mad?* You are dissatisfied with it. It will flop anyway.

- Motivate yourself. Reflect upon how much time and emotional energy you have *already* invested and ask, "Do I really want to throw that away?"

Write your (sales) blurb for the cover, and post a copy before your eyes. That is what you can – and will – create.

A writers' circle or similar is valuable for mutual understanding and support. Often there is at least one person on your wavelength: bliss. Talk about just one of your characters to another author.

But defer the satisfaction of telling all the details of your tale until after completing. You need every bubble of that energy.

For the moment, it is all yours to hug within you. You are like a plastic bottle of fizzy water: turgid. Taut, if tapped, you thud like a drum and are rigid; you repulse any pretenders wishing to occupy your space. You will go where you want.

However, screw off your top to release the gas and the container relaxes into a floppy unexciting, defenceless, dimpled thing that wobbles. A prod easily deforms you, knocks you off course.

- Finish first draft.

- Revise many times. That process, too, is lengthy. You are honing, polishing, ever improving. This is as crucial a stage in your tale's journey as any. Take courage as the end is in sight.

Show to another

- Until now, only you have seen your novel. Now, take courage and show to another person whom you trust and whose opinion you respect. Follow their advice for any revision even if it requires major painful restructuring.

You have done it.
It represents a significant life task.
Congratulate yourself and
await the praise of others.

Nobody can remove
that achievement from you.

You have *done* what others
merely claim the ability to do.

---

8 Poetry

The magic of poetry

I admire poets. I relish listening at readings. I believe that an appreciation of poetry and knowledge of poets' techniques enrich *all* writing. However, I am not a poet.

Poetry is an art and craft of itself. It plays with the sound, rhythm, arrangement and meaning of words in richly varied ways and to richly varied effect.

Poetry is often an expression of elevated ideas and feelings: high beauty of thought, language or artistic form. Poetry heightens feelings, gives pleasure - and stimulates tears. Poetry ranges from solemn to flippant. Poetry is pure concentrated emotion that reacts with something in the reader.

But something about poetry cannot be defined. Poets need no logic. Contrast that, for example, with a bridge that onlookers describe, shaking their heads in awe, as "frozen poetry"; that required design by a civil engineer and years of study of mathematics, science and technology. Poets do not require the methodical chain of reasoning of (narrative) prose. The poet, as if from nothing, creates a new gestalt that is sublime.

- Poets can reach places that prose writers cannot. Only poets can do this, rather like the *Heineken* advertised in the 1990s.

Moreover, once a reader memorises a poem, (s)he possesses it forever: an incorruptible consumer durable. Given such a good press, what is there not to like? It is no wonder that poetry seems to be of passionate interest to many.

Winning Words

First consider the rhyme or doggerel:

> "Lefty loosie.
> Righty tighty."

The creator presumably started with the practical advice: "Left loose, right tight." That helps when rotating taps and (right-handed threaded) screws. That is, to loosen, turn left (anticlockwise) from the top.

Its creator(s) added the 'y'-sounding syllable to each of the four single-syllable words which carry the meaning of the jingle. The result is a structure of rhythm and sound that appeals to our natural propensity to create, perceive and enjoy patterns, and so to make, "Left loose, right tight', more memorable.

Compare this with "Split Milk" by *W.B. Yeats*:

> "We that have done and thought,
> That have thought and done,
> Must ramble, and thin out
> Like milk spilt on a stone."

To me, only the *Yeats* is wonderful. It has something that the first lacks but I do not know what it is.

In 2013, we "saw" what poetry, compared with prose, does to us; scientists observed brains reading poetry using fMRI (functional magnetic resonance imaging). Poetry appears to stimulate cerebral areas associated with memory – "introspection" – more strongly than areas "lit up" by prose.

- Poems connect, somehow, with *your* memory.

If you think that something is a poem, it is a poem *for you*. It may make your spine tingle or your hand pause - or cut - while shaving.

All that does not help you write poetry.

There are many would-be poets but few "mass-market" outlets for poetry. To re-emphasise advice from Chapter 1:

Poetry

- research whether you, realistically, have a market.

For poetry, research with particularly brutal honesty, your investigational muscles on steroids. The word on the street is that nobody, or almost nobody, earns their bread in Britain solely by writing poetry. However, my hunch is that you do not want to write poetry to earn your bread.

> I suspect that you want to write poetry because you love it so much. There is always the *hope* of mainstream publication and fame.

It is, however, certain that you will not attain those goals if you do not try. For many poets, most income is not from publication but ongoing subsidiary rights (quotation, broadcasting etc). Put differently, your few words earn while you sleep: always pleasing.

Favourite poems

Aged eleven, about fifteen miles from *Shakespeare*'s birthplace, at my grammar school, our gowned headmaster taught us for just one lesson a week. Homework was learning a psalm by heart for regurgitation the following week: enough to infuse hatred for poetry into any boy. But it did not. Some of my dearest poems have an ecclesiastical flavour. Witness the power, while standing, mired in mud churned by chill rain, next to the open grave as the vicar proclaims in the English burial service from the 1662 version of the *Book of Common Prayer*:

> "earth to earth,
> ashes to ashes,
> dust to dust."

This may not feature in poetry books but it offers rhythm and a serious (indeed, grave) situation.

Winning Words

More cheerfully, *William Wordsworth* uplifts with:

> "I wandered lonely as a cloud
> That floats on high o'er vales and hills,
> When all at once I saw a crowd,
> A host of golden daffodils;
> Beside the lake, beneath the trees,
> Fluttering and dancing in the breeze."

I also understand why *Xu Zhimo's* poem, "Taking Leave of Cambridge Again," is beloved in China. The first verse, translated into English by Guohua Chen, becomes:

> "Softly I am leaving,
> Just as softly as I came;
> I softly wave goodbye
> To the clouds in the western sky."

It is as well-known as *Wordsworth's* "Daffodils" in Britain.

Characteristics of poetry

Arguably, if you must ask what a poem is, you probably will not understand the answer. Any definition has very fuzzy edges.

However, poetry offers some, or all, of:

- rhythm,
- "feet",
- rhyme,
- alliteration,
- consonance,
- form,
- specific visual appearance,
- metaphor,
- simile,
- structure,
- metonymy,
- allegory and
- vivid language.

Poetry

In English, *rhythm* is the pattern of stressed or unstressed or syllables in a line. This is particularly evident when read aloud. Figure 10 displays five types:

Figure 10 Meter (pattern) in poetry

Name	Emphasis	Example
iambic	unstressed / stressed	desCRIBE
trochee	stressed / unstressed	FLOWer
spondee	stressed / stressed	HOMEWORK
anapest	unstressed / unstressed / stressed	Un-der-STAND
dactyl	stressed / unstressed / unstressed	SYLL-a-ble

(The iamb feels the most natural.) Next consider how often that stress occurs in a line or other naturally spoken unit. That is the number of "feet" between "// s" as content in Figure 11 illustrates.

Figure 11 "Feet" in poetry

Number	Name	Writer	Example
1	monometer	(1970s slogan) *Milk Marketing Board UK*	DRINKa PINTa MILKa DAY
2	dimeter	*Hood*	TAKE her up // TENDerly
3	trimeter	*Coleridge*	When HERE // the SPRING // we SEE
4	tetrameter	Nursery rhyme *(Anon)*	PETER, //PETER, //PUMPkin, //EATER.

Rhyme consists of identical or similar sounding words (e.g. rhyme, rime, chime, time) at the end of lines or other predictable intervals. For example, words A and *A* that rhyme and words B and *B* that rhyme, may occur as in Figure 12.

Figure 12 Order of rhyming words

Line number	Rhyming word	Example
1	A	apple
2	B	tree
3	*A*	*dapple*
4	*B*	*spree*

To some people, an offering is only a poem if it rhymes. That is as uninformed as thinking that a scientist is only a scientist if (s)he wears a white coat.

Alliteration is the repetition of letters or their sounds at the start of at least two words that are next to, or near to, each other. An example is, "The parrot perched on the pirate."

Consonance is the repetition of a consonant (not a vowel), somewhere in a word, throughout a sentence. An example at the end of words is "slither and lather."

Structure is another characteristic of poetry. A small component is the line. A "stanza" is the paragraph; two lines are a "couplet"; three, a "triplet"; four, a "quatrain." A number of stanzas become a "canto."

The image *"form"*, such as the juxtapositions of lines on the page in relation to the white space, is important to some Modernist poets. The substantial amount of white space around the words matters. Some classical Chinese art requires not only a poem, inscribed using "word picture", skilfully brushed, characters: the calligraphy (logograms, not Graeco-Roman letters) - but also a painting. You have seen those scenes, often featuring mountains and willow trees of heart-melting beauty.

Poetry

A *metaphor* is an analogy that some aspect of something is something else, e.g. *Shakespeare*'s "All the world's a stage." This is one origin of one well-accepted sociological perspective: *Goffman's* dramaturgical. Everyday life is interpreted as theatre; actors play specific roles, front and back stage and so on. Metaphor does not use the words "as" or "like."

A *simile* uses the words "as" or "like" about a common feature e.g. "as busy as a bee." A simile is so direct that it (metaphorically) hits you over the head.

A *metonym* calls something not by its own name but by something associated with it. The part is a symbol of the whole. Examples are "sword" for military might, "pen" for "written word" or an image of a wheelchair representing all disabled people. Another illustration is a hairdresser using the trading name: "Snip." Around the 17th century in England, "barber surgeons" combined both roles.

An *allegory* has hidden meaning and features humans such as "Piers Plowman" by *William Langland*. That mediaeval tale is about a man's quest for a moral life and a social satire. It includes dreams and details the lives of "Dowel", "Dobet", and "Dobest" standing for the notions of Do Well, Do Better, and Do Best, respectively.

Vivid imagery paints a powerful picture in the reader's mind. An example is chalk scraping a blackboard.

Categories of poem

Different cultures favour different layouts of poetry. I outline the main forms, with emphasis on the English-speaking world.

Fable
This is a succinct moral tale with ancient origins often featuring animals. Think *Aesop's fables*. One is "Belling the Cat" that ends:

> "The mice looked at one another and nobody spoke. Then the old mouse said: 'It is easy to propose impossible remedies.'"

Winning Words

Haiku
The formal rules of this Japanese form include: five syllables on the first line, seven on the second and five on the last. There is debate about whether exact numbers are essential in English. It should reference time and nature but seldom contain a title. Emphasis changes at the end of the second line. It is intensely image-based and contains a Zen or "aha" moment. *Buson* constructed:

> "a mosquito buzzes
> every time flowers
> of honeysuckle fall"

Light
This is short, personal, contemplative and often humorous. For example, *Wendy Cope* in *Waste Land Limericks*, her parody of *The Waste Land* by *T.S. Eliot*, includes:

> "A typist is laid,
> A record is played –"

Lyric
These convey personal, often emotional feelings in the present tense. An elegy is a sub-category that is mournful or mysterious. For example *Emily Dickinson* writing from a viewpoint of fearing that she is going insane, starts:

> "I felt a Funeral, in my Brain,
> And Mourners to and fro
> Kept treading - treading - till it seemed
> That Sense was breaking through -
> And when they all were seated,
> A Service, like a
> Drum - Kept beating - beating - till I thought
> My Mind was going numb -"

Narrative
This tells a story. For example, *Robert Burns* weaves a tale including drunkenness, a church, witches, warlocks and a chase, ending:

Poetry

"Whene'er to Drink you are inclin'd,
Or Cutty-sarks rin in your mind,
Think ye may buy the joys o'er dear;
Remember Tam o' Shanter's mare."

The epic is a species of narrative. Think *Homer*'s Iliad. Epics are seldom written today. A rare (but Nobel-prize-winning) exception is "Omeros" (1990) by *Derek Walcott*.

Ode
This has, generally, a serious subject, unlike Lurcio's (Frankie Howerd's) introduction in the British TV series "Up Pompeii!!". Think *Horace*. This extract is from *Ben Jonson*:

> "It is not growing like a tree
> In bulk, doth make man better be;
> Or standing long an Oak, three hundred year,
> To fall a log at last, dry, bald, and sere."

Prose poem
This mingles prose and poetry and is a "short short story", "flash fiction" or "microstory" containing, perhaps, 200 words. They are telegraphic but contain the elements of stories including protagonists. *Oscar Wilde*, well within the comfort zone of his classical education including Greek mythology, ends "The Disciple":

> "And the pool answered, 'But I loved Narcissus because, as he lay on my banks and looked down at me, in the mirror of his eyes I saw ever my own beauty mirrored.'"

Satire
John Dryden, the first poet laureate, satirised a protestant. *Jonathan Swift* offered *A Satirical Elegy on the Death of a Late Famous General*:

> "His Grace! impossible! what dead!
> Of old age too, and in his bed!
> And could that mighty warrior fall?
> And so inglorious, after all!"

Winning Words

Sonnet
This has 14 lines. The first four introduce, the second elaborates. A problem occurs in the third; the ending is a twist or afterthought. A Shakespearian sequence is *a-b-a-b, c-d-c-d, e-f-e-f, g-g*. Typically they address love and offer vivid imagery. Famously, Shakespeare wrote:

> "Shall I compare thee to a summer's day?
> Thou art more lovely and more temperate:
> Rough winds do shake the darling buds of May,
> And summer's lease hath all too short a date:
> Sometime too hot the eye of heaven shines,
> And often is his gold complexion dimm'd;
> And every fair from fair sometime declines,
> By chance or nature's changing course untrimm'd;
> But thy eternal summer shall not fade
> Nor lose possession of that fair thou owest;
> Nor shall Death brag thou wander'st in his shade,
> When in eternal lines to time thou growest:
> So long as men can breathe or eyes can see,
> So long lives this, and this gives life to thee."

Note the fertility of just one transplanted phrase "darling buds of May." It became a novel (*H.E. Bates*), a British Television series and a rock album.

Speculative

These are beyond reality. They include horror fiction and the extrapolation of science fiction. For example, *Edgar Allan Poe* offered *The City In the Sea*, ending:

> "There shrines and palaces and towers
> (Time-eaten towers that tremble not!)
> Resemble nothing that is ours.
> Around, by lifting winds forgot,
> Resignedly beneath the sky
> The melancholy waters lie."

Poetry

Tips on writing poetry

I do not know whether, for the poet of genius, the words just appear. *Keats* first drafted, "A thing of beauty is a lasting joy", but then crossed out and redrafted to, "A thing of beauty is a joy forever." All the rest of us can do is to try to say something that will connect with something within readers.

- Capitalise upon the abilities of your computer. Do you need a word to rhyme or find synonyms or antonyms? Many are there, instantly, on the web. Do you need some help in fitting syllables into a formal pattern?

Construct a master diagram with cells. For example, Figure 13 is for the syllables' (5-7-5) of haiku:

Figure 13 Haiku template

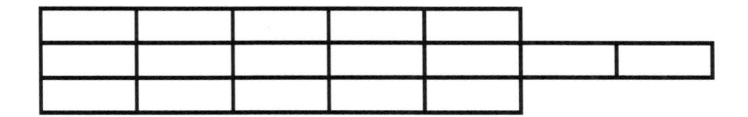

Just populate it with individual syllables of words.

Many resources are available on the web such as worksheets and templates.

Use them. *Shakespeare* only knew spiders' webs.

> *Shakespeare* had no web;
> you have, in sage surging droves:
> see where they pasture.

Winning Words

The general advice on all writing applies to poetry.

But particularly pertinent are:

- You must have *something to say*.
- Poetry has forms and techniques. They need *practice* to gain fluency.
- Study specialist book(s) and/or a poetry course.
- Read widely.
- Make every word count, and be the best possible word.
- Plunder your commonplace book especially for the *vivid*.
- Use the most powerful tense.
- Read it aloud. Your whole body can sense the meter.
- Focus on patterns.

Poets attempt to see novel patterns in English language. This is so basic that sometimes they forget. My take on patterns may surprise, and, hopefully, help you.

- Scientists also quest patterns.

Scientists love patterns and are tuned to being alert to their absence, or anomalies. The Russian chemist *Mendeleev*, for example, saw periodicities akin to musical chords in the characteristics of elements. For generations, the Periodic Table has been an icon of scholarship.

That is a part of "normal science" comprising well-accepted patterns. But very occasionally, so many anomalies accumulate that viewpoint must be changed: a "paradigm shift," using the phrase of *Thomas Kuhn*. Scientists crave and fear that exhilarating time of "revolutionary science" when a new viewpoint emerges with new patterns.

Examples are *Copernicus* with the Earth no longer being the centre of the universe, *Darwin* with natural selection and *Einstein* with matter and energy being interchangeable and everything affecting everything else (relativity). Even plodding chemical manufacturing, where materials are synthesised,

Poetry

depends on adequate control of the process. If out of control, something different is born. That might not rivet you. But it might offer grist for your literary mill, if you look with writterly eyes informed by, for example, *Shelley*'s "Frankenstein."

Open your eyes to the patterns that science offers, such as the fractals of snowflakes, smells of compounds or naturally occurring rhythms such as waves, interference patterns or a drop falling into liquid in slow-motion. Some experimental poets inspire, creating six lines with respective syllable counts of (0)/1/1/2/3/5/8: the (mathematical) *Fibonacci* sequence. That also measures beautiful patterns in nature; witness, for example, flower petals.

Another example is the balls on different lengths of string forming and reforming beautiful shapes over time. One illustration is the sinuous waves witnessed since around the year 1867. *Ernst Mach*, when Professor of Experimental Physics at (now) Charles University, Prague demonstrated how they repeated. Key "pendulum waves" and "Harvard" into *You Tube* and marvel.

- Look at some mathematics, science and technology (such as the provocations in this commonplace book).

Poets seldom search there so low-hanging fruit may await your discovery.

One justification for this chapter's length is the usefulness of poets' techniques outside poetry.

> Do not lock poets' techniques away in a box marked "poetry." Some will wonderfully enliven prose: fiction or non-fiction.

9 Research for writers

Research means search, search again, and continue. Favour sources that are up-to-date, written or approved by experts, accurate and unbiased. Check that more than one person holds a particular opinion especially if the topic is controversial. Published writers, by nature, are controversial. They stick their heads above the parapet. Each says, "This is me and this is what I think."

For mastery of a subject at full professional level 10,000 hours of practice is the accepted norm. That does not mean just doing the same thing repeatedly, without correcting mistakes. It demands reflecting upon the topic and trying to improve. It equates roughly with registration as a learned professional such as in law, medicine or the church or with study to doctoral level. That level is desirable if writing for fellow experts in that field. Even then, the individual is only expert in the one area and may be clueless about anything else; e.g. (s)he may suffer a noisy laptop; upturning exposes the safety pin catching the fan.

Fortunately, the research that writers for non-academic markets require seldom needs the depth required for the academic market. Generally the writer only requires sufficient research for the particular piece written for its intended market. For example, consider foxgloves. A gardening magazine, interested in their cultivation in borders, and a journal about phytochemistry (the chemistry of plants) demanding details about glycosides (foxgloves' medicinally active ingredients), require different sorts of research.

What the writer does need is a jackdaw mind, to *notice* things about the topic. (S)he is like a crunched up ball of self-adhesive tape that ideas stick to that would fall off non-writers. Sensitise yourself for that golden thread, that gossamer-light filament of information that could so easily float away and be lost. Make it stick to you. You will recognise it. You will weave it into a yarn

Research for writers

that will fascinate your readers. You may unearth the information in a tiny footnote in a desiccated academic tome that you struggle to read. So:

> encourage serendipity.

Where will you get information?

Information is of three types: primary, secondary and tertiary.

Primary data

These are the original source, and, for some purposes, the gold standard. Examples are:

> aircraft "black box" after accident,
> artefact in a museum,
> autobiographies,
> centuries-old book within university rare books collection,
> *commonplace book* entry of your personal experience,
> correspondence,
> diary,
> documents from your past (including prints from chemical films collected in photo-albums or digital images on your computer, interviews),
> letters,
> meeting minutes,
> patents (Intellectual Property Office [IPO] for the UK),
> personal records e.g. marriage, birth, death certificates,
> *pan for gold* in your loft or attic.
> pottery shards with drawings from antiquity,
> printout of instrument readings,
> scientific paper presenting new scientific evidence,
> tattoos decorating living human flesh,
> travel to visit the place (e.g. compare Icelandic sagas with the landscape where they are fabled to have occurred) or
> your personal experience, i.e. memory.

Interviews and correspondence with experts electronically, is "free" and important. You have access globally. In my experience, academics, in particular, are happy to advise you and may, unsolicited, offer angles that had not occurred to you.

Secondary data

These are interpretation "one step removed". Examples are:

> article about a location, that "panoramic" photographic pull-outs illustrate, in the *National Geographic* magazine,
> biographies,
> review articles in scholarly publications or
> plaque near museum exhibit.

Tertiary data

These are a high level *over*view. Examples are:

> encyclopaedia,
> dictionary,
> textbook or
> *Wikipedia*.

Classifications are somewhat flexible. They vary somewhat between fields.

Internet search may trawl all three levels. For example, studying an original (unedited) documentary film reproducing a political speech on *You Tube* would be primary, an opinion piece in a respected magazine, secondary and a sentence in a textbook a generation later, tertiary, data.

Keeping records

Before you forget your new information or your memory is corrupted, note down or audio-record your finding. Remember to include details of the source.

One recording method is to use sheets of card. You can sort them.

An alternative is computer software, even something as simple as "sticky notes" for your desktop, or noting information in a *single* file for a particular topic. You may then search that file by key words. Next, copy and paste *all* your *single* files into just *one* master information file (with at least one back-up copy).

- *All* your textual data then become fully searchable. Just insert the required word into the "find" function.

This would have appeared as magic to a writer, struggling with for, example, cards, scrap books, scissors and glue, before our computer age. See *Clarke's* Third "Law" in the Technology section of part two. Humans, today, stand on the shoulders of their giant silicon cousins. Humans include every other writer: your competitors. That raises the bar of expectation.

Tips on where to find information

> Read a text book, even one for children. Text books distil the crudest, propaganda-permeated, information. Witness differences in school history textbooks approved in different countries.
> But do not, necessarily, reject those tertiary data.
> Reading a textbook is often a good start.
> That textbook has done much of the
> hard work of summarising, distilling.

That saves time. Your plunge, deep into a topic, becomes easier. You are less likely to "drown" in a topic that was so inaccessible that you become dispirited and give up.

However, a textbook will present the accepted view and may blind you to a view that is uniquely yours: novel. Others may not perceive that view until you, the writer, signpost it for them.

Winning Words

Capitalise upon the "free" services of your local public libraries and professionally qualified employed ("proper") librarians.

They can obtain public reference copies from the British lending library or elsewhere for you, for a fee. You may be able to pay to join your local university library with its specialist network.

- Use the web. You can go far by using search engines such as *Google,* especially if you include *Google Scholar* or *Image*. Pictures may nudge, or even jolt, you in ways that words cannot.

It pains me as a writer to admit that. *You Tube* also contains original material. Even brilliantly-illustrated text can seldom compete with moving images and sound for demonstrating "Do it yourself techniques," for example.

Do not limit yourself to sight and sound. Capitalise also on taste, smell and touch. For example, explore a traditional market; it surrounds you, gushing data. Ferret out museum or art gallery exhibits that permit close approach; smell may connect you with some gloriously pertinent memory buried in your personal past, instantly.

Professional bodies offer access to authoritative material in their specialist areas. Membership of those bodies is restricted to their professionals and requires a fee. However, they may offer free help to lay people. Such institutions may facilitate contacting experts, including internationally: a one stop shop. But remember their propaganda function. They are biased.

- Contact an "amateur" society in the field, especially if local. It may be worth joining. Alternatively, they may be happy to assist you as a non-member. Many have an outreach educational function, especially if they are charities; their members often enthusiastically assist your writing. Members might even become a market.

Purchase hard-copy books from on-line retailers. They are inexpensive, especially if second-hand. Alternatively, download

Research for writers

e-versions. Many classical luminary works, including some out of print, are downloadable, free, from *Project Gutenberg*.

Consider "dusty sources" such as journal articles, manuscripts and microfiche. Following digitalisation, hard copies in libraries are becoming less important. Rooting around in the dusty stack of an academic library of fond memory is, today, seldom required. But you might examine private papers previously only seen by family members: an immense privilege.

Go there. Today, long haul travel (even with extra taxes and so on) can be comparatively inexpensive; to previous generations it was expensive, time consuming and difficult. Presence is incomparably superior to any secondary or tertiary sources. Being there exposes all of your senses. Make the most of personal two-way interactions and networking opportunities.

> Do not be "snooty" about tourist guide commentary. The least able possesses many times your local knowledge: potential gold.

Consult the fountainhead. Contact *the* expert. Luminary figures may still live and be happy to talk to you. Telephone the individual. Go to see him/her. Interviewees often appreciate some gift as a token of your respect and appreciation. If you wish to record, first ask permission. Recording and not recording have implications. For example, recording protects you from accusations of misrepresentation but your interviewee may say less.

- Research can be one of the most enjoyable parts of writing.

So enjoy immersing yourself in your topic.

- Find that novel perspective: the one that bites your editor on the nose.

Winning Words

10 Introduction to the data bank of provocation

This chapter introduces part two of this book. It outlines how constructed, what it is and is not and, above all, how to use.

People love collecting things. My data bank was collected from four sources:

- my commonplace book,
- my sociological journal,
- maxims for successful journalism and
- *Google's* "big data" top ten *zeitgeist* headings.

> Most telling for understanding my data bank are centuries-old *cabinets of curiosities*: the bizarre with a flavour of *Barnum*'s freak show.
>
> A good cabinet gathered an eclectic collection.

Ideally it would include: astounding plants and stuffed animals such as the mythical beast of a crocodile, a foetus with two heads, startling rocks and gems, tribal artefacts and sculpture.

1 Personal commonplace book

Commonplace books collect the unusual, even quirky and the ... well ... notable. They include quotations, reports of happenings especially emotional, proverbs, interactions, sayings and observations. They may have a flavour of scrap books, thesauri, Christmas miscellanies, (web) blogs, *Brewer's*

Introduction to the data bank of provocation

crusty *Dictionary of Phrase and Fable*, travelogues, *vignettes* and intimate diaries.

They have a long history from 15th century England. *John Milton* and *Francis Bacon* are famed early recorders. Universities such as Harvard and Yale have promoted commonplace books as reflexive aids to an individual's educational journey. In 1949, *W. Somerset Maugham*, who trained (starting in 1892) as a medical practitioner but became a literary man, as inspiration to stimulate those who were short of it, offered "A Writer's Notebook." Character *vignettes*, plots and musing were included.

Authors often value their notebooks so highly that they view them as almost sacred objects with magical powers: talismans.
That may be because, repeatedly, they unplug writer's block.

A few apt words trawled from their depths can sprinkle star dust on an otherwise pedestrian offering.

They confer subtle power like a rare spice.

Your piece leap-frogs from the waste bin into the editor's acceptance pile.

Commonplace book writers are not alone in such adoration. Ethnographers, after years in the field in a strange society, often view their field notes, taken in the field but still at their fingertips, with reverent, almost religious, awe.

It is important to understand their reason. Their notes are a *thing*, physical evidence of their impressions, their abstract thoughts. They record what shocked them, what made their eyeballs bulge. The shock of the new is anthropologists' stock-

Winning Words

in-trade. Without it, they cannot observe. Or, as *Arthur Conan Doyle* made Sherlock Holmes say to Dr Watson:

- "You see, but you do not observe. The distinction is clear."

Anthropologists and detectives need *observation*. So do all artists and scientists - although they observe through disparate prisms. The writer who cannot observe is paralysed. Arguably, commonplace book writers need observation most of all. Their very name suggests why. They take the *commonplace*, the ordinary, that anybody can see, and transmogrify it into the extraordinary, the strange.

> Your reader thinks,
> "I never would have thought of that!" or,
> "Yes, it's *just* like that for me. Another person feels the same way! I am not alone."

However, today, commonplace books are seldom published. One in the public domain is from personal statements by members of *Alcoholics Anonymous* recovering from their habit. They learned from others; it was a motivational aid. (See: *Trysh Travis*. Handles to Hang on to Our Sobriety: Commonplace Books and Surrendered Masculinity in Alcoholics Anonymous *Men and Masculinities, October 2009; vol. 12, 2: pp. 175-200, first published on 7 May 2008. Travis* is a feminist sociologist.)

I wrote my personal commonplace book over four decades in 42 countries. If nothing else, it covers wider travel than those of the wealthy 19th century gentlemen (mainly) who undertook their grand tours and returned with commonplace books of sites that were expected to improve them. Our planet has shrunk: today, many workers and holidaymakers travel intercontinentaly.

Roget, in 1852, arranged his thesaurus in a way that reflected the knowledge and thinking of his day. He offered a "tree" of six areas (abstract, space, matter, intellect, volition and affections)

Introduction to the data bank of provocation

branching into over a thousand "branches." His contemporaries thought his arrangement utterly obvious.

Today, the size of knowledge has exploded. We live in a global world with more mingling of radically different ideas. Rather than existing rigid divisions, they have mingled and recombined in all manner of novel ways. The very continents and our perceptions shift. The very architecture of our knowledge may be sliced, split and re-mingled in countless ways. (See *Foucault* in Chapter Two.)

- I have melded, split, and offered some categories that I felt *modern* writers would find most useful.

You will not find "writerly" headings such as "the human condition." Arguably, that would embrace most entries.

- Instead, it is analysed into bite sized chunks (e.g. class and status, location inside, love people, sex and viewpoint) that you can extract as required.

My commonplace book has flaws. I wrote it with an eye for what I might use to provoke my writing. As explained shortly, to maintain anonymity, I excluded much from this data bank. Despite that censorship, part two of the book in your hand or computer does retain many of my cabinet of curiosity's most useful bits for writers: *the best bits*.

Note that my commonplace book spans four decades. During that time, attitudes, public mores and behaviour have changed significantly. It is unfair, even cruel, to judge the behaviour or an attitude of an individual of four decades ago against the norms of today.

Occasionally, when essential, I include a year. One example is the buying power, today, of an amount of cash. Another is the context of a particular attitude, such as towards "children outside wedlock," that, like that phrase, may seem dated to modern British eyes.

Books, newspapers, magazines and journals, from popular to learned, informed my commonplace book. A minor source was notions, characters, locations and so on from films and plays. They were fiction. The interpretation from seeing to observing was my take on those dramas. However, my reporting of that take was non-fiction.

2   Sociological Journal

Another source is my personal Sociological Journal (1995–2013). It includes references on technical matters such as class, status and culture. I have used my sociological imagination particularly informed by papers in *Sociology*.

I trawled my sociological journal for particular takes on customs and so on for non-fiction articles. I discovered that, after developing a particular viewpoint on one field, I could apply that viewpoint to another. Put differently, if you had published copy, after reworking and rethinking, it would fit elsewhere. Indeed, that second version may be enhanced.

> More than one payment for each piece of writterly sweat appeals to writers.

Plagiarism *of your own work* is, presumably, impossible.

3   Accepted journalistic maxims

Formulae for profitable writing were borne-in-mind, notably:

- The three Ls ("lust, loathing and lucre"),

- The plan-of-a-plan "blueprint" (see "Fiction Book" chapter): "My God, said the duchess, I'm pregnant. Who did it?" (i.e. religion, class, sex, mystery) and

- "If it bleeds, let it lead" (a news media maxim).

Introduction to the data bank of provocation

4 Google big data zeitgeist

The big data *Google* 2013 zeitgeist of the top ten web searches were also born in mind during analysis. Even if not attached to any scientific or other theory or intellectual crutch, *Google's* numbers are so gargantuan that they must carry some validity.

I am aware, however, that numbers alone are insufficient to compile a list of useful headings for writers. Numbers alone may tell us nothing about meanings or purposes and may mislead.

I omitted any top ten search result headings where they appeared not evident from my data base excluding *Google*. One reason is that, under those headings, I could not offer personal entries useful to writers.

Of course if you insert a search term of your choice, into a web search engine, much is available, "instantly" and "free." For example, try the word "inspiration." I have just recorded 173 *million* hits. That is too many for writers on deadlines. Adding modifiers (e.g. Boolean function) will cull the number to a more digestible total. Put "term(s)" between speech marks "....". If wish to exclude from a specific area add "-" before term(s).

Remember the power to search seeking images and not words. Images may be easier to scan and inspire more.

Maps and satellite images will spirit you across the planet at a click. Even walking down streets is an instant possibility.

So is plugging into snapshots of ordinary folk that their minds have processed, viewing from space the *aurora borealis* encircling the pole, like a crown flaunting diamonds spiting multicoloured fire, a myriad writers' blogs, *Wikipedia,* viewing a site on Mars, constructive mutual criticism in a writers' circle forum or a newborn baby crying.

You may even look back, in wonder, to the universe when it was young: 14 billion years ago.

Winning Words

> An earlier generation might well have thought such sights magic.

It is easy to feel weighed down by the instant gratification of such riches. What is there left to say? Why bother to write anything? Instead, think of web resources as giant shoulders. Stand on them and you *see* further.

- It is your subjective, writerly *observation*, of those sights, your take of them, that you can offer. That is your contribution. It is unique.

What the databank is

I scrutinised all four of those data archives. "Fresh" eyes searched, ever and again, for categories of *practical use* to modern writers; that is, the eyes were "writerly." I used elements of the "grounded theory" approach, a well-accepted, qualitative social scientific research method. Just 55 categorisations emerged from the data.

> I was most impressed and humbled by the simple powerful vivid language of ordinary folk.

I have respected their anonymity by making them unidentifiable. I used techniques for anonymity, standard and well-accepted in sociology. They include omission (or jumbling) of dates, names (where used these may be changed), gender change, and fact and fiction are intertwined in that an entry ("fact") might refer to an arresting figment of fiction from a film, for example. Phrases used may be modified to others of the same meaning.

Depending upon background and education, individuals will extract different understandings from the same data.

Introduction to the data bank of provocation

Remember that I was a sociologist. I emphasised, for example, sociology instead of psychology.

I was *also* educated as a natural scientist: an unusual combination. It is pertinent, today, given the prominence of science and technology in our lives, and the commercial success of science (based) fiction.

Further, until recent retirement, I was a pharmacist: a health professional. I benefited from "insider" knowledge, special interest in professional status and so on. My resulting interpretation, *as that combination*, provides a most unusual, possibly even a unique, "take."

The resulting data bank is idiosyncratic and quirky. Remember those cabinets of curiosities. They tend towards "the most" of this of or that. There lies their power.

- I hope that this data bank will provoke – *goad* – *your* creativity.

What the data bank is not

I would expect, say, an academic, with a life-long focus on English literature, to trawl a different catch.

However, some of the entries in my commonplace book seemed (to me) so splendid that they embodied their individual "stamps of excellence," although I had not noted original sources. I discovered those later. To my embarrassment, they included many d̲ead w̲hite E̲uropean m̲ale (DWEM) luminaries of literature and other intelligencia.

Some sociologists rail against quotations from dominant figures. They exert a sort of power and control: a dead hand, like an ancient treaty binding nations, that overrules the wishes of the living. In defence, I know little about English literature; I noted the quotations *because* they seemed so powerful. They gushed "stand alone" excellence without their authors' names. However, readers should be alert to my re-uniting the quotes and famous names. Guard against feeling that they *must* help writers *because*, a famous literary, or other luminary, wrote them. Ratchet up your cynicism if literati say a quote is wonderful and expect the reader to agree. Those earning their bread by knowing about "literature" would say that (to misquote *Mandy Rice-Davies*). They protect their turf. Maybe famous names encourage us to place the quotes on *too* high a pedestal. I indexed them, in part, because readers expected it.

> My cabinet of curiosities does *not* reproduce the accepted literary canon that is claimed to be "good for you": the aspiring writer.

Surprises

They included:

War
This section seemed long. However, I was born just two weeks before the Japanese surrendered in World War 2, so have never been conscious of war on British mainland soil. My experience has been of peace, even if a fearful nuclear-tipped one. So all the rest of the data bank is about peace.

Courage
Courage is an important theme for writers. However, that section is small. That is because I have no personal experience of the physical courage required for, say, armed conflict. The courage I admire in others would be impossible to keep anonymous if written down. During my professional life, I was privileged to meet many patients; the courage of some would be unethical to report. They might be identified, and distress result to them and/or family members.

Specific headings

Some categories offer particularly succulent grist for writers' mills.

Behaviour.
Human perception, according to *William James*, an early psychologist, seems a "humming buzzing confusion." Human perception and behaviour are connected. Writers feast upon

Introduction to the data bank of provocation

them. Humans offer many views about why they behave. One debate is the importance of:

- nature (such as inherited: cannot be changed) *v.s.*
- nurture (absorption of a particular culture that is passed down generations).

Behavioural biologists, psychologists, sociologists and theologians of many faiths offer many accounts. They are confident but disparate.

But, for writers of fiction and non-fiction, *one* framework, simple enough for everyone to understand, for coming to terms with behaviour is a boon. I find the sociologist *Max Weber* offers the most *useful* framework. He (Weber M. *Wirtschaft und Gesellschaft*. 4th ed. Tübingen [original German 1922] 1956:1: 1-14) proclaims that there are only four reasons for human behaviour:

> 1. Self-interest (egotism). You behave because it is in your personal interests. This is the most common.
>
> 2. Altruism: interest in another. Rare; e.g. charitable giving is only altruistic if anonymous. An identifiable giver benefits from increased status so is egotistic.
>
> 3. Tradition: habit ... "enormous flywheel of society" (*James* again). You behave as you have always behaved.
>
> 4. Affectivity: you just like it, such as putting sugar in your tea; you have a "sweet tooth."

They seem to cover everything. I have yet to find a behaviour that those four omitted.

Children and generations

These help fix youthful impressions in the mind and on paper. They may be particularly valuable to those who have taken the "grand tour" of child to parent to grandparent. Such entries refresh memory of the fires of youth before too many frailties of body, mind or external circumstance degrade writing ability.

Class and status

This section is deliciously fruitful for writers.

Famously, the British are exquisitely sensitive to class issues. Class is *material*. How wealthy are you? How fat is your wallet? How much is your property portfolio worth?

Status (prestige) is *symbolic*. You gain status in two ways. One is *conspicuous consumption* of your wealth. So class and status tangle together. For example:

- How many hundred acres constitute the landscaped parkland surrounding your mansion?

But consumption must be *stylish* and not "naff" or "kitsch".

The second way is that things other than spending wealth also confer prestige. An individual may also receive honour directly. Illustrations are answers to:

- Was there a RAF flypast at your wedding?
- How highly do others regard you?
- Do others think you are beautiful?
- Are you a model/film star?
- Have you published anything?
- Are you a graduate?
- Can you waggle your ears?

Occupations form the broad base for many modern official socioeconomic classifications. Higher professionals (such as medical practitioners) are at the top. "Super professionals" also exist: the elite within their elite group such as judges amongst

Introduction to the data bank of provocation
barristers. Layers underneath include routine occupations down to the long-tem unemployed.

One recent system ranks:

- the elite,
- established middle class,
- technical middle class,
- new affluent workers,
- traditional working class,
- emergent service sector and
- the precariat.

(See Savage M, Devine F, Cunningham N, Taylor M, Yaojun L, Hjellbrekke J, Le Roux B, Friedman S, Miles A. A New Model of Social Class? Findings from the BBC's Great British Class Survey Experiment. *Sociology* 2013 47(2): 219-250.)

Curious to discover your place?
Take the short test on:
www.bbc.co.uk/news/magazine-22000973.

Fascinating grist is whether, today, groups are more mobile or rigid compared with feudal times. Then, groups knew their place (squire, labourer and so on). Some historians think that your status position remains dependent on our ancestors of three centuries ago. The "real power" in Western societies, at least, remains with "old money."

Smell
- A smell data-bank is valuable if the writer wishes to enliven by describing at least three senses.

Interestingly, smell and taste are chemical senses. Actual molecules are essential for nerves to fire. You cannot taste without a sense of smell; they interconnect. Food and drink offer numerous examples of chemical senses, aflame.

Many animals possess senses that humans lack (e.g. echo-location in bats and dolphins; magnetic in sharks). Some philosophers argue that, *in principle*, because that impression must be filtered through human bodily and intellectual apparatus, humans cannot understand *what it is like to be* those animals. That may matter for possible contact with (extra-terrestrial) aliens.

It may in principle be impossible to write, meaningfully, about such senses that protagonists enjoy or curse. For example, powerful magnets may "blind" a shark. But if *you* could *carve* a way, you would, truly, be writing something novel.

Technology
Technology is particularly interesting when it speaks of change. An example is a candle and stick telephone that was once the cutting edge compared with a modern smart phone.

- The same individuals live through, and must adapt to, a torrent of novelty.

Machines now have their own intelligence that can surpass human intelligence in some fashions. For example, a comparatively simple computer, possessing the brute power to compare all past known chess moves with many possible moves ahead, can outwit humankind's best chess grand masters.

Moreover, the computer is improving while humankind is not. Computers are increasingly interconnected, co-operative in their gigantic web. I find those perspectives awesome.

Introduction to the data bank of provocation

How to use Part Two of this book

- Do you wish a light read? Just browse and enjoy.

For serious study:

> - Decide which heading in the "List of Contents" is closest to your present focus, concern or suspected area of writers' block.
>
> - Go to that heading.
>
> - Items listed below are your help list.
>
> - Dip in.
>
> - See what emerges.

For example, you may have characters with particular appearance, behaviour, nationality, age, status, class position and viewpoints in locations. They find themselves in particular situations. Illustrations abound. For example, the unexpected section gives many examples; combining them could yield many plots. However, by convention, "the unexpected", unless forewarned – in a full-on yet nuanced fashion - cannot dig heroes out of problems. That is considered cheating.

This device is also valuable for non-fiction. Spicing up, or varnishing, with a few notions may add fire to your non-fiction. An example is an article about controversial organisational change. An editor thought my adaptation of the Irish proverb about splinters and sliding down a banister was so apt that he repeated it using a large typeface in a box.

The data bank contains almost 5,000 entries.

- One, unmodified, just might exactly hit the spot for you. If so, I wish you well with it.

However,

- entries offer, by combining any two, about *eleven million* unique combinations.

Consider those as *11 million* twin intersecting planes in the 3D cross of Figure 4.

(There are, "fairly accurately", 4,666 entries. They represent an *astonishing* 10,888,111 possible different pairs of entries, order within each pair being ignored.)

Insert your own inspiring, quirky, even gently mad, idea into the collection. Suddenly, into the world, a new gestalt (remember Figure 3) will erupt: *yours.*

I do not know what it will be. If I did, I could be a wealthy global best-selling novelist.

- *You* will scribble down *your* glittering notion, furiously. It should comprise a thick rich description. Maybe humankind has never heard your notion before.

> Hopefully, while the wind howls outside, inside, by the roaring fire and sweet wood-smoke of the chimney breast, youngsters and old-timers will lean forward, engrossed, to hear
> *you* tell *your* new tale.

Part Two

Commonplace Book

Data Bank of Provocation

Academe

The portion of graduates with a first doubled over ten years to one in six (2013).

An Australian vocational education and training college advertised using three vehicles photographed in a car park, labelled "dentist", "lawyer" and "the guy who built their houses." The first two had inexpensive local cars; the last a foreign (expensive) *Porsche*. The tagline was "Don't just build their trade skills; they also build their lucrative future." Put differently, training to be, say, a builder, electrician or plumber, compared with a more academically learned professional, results in higher income.

Proverbially, knowledge is golden. But since the web, much of the world's knowledge has become instantly available, "free" at the stroke of a finger. So that proverb now has a different meaning. Knowledge has become more democratically available and, arguably, its value degraded.

Alan Stiltoe was one of the last of the auto-didacts (self-taught). He worked in a bicycle factory but read *Nietzsche* and other philosophers in the evenings.

Universities should make your head hurt. That should continue all your life.

Ancient idea: "whiskery."

He's a perpetual student.

For a lecturer's position, it's not how good you are. It's how many publications you have: the minimum is four (2000).

Academe

Education is the movement from darkness to light.

They plan (2013) to convert the site of the first institution of higher education in Athens, where *Plato* taught, into a shopping mall.

Lecturer greeting engineering undergraduates in the 1960s, "Good morning, gentlemen and lady."

In pride of place in the council chamber was a tapestry of academics in the brilliant plumage of their ceremonial robes. Similarly, images celebrating valiant soldiers sport shiny medals and colourful ribbons.

"Always store on your shelf a whole series of problems for students to investigate."

Her paper was cutting-edge and had a career-defining impact.

Genius may twist threads into a tapestry.

"Would you just look at that," urged his wife.
On graduation day in Portugal, the handsome young man clutching his guitar, surrounded by a gaggle of gorgeous girls, sweated in his heavy gown. It looked tattered. The custom was that, for every significant event, such as leaving his family, gaining the right friends, or a love affair lasting more than one month, the cloak was torn and repaired. For each type of event, there was a designated part of the circumference. The thread was of the faculty's colour.
"What faculty is it?" asked the onlooker.
"It is pharmacy."
Husband and wife had been pharmacy students long before.

Thought grenade.

Winning Words

"Education is ruining our culture. We send our daughter away to university and, when she comes back, she does not want to be wife number four."
(South African).

"We change things slowly by education. I was an activist. My children have degrees. Advancement is by education."
(Another South African)

The gardens had been cultivated for five centuries. Participants congregated from all over the planet. Fine food, wine and grand stories flowed.

"Everyone is taught Marxism/Leninism at school and must study their philosophy at university. The society breakdown is happening in the West now, as *Marx* predicted in London in the 19th century."
(Russian)

"How do you get a lawn like this? "asked the American.
       The Briton answered, "Seed, mow, roll. And seed, mow, roll again. Do so for 600 years."

Education is, simply, the soul of a society as it passes from one generation to the next.

Xian (China) possesses 40 universities (2008). Halls of residence have dormitories with twelve students in each room. Students always eat outside where there is more room.

The professor, the great man, was over the moon; the paper buoyed him up.

Bemoaning change in the pharmacy syllabus to remove most of the dispensing: "We did all sorts of interesting things like making different sorts of emulsions – I can still remember the ratios. It's gone off now."

It is necessary to jump from the textbook page into the practical jumbled world.

Academe

Oxbridge is fabled to have a different class of map of the world (projection). Instead of looking up at the institutions of power, you look down upon them. You can see the way into them and the links between them.

Modern science is founded on the verification of hypotheses by experiments. The (London) Royal Society's first curator of experiments urged, "To be Directed by the Great Schoolmistress of Reason, Experience. And not to be ruled by groundlesse fantcys and conceits."
(Robert Hooke)

Messing with your mind.

Everything you have been taught by school or book or song or rhythm.

Lecture had become boring:
"It's interesting, but not very."

Old professors do not die. The merely lose their faculties/fade away in a scattering of footnotes

Surgeon's training: watch one, do one, teach one.

The complexity and vastness of mountains is a metaphor for limitless human imagination.

Knowledge is important because it humbles and inspires.

Ancient emotions and modern understandings.

It is no co-incidence that the first teashop was in Oxford. Academics, working late into the night, realised that tea could keep them awake.

They are dancing on the head of a pin.

You have to admire those studying in evening classes or for part-time degrees. After a day's work, they are tired, find it harder to absorb, arrive in twilight and leave in darkness. They are like wraiths.

Winning Words

"The company will pay half the costs of my MBA," she said.
"Do it," he replied.

"He would climb to it, if he climbed alone, and there he would suck on the pap of life, gulp down the incomparable milk of wonder."
(F. Scott Fitzgerald)

Originality is judicial plagiarism.

The visiting lecturer stunned the undergraduates, not least because his paper aeroplane hit an academic in the front row on the head.
They asked their internal tutor, "What do we have to do to be able to think like that?"

"Full marks for … Slightly fewer marks for …"

Ideas' entrepreneur.

Undergraduates until the 1960s had to swear an oath to the librarian to keep books well (Dublin).

Kaleidoscope thinking.

Discoveries of other pilgrim minds

New PhDs with their red-faced gowns, floppy hats and black medieval bonnets with double gold tassels, "You've got your tassel on the wrong side."
A new batch of multicoloured gadflies loose.

Cambridge is the city of perspiring dreams.

After 2 ½ hours of thesis defence, challenging almost to the point of aggression, he felt weepy and like a wrung-out dishcloth.

Criticism of teaching methods: elderly eminent professors cried.

It is well to lie fallow for a while.

Academe

Heavily larded with ...

Sailing uncharted oceans of thought, alone.

She told the professor that she did not agree with his research findings. She found herself chairing the meeting in which he presented his findings.
    She said, "I've made my views known, I will stand down."
    The six people in the audience of hundreds who knew the subject crucified him.

I did not want to know that my pilot had got 99% in his exams in electronics, 15 years ago; I wanted to hear that he had flown that plane a lot recently and always landed safely.

Professorial attitude: publish or perish.

Polish the endowments of the young.

"That sort of student is so bright that you don't have to teach them. Just sit them in a corner with the right book and they will soon have left you behind."

Academics often sport sandals or even exposed toes.

"Have you noticed that the physicists are gaunt while the chemists are chubby?"

Female professors over forty favour hair tied back taut in buns; they may even seem waxed.

He had being chewing over how to represent the numbers pictorially for months. Eventually, at 3.30 am, he discovered it. He punched the air and hooted with delight, tears streaming down his cheeks. He realised he had not stopped to empty his bladder. He folded up, bursting with pain.

A little knowledge was a dangerous thing. A lot was lethal.

Skill without imagination is mere craftsmanship or wickerwork baskets.

Winning Words

Helicopter perspective: take both the wide view and zoom.

"The Rottweiler of academe."

(Discipline) engraved through them like the letters on Blackpool rock.

Aged

The arc of life.

As you age, you need longer and longer to prepare your body for the day.

"Hasn't he wrinkled up?"

Elderly people, gathered together, tend to discuss their ailments: an organ recital.

He exposed his tartar-encrusted teeth in a fatherly smile.

Old age is when you prefer Epley's manoeuvre (to correct inner ear problems causing dizziness) to sex.

Age is like a horror film: a cheap video nasty. You know they have saved the worst until last.

Old men are frail and their voices quaver.

Recently retired:
    "I am now officially a useless old git."
    To compensate, he bought a 155 mph *Yamaha* 1,200 cc motor bike.

We degrade in different ways, my beloved and I.

Maoris describe ages of man not in years but in characteristics such as: dripping nose, hairy ears and asleep genitalia.

Appearance

It uses more muscles to be impassive than to smile.

Nut-brown old men ploughed indeterminately back and forth. During a few hot days a year, the water heaved with youngsters darting around unpredictably,

His eyes seemed to squint. Maybe they could not help it, having been under those scraggy bushy eyebrows for so long.

Škoda: cheeky little thing.

Humans are hard-wired to adore big eyes and a pug nose.

The walker at dawn pulled white socks over trousers.
  "It's my visibility and fashion statement," he said.

Elizabeth Taylor had the genetic mutation of an extra row of eyelashes (distichiasis). They framed, particularly strikingly, her violet eyes.

"... no matter what complexion."

Bookishly handsome.

Most generals have square jaws that stick out.

"They wore these sateen blouses. You know what I mean."
  The other man did: soft to the touch, unnatural sort of shine, cotton before cheaper, completely artificial *Rayon* replaced it.

Style? Merely a snare, delusion, window dressing.

He always wore a hat but was not bald.

Appearance

"I like hats," said the ex-RAF officer.

The olive oil dish for shared dunking leaves everything shinier: fingers, lips, life.

Silverback.

Waitresses were interesting, having a long apron at the front and a short skirt at the back.

"For a *Zulu* loincloth, any animal would do, but a warm and fluffy homestead is preferable."

In the cut-price store were only hair oils, straighteners and bleaches; no lacquers.

"I must just put on my war paint (makeup)."

He'd moved on from apple shape; he was now a triangular block of *Toblerone*.

Wording on tea shirt, "This bitch bites."

To maintain a beehive demands vicious painful backcombing.

"How do you look so young, so strong? What do you eat?"
    What a sweetie! What a babe!

Do tattoos, earrings and chips define my countrymen abroad?

Women, in a man, appreciate taut buttocks.

The New Year's party gave permission to wear silly conical hats, masks under or over glasses, streamers and blowers that uncurled to poke cheekily.

Some men with black hair do go grey young.

Skin interestingly decorated with freckles.

"Oh, you're all furry," he said, kissing both bearded cheeks in the Italian style.

Winning Words

City dwellers think it is important to look stylish; generally country dwellers are less concerned.

Air stewardess stereotype: tall, slim, blonde, hair pulled tight and kicked upwards in a ponytail that swished.

She was bronzed all over, but fainter towards the soles of her feet; presumably they saw less sunshine.

You could tell which of the more mature male air stewards had face lifts. They looked like frightened ferrets.

He was so tanned that he gave out a low level of heat like a lava lamp.

It was disconcerting to travel for a hundred miles behind a giant *Orville* and *Tweety Pie*; nine-year old boys were inside. It was OK if they did not wear the heads.

His face, like those of *Rembrandt*'s sitters, had been lived in. The eyes had seen laughter and sorrow, like all of us.

The most dubious enterprises present the most attractive and personable public relations fronts.

The yogurt ice-cream dripped: eight sticky streaks already adorned his trouser leg.

On her hen party, the thoroughly modern Miss wore a pink peaked cap with antennae, a moustache, white cricketing shorts with an L plate and rather oversized kneepads. Two punts were full of pink caps, already well-oiled. It would, perhaps, be unwise to be afloat under the polewomanship of the head hen.

(Celebrity) is 65 now and looking good. You need two things for that: good health and money.

Old sagging skin of vampires becomes taut and fresh as they suck out the young blood of their victims.

Clothes are all.

Appearance

"She isn't quite as pretty as she thinks she is. She has dressed up seven years too young and four inches too revealing."

Her husband was less edifying.

That suit had once radiated power. But now the belt hung down at the front and his gut bulged over it; he tottered forward with its weight.

"You're leaking."
"I'm sweating like a dyslexic on countdown/pregnant nun."

Cynicism wrapped in a yarn.

Prim and tight-buttoned.

The greatest culprits for staining teeth yellow are tobacco, coffee and red wine.

Old people have big ears. That is because they continue growing after other parts have stopped.

Devastating lacquered elegance.

Child describing a bald man with a beard:
"His face is upside down."

Their tonsure, how they cut their hair, identified them.

There was something about his face, the look of the eyes, that suggested surgical reconstruction.

On one wrist was a watch and bracelet with big green polished stones; another bracelet with green stones encircled the other wrist.

"What do you think, boys?" she asked.
    The boys, aged 61, 71 and 58, wore beards, greyish, white and fake brown, respectively.

After shaving, his face looked like a desert war zone.

Winning Words

The white cat was dirty: she had been under somebody's sump.

Tinsel up *v.s.* sexed down.

A "spiv", glamorous, shallow, all show – but charming.

Ugly duckling meets proud peacock.

Americans liked … . She has a womanly body shape and is posh.

Goatee beard, yellow, carefully cut.

He had an English tan and teeth (i.e. pallid and crooked).

Maelstrom underneath.

Fantastical.

The striated muscles of her supple back rippled and rearranged themselves.

Clearing mother's house after funeral; in the drawer, respectfully preserved, were his "Buddy Holly" spectacles, the old spare pair that he kept before marriage.

Many redheads, some so vivid that only a bottle could endow.

Where the vacuum cannot reach, dust balls settle.

The sun had left her hair and grey invaded.

His tie always seemed to get in the way. The splotch, that he assumed was juice, showed no sign of evaporating. Oh dear: it was oil, not water; there was also another splash. He washed with soap and water, dried overnight and squashed in the trouser press. His only tie was not pristine but would have to do.

A plate large enough for the course to be laid out as a work of art.

Appearance

Two years ago hair cut severely short, reserved. Now soft long curls tumbled over her shoulders and she oozed confidence and happiness. Was she in love?

He pulled the long hair from his throat and teeth. The hair was not greyish and coarse like his or dark and fine like his wife's. Where had it come from? The restaurant kitchen?

Alarmingly white set of false teeth.

Only the bi-focal line on his spectacles revealed his age.

The Queen of the May was crowned with forget-me-nots (*Myosotis*) so that she forgot-you-not.

Fake blonde.

Glaciers look dirty because at the centre of each snow flake is a speck of dust.

The long hair, the sprouting moustache, the broken English: how like *Albert Einstein.*

The minder had no neck.

In 1900, only actors, actresses, film stars and "fallen women" wore makeup. *Max Factor* (junior) made for the film industry and then the masses. Invented the words: "make-up", "pancake", "eye shadow."

She had a film of almost white down on her face that made it seem luminous.

At "(*Name of pharmaceutical company*) House", the groomed "reps", came and went, with their rectangular black brief cases and *all* the women wore brief skirts.

... rested the A3 pad, on which he had drawn a diagram, on his paunch.
    "Look! I always knew that ... had developed that shape for a reason! He's a portable visual aid!"

Winning Words

In the baths at ..., compared with ..., a tauter class of bottom.

It was so hot and difficult that, as he pushed the lawnmower and panted, drops of sweat arched from his upper lip.

"Save our jobs, for ...'s sake," said the poster printed onto the tea shirt; ... would not have minded.
    But it was a bad photo and when a buxom shop steward wore it, he had a huge forehead and a tiny chin.

Groin-polished turnstiles of the underground.

Her hair was so black that, in the sunshine, green glinted like the shimmering on the wings of a raven.

Little men, to compensate, are bumptious.

Dingy, dilapidated, even dangerous.

In the slanting sodium street light, the rain droplets on the roof of the red, newly-waxed car resembled goose pimples.

In their photographs on their bus passes, they looked about ninety and as if they had suffered a fright. Automatic booths always did that to people.

Man with buck teeth:
"When I meet someone, they do not know whether to shake my hand or feed me a sugar lump."

His jewellery was made from *Craptonite*: sewage sludge incinerated at a high temperature. It became vitreous and machinable.

The luminary actor, as a tactic, placed a small ticket in the "cleavage" of his buttocks and tensed his muscles (gluteal) to hold the ticket; that necessitated a "mincing", "limp-wristed" sort of gait.

It was the older women who had see-through blouses and their bras were heavy duty cantilevered jobs.

Appearance

The women carried goods on their heads in black bin liners.

Face like a new moon.

"No flashes," said the sign by the *Mona Lisa* – but they flashed.

A cigarette was *always* inserted into the statue of the fat lady.

"The snuff box": the hollow between the thumb and the outstretched trigger finger.

Nature had been niggardly.

Besmirched.

Hand gestures: open means person of the people, steepled means analytical.

You can camouflage body language but not eyes. Poker players wear dark glasses and sit in a dark corner. Jade traders sit against a light window.

Crêpey skin.

The sort of person who could eat a whippy ice-cream without it melting and dripping over his hand.

"Put your mouth in," (smile) before public performance.

Wisps of hair that had been doing valiant but fruitless long-distance work over the top of his head.

Coffee advert: executive tart.

A man like a fork lift truck.

The blond young man had a moustache, a darker beard, unshaven like an animal coat. The hair went down his back, disappearing under his collar. Did it join with a coat of hair on his chest?

Winning Words

The old seaman became less red as you eyed him upwards. He had a fluorescent orange anorak, an orange-grey beard and a faded pink cap.

Young couples, wide-eyed and confident.

He donned his social identity: trainers and jeans.

Tidy clean-shaven lively young salesmen, cloned.

The middle-aged man had grown a paunch of slab-like solidarity.

If you described yourself as an animal, what would you be? Tiger, crocodile or slug?

Chimney sweeps used not to wear gas masks; now they do.

The large hedgehog stood in the road. It did not appear squashed. It moved its front legs but got nowhere. It barked like a puppy dog, a strangled agonised cry.

The globular man was shaped like a berry and wore one earring.

White woman in a country with black inhabitants: "The children kept pinching me hard; they thought I was a lump of lard and would change shape."

A very little black dress and the face of a child.

"If you are photographing ... you will need a wide-angle lens."

He was chewing like a bullock in sweet grass.

"A ten thousand camel mama!"

In the middle of the concrete-encircled roundabout was a trail of soil (dislodged from the inside of wheel arches). He looked for the car with the dent. There it was!

Appearance

Only then did age grant him the patina peculiar to men at ease with real power.

Bedraggled as used dental floss.

"every tooth seemed like an inestimable pearl ... two rows of orient pearls between parted lips ..."
(Nathaniel Hawthorne)

The men were so fat that their eyes were almost closed.

It is really not fair that some women should have the luck of looks and others not. You must agree.

A girl with a military looking uniform sporting gold braid and a short skirt served the soup.

Sweater swathed lumpishly against the weather.

She liked the order of the clean washing blowing on the line; he liked a row of clean milk bottles.

"His general Contour suggested that possibly he had just swallowed a full-sized Watermelon without slicing it up."
(George Ade)

He's a great vat of shrugs and pouts and deadpan stares.

The lens of the overhead projector was filthy. No-one could have cleaned it for one or two decades. He cleaned it with his handkerchief.

"This juiceless and ravaged semi invalid with the shuffle and the ancient wheeze."
(William Styron)

He crossed his legs at knees and ankles, leaned forward and sweated. That's nervous.

The stable girl had been unaware of the manure on her boots.

Winning Words

The men who have taken the hardest rubs in life are the shiniest.

All the female swimmers who were pensioners wore brightly coloured bathing caps.

Middle aged woman, her fecundity faltering.

Majestically pregnant, her belly like a 16th century galleon in a trade wind.

When joggers look in the mirror, they do not see what others see; they see themselves in relation to an impossible ideal.

She surrendered her bulk to a wicker arm chair that, out of sheer fright, burst out a salvo of crackling.

You could tell the bright ones: finer features, purposeful movements, calmer; boys lacked ear and nose rings.

In church he peered down into his hands. A tiny mirror was there.

His tangled straggly black beard was a way of expressing individuality.

Don't take much notice if one person calls you an elephant but if they all start feeding you buns, get worried.

"Out of timber so crooked as that from which man is made nothing entirely straight can be carved."
(Immanuel Kant)

To detract his opponents from what he was saying at the meeting, he wore a huge tie with a star shell.

The pavement vendors threw their wares into their car boots when the police siren shrieked.

Telephone call to a meeting organiser:
"The usual way of recognising a speaker is for him to carry a ...; I won't do that. I am a dwarf with a hump."

Appearance

The bishop: a tall man with great glittering eyes.

The old (38 years) king's jerkin was two metres around. He could not climb the stairs.

Whole families fat or thin.

Matrons with complex coiffeurs swam sedately, careful not to wet them.

The museum exhibit spoke to him through the centuries. There was the dark grey bald-headed man in bed with his *Frau* with a silvery bun and a bed pot under the bed.

Compelling image of a brilliant mind within a broken body.

The softest thing about him was his teeth. He might find it hard to settle.

Who can resist looking at himself in the mirrors on columns of department stores? But furtive; only in hairdressers is lingering allowed.

The appearance of plants in old age is rarely an adornment. They have middle-age spread or become increasingly scrawny and withdrawn, like people.

Rugby player with feet so wide that he needed specially made boots.

Deep wrinkles, furrows all over his bald head.

The pleasant ingenuity of advertising depends upon an unvarying and simple message: buy it.

"I am bleeding through the ears. I have never been lied to so much."

Gold chain around her ankle.
"How long have you been on the game, love?"

Winning Words

He looked perfect outside but inside was twisted with pain and bitterness.

Teetered on high heels.

The exercise guru said, "You have earned that sweat. Wear that badge with pride."

Why did elderly women wear black gowns when black absorbed the sun's rays and must have made them hotter?

Bushy prickly moustache, but grey.

Traditionally, male politicians bare torsos on holiday.

"The day you wear that hat is a bad hair day."

"To look young it helps to be slim and smile a lot."

Shoes sporting shiny buckles like a "spiv".

Uniform of birders: green wellies, oiled anorak, wind cheater, woolly hat, gloves without fingertips.

His whiskers were so bushy that they gave the impression of being grown under glass.

Appearance

"I like to play them in my hands," the expert speaker said.
    He was gushing, flawless and the listener felt like weeping from the expert's prowess.

He was dressed from a Savile Row window and oozed gravitas.

"He looks as though he'd been weaned on a pickle."
(Alice Roosevelt Longworth)

"It is with narrow-souled people as with narrow-necked bottles: the less they have in them, the more noise they make in pouring it out."
(Alexander Pope)

A photograph is a trace, something directly stencilled off the real, like a footprint or death mask.

She was sitting the way a woman sits when she is about to go home

Art

An opera is a performance where plump women wear tea-cosies, trees descend on string and the eyes prick with tears.

Dali had an anatomical revelation about *Freud*'s brain. It was a snail that a pin could extract.

Film crew about camera angle, "I'm cutting in tight."
"Look at John. Don't look at the camera. Pretend that you do not know him."
Liked shooting through (gas) open flames of central hearth.
"These arty types like that sort of thing."

Early aristocratic visitors to the (English) Lake District were not content with nature as it was. It needed enhancement to make it more "painterly." They viewed it backwards, framed, and in the mirror of a "Claude glass", sometimes adding a coloured filter to make the colour more appropriate to the season.

American film directors may create a sensible and thoughtful film. However, generally, by the end, they think that their audience will be so bored that they are asleep; to wake them, they must have guns and explosions (British perception).

Platinum (photographic) print.

A picture is so much more real than a photograph because it goes into your eye, you feel it with your brain and heart and it comes out of your hands.

Art

The clarinet has a little tap to empty the distilled water (and grease) condensed from breath.

Alone (except for the dead bodies) the artist brought in her long sheet of paper and drew, in black squid ink, life size, the giant squid.

The very names of some pigments (e.g. *"lapis lazuli"*) are poetry.

In the Middle Ages, paints stored in bladders without labels; the artist did not know the colour until opened.

1950s British design is mired in nostalgic romanticism.

After World War 11, poverty led to the austere use of the meagre materials available. The result was simple design.

The artist is amoral (not judging right or wrong, unlike *im*moral) and derives as much pleasure from virtuous as corrupt creations.

1950s Dracula films have a heightened, "picture postcard" colouring.

In the vocabulary of the Moors, white was alpha (the beginning), black was omega (the end), yellow was sun, green was life and blue was paradise. Those seemed to cover most angles.

A chromo(lith/graph) of four pears printed in *Brussels*.

The ultra-violet (UV) lamps lit up his trousers in the art gallery, but not the face of his watch. Time had disappeared.

In photography, sunshine, tripod (and *Photoshop)* contribute much.

The classical Chinese picture has four elements: sky, earth, calligraphy (poetry) and, in red, the seal of the artist.

Winning Words

Gaudi spent his life creating rounded living shapes. An angular inanimate tram ran over and killed him. He died, unrecognised, in a hospital for the poor. The Vatican beatified him, so it came all right in the end.

An imposing canvas of MPs in the House of Commons. Just one, wearing red, stood out: a soldier. Adding a dash of red to draw the eye is artists' (e.g. Constable's) cash cow.

The man and the woman were bulbs growing in a pot of the same soil, their long hair twisted together.

"Damn'd face painting."
(Thomas Gainsborough)

He could not remember queuing for one-hour for any show but *Picasso* delivered; it was worth it.

Picasso never paid for any meals, although he went to the swankiest restaurants. He always paid with a cheque. Would you cash a cheque if *Picasso* had signed it?

Vibrant nostalgia in colourful lush canvases of sugar plantations amidst jungle.

Any artist needs a stubborn and a strong internal compass.

Leonardo was an early painter to depict so that eyes seemed to follow you around the room.

All good art tells us something about the way that we live our lives.

Art

There was not even one artistic bone in his body.

Nicosia cathedral: icons painted with natural pigments (e.g. walnut shell or pomegranate) onto fresh moist plaster. They bound together and lasted for centuries. Artists were no longer permitted to re-paint. Some had changed Roman into Turkish soldiers.

There, hanging on the wall of the Mauritius gallery was the original of the picture of skaters he had only before seen on Christmas cards.

Astronomy

When young, he had constructed a telescope with a mirror six inches across. He had dreamed about big observatories with huge mirrors and object glasses, such as at Lick. He was, at last, in a famed observatory at Mars Hill, *Flagstaff*, Arizona.
    He looked through a little telescope in the forecourt,
"How do I adjust it to make it sharp?"
"You can't. It's meant to be fuzzy like that."
    Then he entered the big dome. This was the very spot where *Percival Lowell* had claimed to see channels on Mars. The dim interior lighting was red and the sky a rectangle of black though the slit opening. He peered through the massive eyepiece of the big telescope boasting a lens 24 inches across. The fuzzy patch resolved into myriads of stars. His eyes moistened.

This is the closest to hallowed ground in a subject without saints. (The 100 inch reflecting telescope at Mount Wilson where *Edwin Hubble* discovered that "nebulae" were galaxies like our own. The Hubble orbiting [space] telescope is named after him.)

Comet Halley: magnificent against the foil of the velvet black background in binoculars.

Supermarket staff put up the "Gone to see the eclipse. Back in five minutes," sign.
    At 11.18 a.m. all the backroom staff, such as the bakers, crowded into the glass entrance lobby. A thin crescent was overhead through cloud. Excited voice, communal gasp. Sudden chill. All too soon, the five minute sign had to be removed.

The star "Lucy" (after the song by the *Beatles*) has, at its centre, a diamond 4,000 km across.

Astronomy

Disaster! Tripod topped over during a gale and dug into grass. The motor still seemed to work. But the fabric cover was torn and adventurous snails crawled over it leaving slimy trails.

Put your money where your mount is.

Your wedding ring and you are stardust. Atoms and men are the ashes of the nuclear reactions of stars. Put less pleasingly, you are nuclear waste.

Amateur astronomy's tribe has two main sects: "screen scanners" and "visual observers."

By his bedside, the boy had set up his flimsy camera tripod, and lashed on his telescope using string. He had constructed it from a spectacle lens and magnifying glass held together with a cardboard tube. He spied that Saturn had a bump that might be a ring.
    Voice hushed with wonder, he whispered, "Wow."

School visit to a local astronomical society:
A lad, usually not interested in anything, asked a question. A spark was ignited. Who knows where it might lead?
    Afterwards, the teacher said, "You know, you've interested him. Never seen that before. We can work on that."

"The first gathering of an amateur astronomical society was photographed around an old brass telescope. He recalled early club meetings being held in his house because he was put to bed early to accommodate them." (1945)

About eclipse: "Something is wrong with the moon. It should not be lying on its side like that."

It demanded an extreme lack of practical ability to fit the finder mount backwards.

Winning Words
Fabled observatory; telescope of legend.

Galileo had a bit of bother with the inquisition.

At the exhibition, about 85% were male and 15% female; a majority wore anoraks.

Patrick Moore was there for a book signing.

As many telescopes crammed the hired sales space as it would permit.

We live on a knife edge between fire and ice.

Some way outside *Alice Springs* was a site so dark that stars were brilliant against coal dust. The Milky Way being formed from milk spurted from a Goddess's *(Cassiopeia's)* breast pierced by an arrow, really seemed plausible. A fire pit offered reddish embers; dim red lights led to the observation area. That offered a line of short *Maksutov–Cassegrain* telescopes on stout pipes, binoculars, a red flashlight and laser pointer. Magical tales of myth, legend and scientific "fact." But the last, by far, was strangest.

"Goldilocks" zone for habitable planets: neither too hot nor too cold but just right.

His favourite image was the Hubble deep field. In that tiny area of sky, appearing black to the naked eye, whose light had taken almost the entire age of the universe to reach us, galaxies were scattered as dust.

With naked eyes or binoculars, our nearest galaxy, Andromeda, appears a faint fuzzy blob, smaller than the full moon. We only see Andromeda's core. When imagers enhance its brightness, it appears six times larger than the moon. When Andromeda's light started on its journey to your eyeball, dinosaurs ruled the Earth.

Astronomy

You, I, and everything around, only comprise about 5% of the universe. The remaining 95%, (2014), astronomers assure us, is "dark matter and energy." Estimates appear to be rising. What do we know about that 95%? Nothing. Is a completely new model of science overdue? However, it would not only have to explain dark matter/energy but also our "normal" universe – and do so better than our present model.

"Where is everybody?"
(Enrico Fermi)
Only recently have we become certain that many stars have planets. Theoretically, even back-of-envelope calculations estimate that life is everywhere, but humanity has not yet contacted it. That suggests the Fermi paradox. The universe has many civilisations. Why have we never communicated? Maybe we have. Both musings, that humankind may be alone or not alone, are awesome.

Numbers about the size of the universe with so many noughts are so ... astronomical ... that, perhaps, only metaphors help us to understand. Thinking of Earth as just one grain of sand in all its sandy beaches may be one starting point.

Behaviour

Shake him until he was all frothed up.

The thirtyish career woman suddenly realised that her biological clock was ticking: she wanted a family.

> "Things alter for the worse spontaneously, if they be not altered for the better designedly."
> *(Francis Bacon) 17th century*
>
> "Failure to plan is planning to fail."
> *(Mantra of civil emergency, and other, planners) 20th century*

Do not use the past as a mallet to hammer the little pegs of the present into the ground.

Slattern.

The meticulous man, whose spectacle lens had fallen out, checked, and if necessary tightened, their screw on the frame, every Monday - after trimming toe-nails.

... was career-limiting.

"He was so laid back that he was horizontal, or, possibly, dead."

He was crumbling: surviving on three hours sleep and half a bottle of brandy a night.

Adrenaline rush: his brain's primeval limbic system that he shared with lizards ruled. Its uproar for survival, food, alcohol,

Behaviour

sex, rewarded with pleasure chemicals. They could not be refused.

The organised man had tie racks displaying ties too colourful, narrow or wide, conference, school, funeral (black) and bow ties. But he always wore the same three.

Laugh like a horse's whinny.

"I do not eat chocolates or drink but I have this one weakness. I must go outside and smoke."

He recognised his long-lost school friend's habit of touching spectacles and eye with the finger of one hand. Years vanished.

Afterwards, he had a necessary and mildly pleasurable bowel movement.

To avoid getting wet feet in 1 ½ inches of stream water, walk balancing on your heels.

Public altruism is giving ourselves emotional sweeties.

During World War 11, women down the air raid shelters often did not have periods but they re-started once the war was over. The body knew when times were right.

High stepping ferocity; *stamping* of the dance, hands clasped to other dancers, drum beat behind. *(Africa)*

"Do you want a clue?"
    "I'm too tired for games. Just tell me."

"It's a big ask."

To reduce the number of journeys, he loaded three 25 kilogram bags of gravel onto his sack barrow. It creaked and would not budge.

Zodiac (inflatable boat) arm grip is hand to forearm, firm and mutual.

Winning Words

Could that be the roar of a crowd watching football in the railway station? No, too loud. Grizzled with curiosity, he could not help himself walking towards the roar: a medley of shouts and cheers. Umbrellas waved in the air. He could not see so held his camera aloft to capture a picture and view it. A balcony was bursting with bodies like bees in a hive. Police flaunting fluorescent yellow tabards lined the stairs.

The *Tannoy* blared, "This is a police message. There is a serious health and safety hazard. All persons not waiting for trains must leave immediately."

It was repeated one minute later. Then a softer female voice in more friendly language. That was clever. They had been reading their psychology books. But was it as prelude to Mr Hard Man again and his harsh official reading of "The Riot Act" after which people could be shot dead? That Act of 1714 forbade the riotous assembly of more than twelve persons; last used in 1919, it was repealed in 1973. But this author's lay hunch is that something like it remains.

Hissy fit.

Young men swagger; old men totter.

"If you hector people too much, they clam up."
The gently put question with the potentially lethal answer is better.

Speakers' voices:
- authoritative, plutocratic, smooth and sermonic, even worshipful,
- monotone mumble to one slide hiding a solid block of tiny text,
- musical, warm like creamy custard with the magnetism of a nubile girl,
- desiccated old stick but sparkled with splendid sound-bites and
- formulaic and factual but experienced, enthusiastic and fascinating.

Behaviour

He scowled at five wasps buzzing around an outside table.
"If a wasp stings, one hundred wasps will die," he proclaimed theatrically.
One stung.
He started whacking with his newspaper. "99, 98, ..."

In the London underground, if the doors close on you, without help, they seldom open. The haversack of the girl caught with half of it outside. Four pairs of hands helped force the door open.

What is the umbrella etiquette in a crowd in torrential rain?
To avoid collisions, do you raise or lower your umbrella? Or tilt it?
"You are lethal with that thing. With your height (tall) you can only raise."

"I got the job!" she said and danced a little jig.
Her clothes parted in the middle to expose her midriff. She had a taut little tummy.

Those who dispense good advice are often too old to behave badly.

"I never miss a chance of getting my hands on a man," said the Women's Institute (WI) Branch President, adjusting the speaker's lapel microphone.
"I'm enjoying it," he said.

"I've tried *Prozac, Ritalin,* psychotherapy and religions – but still the cheerfulness keeps breaking through."
(Leonard Cohen)

"We took the top off the village sewage treatment plant and stood on the rotating arms."

Snuffles of satisfaction.

She flounced in.

"G'day."

Winning Words

He scratched his head; he was not a very practical sort. It seemed that the more stylish and expensive the sink, the harder it was to suss out how to open and close the plug hole. He discovered that pushing it once opened it, pushing it again closed it, pushing again opened and so on. That discovery took ten minutes.

He is as twisted as a corkscrew.

In Mediaeval Suffolk, it was bad manners to scratch the fleas on your arms or chest before your master's table.

Locals rapidly knew what was really going on in the city by word-of-mouth. *(Moscow)*

The bikers revved their engines and chatted to each other. One engine exploded.

The banners flapped. The drums banged.
 The loudspeakers screeched, "Save our NHS!"

Weave a web of cunning.

Sliding into sloth.

Chomp on the sap of life while you can.

"Hell hath no fury like..."
(After William Congreve)

The girl plonked filthy trainers on the train seat.

We zig while others zag.
(paraphrased from William Congreve)

They had nothing else to do so rested their heads on arms and went to sleep.

After a Tsunami-like sneeze: "Your sneeze! You gave me a shock."

Behaviour

Occasionally children from remote stations visited their broadcasting school at *Alice Springs*.
"Quieten down. You don't need your outback voice here."

Civil defence advice at the back of telephone directory:
"If earthquake 'Down, cover, hold';
If volcanic eruption, stay indoors, wear mask or cloth, avoid lava flows;
If tsunami over 35 metres in height, go one mile inland."

Loving yourself is the start of a life-long affair.

"We must stand up to the bully countries who think that they speak for the whole world."

Veg out.

Sometimes you can treat life ever so lightly and still make an impact.

"He exercised so much that he even had muscles in his spit."

Fortunately there was nobody at the funeral who it was necessary to punch on the nose.

"Oh! I should not have said that ... the words just fell out."

Shave with the grain of your skin to avoid razor burn.

"My favourite activities are stamping and squirting."
Stamping uses a date stamp and ink. Squirting uses low viscosity lubricating oil from an aerosol can.

I was so stimulated that I was as limp as a noodle. (after vigorous exercise)

We have ways of making you lock your trolley in an ordered straight line for us so that we do not have to. Would you like your £1 coin back?

Winning Words

When you are "slagging someone off", make sure that you have replaced the telephone receiver.

The incredible sulk.

It's the doing that keeps me cheerful.

We have become doers, not beings.

Callous to the extent of being ossified.

"You have a serious deficit (leaving your wife alone on holiday). You will have to do something really special to compensate. I will keep my fingers crossed for you."

French wedding: multi-coloured balloons bounced. Locals lined the path between the town hall and the restaurant and cried "Good luck" in English.
    Street cleaners stopped and clapped, "Bravo!"

"You are talking to me under a misapprehension. You assume that I care."

Listening forensically.

Emotional constipation.

Bad mouth him.

"I wonder if he is too controlling."

"So much smoking. Don't they have public health campaigns here?"

"She is a drama queen."

Zip her lip.

"Detrain at this time."

"Yee ha!"

Behaviour

Embroiled in controversy.

Notice: "Please do not empty your dog here."

"He's never here for us as a manager. He just goes into his office and closes the door."

Grandson, father and grandfather walked one behind the other, holding their hands behind their backs, identically. Just like *Pooh* Bear.
(Character of *A.A.Milne*)

Pit bull terriers have tails so muscular that a thump can bruise your leg.

A smile got you a free doughnut.

If you are stoking the fire, do not look at the mantelpiece.

To succeed on your first date, know the meaning of flowers (not just boring roses); all women do. Clean the car and hang air freshener. Do not show off the stereo by playing it too loud.

She bottled and stored herself away like summer fruit.

It's only the unreasonable people who achieve progress.
(after George Bernard Shaw)

He steepled his fingers and sucked his teeth.

Female pharmacist's take on male patients who retire:
"They start off, I am the high-powered business man, but after six months they are more relaxed, chatty and lovely."

"I told him that he was a naughty man; he was not used to that."

People skills of a porcupine.

"When I said goodbye to my house, I howled."

Wrapped in anxiety, she squeezed the bubble wrap.

Winning Words

He jerked from his sleep: hedge branches. He was travelling through them. In the big car he felt calm and cocooned but urgent effective driving was essential. He swerved and braked, crossed the carriageway and hit the hedge on the other side of the road. He swerved out of that. He hoped he would hit nothing hard. Thank goodness no lorry was in the way on his erratic path. The car behind hung way back. He felt so silly with the back bumper hanging and scraping the road. At least he lived. But that evening he shivered uncontrollably.

He delivered a political election leaflet door-to-door.
    "I am your tooth fairy."

Verbal mugging.

"Space really screws you up."
(Kevin Fong)

You are a fish and I am a maggot of attraction.

The plane circled around and around.
    "We cannot land because of the fog," said the captain, "We will have to leave now and fly back to … because of lack of fuel."
    "This is my worst flight ever," said his neighbour, well travelled in the world of oranges.
    They would lay on a bus service.
    They tanked up from … with comfort food. It is surprising how much chocolate you could buy for £10. He felt arteries clogging with cholesterol.
    The driver said, "Wait for six minutes and I am allowed to drive for five hours without stop. Who wants that?"
    Many hands shot up.
    The destination airport was shut.
    "Where can I get a taxi?" asked the girl student in despair.
    "This day is a disaster," said another fellow passenger.
    But the Dunkirk spirit had kicked in. How would a bus full of Italians have behaved?

Behaviour

Would you give up your little finger to save one million people who live in ...?

"What I like about ... is that, again and again, he has managed to re-invent himself."

At the ticket desk a bored youth looked at a picture paper.

The micro-gravity of space produces, "not just bone demineralisation but also muscle atrophy, impaired co-ordination, cardiovascular deconditioning, altered hormone levels, orthostatic intolerance and even hallucinations."
(Andrew Haynes)

The grunt during tennis service was like a crow squawking while descending upon carrion.

How many times a day did women see that look?

The Czechs watched the video of their velvet revolution in silence and left sombre-faced and subdued.

About a freezing shower:
    "I've just had a cold shower. Lovely",
    "You're joking."
    "Take it first on the back of the neck. Then go in slowly. You'll glow afterwards."
    It worked. ... had learned in the army.

"I go after the wrong sort of man: those who put me down and ignore my wishes."

"I thought he was a quiet man but when he had the stage he turned into an actor."

The water in the swimming bath was so hot that you could only lounge and not exercise, but the showers were ice cold.

He bristled like a hornet hyperactive on the pollen of oil seed rape.

"I need to go make wee-wees. Which way is it?" (toilet)

Winning Words

Response to gushing appreciation at retirement: "If you are not careful, you will break your butter knife!"

(I can) "sting like a bee."
(Muhammed ali)

The small urchin kicked every closed shop grill; maybe he disliked the people inside.

His mouth was a slipping clutch.

"A closed mouth gathers no foot." (If you do not speak you are certain that you will not say anything embarrassing.)

She wrapped around him like a flag around a flagpole.

It is "better to light a candle than to rail against the darkness."
(Peter Benenson)

"He who was once burned by soup will even blow to cool yoghurt."
(Romanian proverb)

The station master, with silver braid on his cap, explained why the train was late, "I'm sorry, sir, but there was a gentleman who was so tired of life that he had to end it under the 5.05. ... train. We get about two or three a week."

Public toilets crowded with old men standing before the urinals, dribbling, waiting and cursing their prostrate glands.

The mad, the sad and the bad.

When *Mailer-Daemon* returned an e-mail, it made him mad (demonic).

Sole self employed business people who loose their internet connection go wild in despair, because they have disappeared.

If life deals you lemons, make lemonade.

Behaviour

She caught the red carnation thrown by an opera singer at *Le Figaro*.

Taking an oath is a fearsome thing. It covers every part of you and if you break and then open your fingers, every part of you slips through and away.

"Be excellent to each other. Party on, dude."
(Chris Matheson and Ed Solomon in film: *"Bill & Ted's Excellent Adventure")*

His sons dissuaded their 76 year old father from taking a fifth wife by buying him a colour television and video.

Minor social peccadilloes need an apology; major, repentance.

Elderly widows like bus journeys because there is someone to talk to; they are lonely.

The elderly man, surrounded by women, said, "It's like being in a cage full of canaries, all twittering."

Actions have consequences. You may find that you are only cutting one head off a hydra.

Skateboarder on Californian seafront:
"It's good. But you are paying for this with your blood."

He preferred his umbrella plant to people. It did not sulk, throw memos or slash tyres.

Sat so long that bum numb.

Filled with baffled and unshedable tears.

"Don't you think that she's got her tail up today?"

"The game ain't over till it's over."
(Yogi Berra)

Winning Words

In the residential home for the elderly there lived seven women and one man. He came in saying that he had just (tele)phoned his wife; she had died two years previously.

Hills upset natives of Norfolk.

The optimist fills in the crossword using a fountain pen.

His mood was dark and concentrated like an *espresso* coffee, not light and frothy like a *cappuccino*.

Raddled with nerves.

He sat on the WC and played the knocking of air in the wash basin tap like an organ.

Running around like a flea in a fit.

The autistic swam, on his back, underwater. At first, he alarmed the lifeguards.

In *Paris*, when the pedestrian light was on green, the cars stopped, eventually, but with bonnets over the zebra crossing, threateningly. Their engines revved in anticipation of the next ten-a-breast race.

No government does any long-term planning. But at least you can attempt in your private life (say 5–10 years).

"Seen the Quisling lately?"

She flung a look that would have opened an oyster at sixty metres.

A slice of the sloth.

"Don't even talk about it at the pillow."

Before entering the prison, emptying your pockets was compulsory. Lucifers, batteries, car keys and watches were deemed contraband.

Behaviour

Cordial distain (scorn).

On a river boat toilet:
"Gentlemen, please stand close. You may not be as long as you think."

"How are you?" produced paralysis.
    Did she really want him to recount every ache of body and spirit?

Let him taste the sterner face of ... hospitality.

Parents do their best. For example, builders live in huge houses and build houses for their children.

The radiation from their interaction could fog film.

To wife: "In this great fish tank of ours, weren't you lucky to hook me."

Learn to say "No." Let others collect the Brownie points and heart attacks.

When wondering whether to re-enter the fray with an unpleasant protagonist who had, for awhile, been quiet: "Don't wake a sleeping dog. It may be in a temper."

"We have given up writing on the dates of weight checking of fire extinguishers on their attached labels. It's because people are inveterate peelers."

Grandpa always increased the television sound; he must be deafer than he admitted.

Nature has left this tincture in the blood: that all men would be tyrants if they could.

Barnacles of regulations.

It was the ordinary things that made tears flow.

What a tidy person. On the wash basin, he placed his soap, moulded like a puppy, upright, until the soap had so dissolved that it would no longer stand upright. If the last user had abandoned it in repose, he repositioned it to attention.

He began before he had teeth.

He drove on, fortified by the comfortable fast car, stimulated by four strong coffees and aroused by *Tina Turner* on too many decibels to hear the ominous noise.

The natural propensity of anyone is difficult to overcome.
Will not both jackal and kingly dog howl and gnaw boot straps?

What's wrong with being obsessive? It's only the obsessive people who are really good.

Poetry readers adopt intense prissy voices.

She injected tungsten into his spine.

Conservation about a young female clerk who had moved office and had a baby (1990):
"Oh, I did not know she was married," he said.
"A bit behind the times, aren't you?"

If a car will not start, everyone should stroke it and say, "Nice car. We love you."

"Margaret Thatcher is a mad woman and probably possessed."
(Saddam Hussein)

"Speak softly but carry a big stick."
(Ancient proverb, probably African)

About organisational change: "Beware the repairers of gates that are not broken."

"Get thee hence, witch!" lifting up his hag stone (has hole) threaded onto a sinew around his neck.

Think before ink.

Behaviour

The public stole from an NHS hospital: gold fish from a fish tank, water lilies (and the black plastic refuse sack to store them) from a pond - and the fairy from the Christmas tree.

Carpenter's rule: measure twice, cut once.

Asbestos nerves.

He was so tired that you could sew his nose to his toes and trundle him around town like a hoop. He would not wake.

A compulsion as predictable as bees building a honey comb.

A good sneeze is succulent and satisfying.

All the really important deals are made in places with limited access e.g. toilets, golf courses.

Why did the single beds in the nurses' residency keep collapsing? The manufacturer had never met it before.

A dog always holds something back for the emergency scenting of that crucial lamppost.

Biology

Running barefoot on grass is glorious but their *blades* can cut. Into their sharp edges they have concentrated glass.

A memory stirred and he pointed his nose at a star. When the husky howled, it was with the voices of his ancestors.

The pit-bull terrier cannot help the killing mechanism coiled within him/her.

The dog's growl was so gruff that just listening to it gave a sore throat.

The Dalmatian "Breeze" thought that the ball, with its leather skin and rubber inflatable guts, was a rabbit.

"Meme".
(Richard Dawkins)

Leave any (temperate) land for ten years and it becomes a forest.

Humans share 60% of their DNA with bananas.

The fig flower is internal. A wasp lives within to pollinate the fig. If you are a strict vegetarian you should not eat fig. It contains animal flesh: the wasp and its progeny.

Some gypsy moth caterpillars consume foliage high in phenolics. That reduces transmission of a polyhedrosis virus and facilitates moth outbreaks.

Tree stump covered with glutinous pale yellow fungi: "It's mushroom central!"

Biology

"Slippy glueish juice":
Description of the Harebell (*Campanula rotundifolia*) in the "Herball" (1597).
(John Gerard)

Cocoa nuts have mucilaginous sweet pith (glucose). The seeds were purple within and poisonous to chickens.

Trees grazed by giraffes develop more tannins. They taste unpleasant so are less likely to be eaten. Pheromones transmit that message to nearby trees. Then, they also, develop tannins.

To germinate difficult seeds, pass through the gut of a bird e.g. chicken, and sow droppings. When the dodo became extinct, so did several plants on which it fed.

The "dandelion season" of cheerful yellow flowers, drifting seeds and coarse uncut grass.

Strombolites: ancient life form.

Gargantuan masses of epiphytes in the rain forest, thrusting towards the light.

"We love trees because they are the lungs of the city. They clean our air. We have a national tree-planting day." *(Singapore)*

Wading through wildflowers; bees hummed all around, feasting upon clover.

"All this," she said, gesturing at the wildflowers, yellow, red and blue in the sunshine, "We planted none of it. It is nature's bounty."

Leaving his hand, the inner part of the bulrush slithered out of its root, like peeling an onion skin. How soft and succulent within.

The silvery bark felt as smooth as it looked.

Bulrushes are botanical rabbits: beautiful to look at but they breed too much.

Winning Words

Barley straw banishes algae. Hydrogen peroxide (H_2O_2), poisonous to algae, is slowly released.

Extremophiles near steam-vents on the ocean floor extract energy from sulphides at 400°C, in total darkness.

"We call the fig tree *(Ficus carica)* the 'hypocrite tree.' It looks mature and ripe from far away, but its looks can deceive."

Sunlight warmed the *Buddleia* and its butterflies.

In the meadow a month ago, the sap was swelling and grass had reached his chest. Growth was now calmer, less frantic.

Trembling aspen *(Populus tremoides)* are one large organism connected by its root system.

A soft green branch is sufficiently pliable to plug a gap in a hedge.

He was called out at 1 am after the alarm went off: the cause was a moth.

The swan, on landing, was wiffling (rapid, side-slipping zigzag descent).

Herring gulls pecked at the corpse of the stranded whale.

Water butt teamed with wriggling hair worms

On the roadside, the long swans' necks twisted around to monitor passers-by. Between the parents nestled grey goslings.

"(Human) amniotic fluid? It's basically, wee."

The appendix is not "useless." It is a safe haven containing "good" bacteria. If the rest of the gut is emptied of such bacteria, for example by flushing with a specific infection, the appendix can "reboot" and recolonise the rest.

Biology

Suffolk colt big working horses are more endangered than giant pandas.

The mud came alive as tiny flies hopped into the water.

The crow would not leave the buzzard alone. Although the crow was smaller, it flaunted a heavy-duty beak and mobbed the buzzard repeatedly. The two vicious black specks jostled in the blue sky.

Your robin in the garden might seem friendly but protects his territory ferociously because everything (food, nesting material) is there. Seabirds lack that security; instead, they capitalise on the safety in numbers of a flock.

Gnats are the first visible animals to colonise cooling larva flows.

Puffins have elegant sharp markings like clergymen of high rank.

The sperm whale's head is full of spermaceti; that contains liquid triglycerides. They are a better conductor than water for focussing echo-locating waves.

A deafening squawking; it must be of a large flock of big birds. But he could not see them. Eventually looked overhead. Ragged "V-shapes" (skeins) of pink-footed geese headed eastwards to the continent, enjoying a good gossip.

The giant squid was longer than a London bus and had suckers. The colossal squid that lived deeper was longer and boasted rotatable hooks.

The rocky stacks, projecting from the sea, seemed frosted with icing sugar but were seabirds and their guano, lined like milk bottles. *(Boreray)*

Wasps clustered around the fluorescent tube while on at 3 am. On switching off, their buzz ceased immediately.

"Oh! It's a moth. I shall have to leave the room. Get rid of it, can you?"

Winning Words

"It is stork central!"
Nests crowned chimneys, electricity pylons and church towers.
Big flappy Mr Stork returned carrying a large stick. He tried placing it in various places. Mrs Stork took it firmly.
"This is where it goes."
He did not demure. (Anything for a quiet life).

Spread like nits.

Interconnected cellars made a bat hibernarium; six species frequented the grounds.

The morning collection of ducks, rabbits, squirrels, and a young deer trotted by to check for any food scraps.

Big emperor dragon flies flutter overhead; big round brown sticky "poos" (faeces) splatter below.

Sudden pain. A drowsy, late season wasp had stung. It should not be blamed. If I was being swashed, I would sting – if I had one.

The otter poured itself into the water and instantly disappeared.

The birds, the fish, moved in patterns older than history

A dozen seaside stalls offered chips. Huge rounded seagulls flocked overhead. Splat, splat, they bombed. How liquid.

The liqueur glasses sported lids to exclude insects getting in.

Wigs had combs so you could scratch underneath. Pendants that were flea-traps were popular.

"I ate leaves today. They gave me wind," said the *Tyrannosaurus*.

Biology

Allegorically, in the hold of *Darwin*'s ship, the caged birds beat their wings against their bars, at the time of their migration.

Moorhens run with such huge funny feet and their necks stick out as if to hit the finishing ribbon first.

The little newt died of concrete poisoning.

If a politician visited, the zoo always brought out the same old male koala. He had the same trouble that old men have. Every time he wetted over their smart suits.

The bee, in the ultraviolet, sees a different world, with markings leading to the nectar.
    Flower colours and ripe fruit say, "Free meal here."

It would, perhaps, be understandable if a fox broke into a chicken coup and ate one chicken. But to bite the heads off a dozen chickens and leave the bodies is more difficult to understand.

Across the little lane, a stream of running rats, four inches across, scampered.

Her pet rat was very clean but would sit on top of the curtains and chew holes.

"There was a big old(e) moth in there."
    "What colour was it?"
    "Brown. Looked like a bat to me. I wanted to swash it but the police man cupped it in his hands and took it outside."

The nest lay deep within the bonfire. The parents could not fly in but must land and scrabble. He could just see the V – shaped beaks of baby blackbirds. Fledging was overdue; then he could light the bonfire.

Hedgehogs eat eggs in the nest and leave a mess. Stoats roll eggs away and bite off the ends.

Pheasants, standing and gossiping to each other in the middle of the road, are not very streetwise. Maybe humans, who reared and fed them, were trusted.

Winning Words

Upsetting such a huge hornet might be unwise. It seemed as wide as a moth. If he hit it with the fly swat, the creature might live and be cross. Instead he applied an industrial dose of fly spray. But it still moved an hour later so he swashed it using the spay can.

The two toed, compared with the three toed, sloth is an exhibitionist adrenaline monkey.

He swung his head upwards to view the Canada geese, "When I see how much they 'poop', I am concerned when they fly overhead."

Human brains are fussy feeders, accepting only glucose.

Fish from minnow to tench.

To mites your hair is just one large oily bon-bon.
(Many tiny creatures live in the forest of your hair and fat-secreting glands.)

The scientific name for an animal that does not flee or fight its enemies is "lunch".

Relatives vary. Compare the little Asian otter with the South American one, six feet long that preys on Anaconda snakes.

The transparent mite *(Demodex)* is so huge that you can almost see it. It lives at the base of eyelashes of about half of people. The older you are, the more likely to be infested.

If a cougar (mountain lion) stalks you, make yourself look as big as possible. Wave your arms about. Throw sticks and stones. If cycling uphill, stand on the peddles. If attacked, fight back.

He peered at the jar of lake water containing 28% salt. Inside swam halophiles: shrimps, the sort used to feed tropical fish.

All skin visible is dead. Much London underground dust is fabled to comprise female skin that tights grated off.

Biology

Within the topmost tower of the temple roosted a white-backed vulture and its chick.

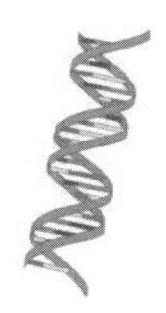

I must love "Lua" and so must you and not just for her poetical name. She was the mother of all mothers, the mother of us all, all that is of flesh or leaf or any other living thing. "Lua" stands for the last universal ancestor to life of Earth. "Lua", the earliest life-form, started to replicate "herself" about 3.4 billion years ago in the primordial soup. (The age of the universe is about 13.8 billion years.)

Octopi suffer. Before experiment, anaesthetise them by immersion in a solution of urethane or ethanol.

The "hot plate test" remains one standard method for observing pain, or its absence, (such as after giving a dose of analgesic). Place a rodent on a plate and heat it, slowly. When the rodent lifts up a paw to blow upon it, that paw is uncomfortably hot.

Ducks float downstream but fly upstream.

What fecundity, what plumpness, in a wild flower meadow with grass waving to his nipples. What lawnmower fumes, how exhausting, to keep a footpath open at two cm height! How exuberant the contrast between the natural height and manicured path!

A giraffe may kick in any direction; one kick can kill a lion.

After "germ theory" was accepted, the home environment swarmed with small but powerful demons.

A blowfly goes into a bar and asks, "Is that stool taken?"

Winning Words

The human cell line in the lab. had squeaky contaminants (rats and mice), so the research, and the papers upon which others would rely, was flawed.

The little tit flew into the conservatory. A huge speckled sparrow hawk followed. It swooped out with fluttering; a few of the tit's feathers fluttered down. Sanctuary had failed.

The band of iron girdling the lawn commanded, "Stay inside and behave yourself."

Bats "click" in the ultrasound; humans need a machine to hear.

There, through a crack, deep within the porch, grew impudent leaves.

The blanket weed had been growing for months, just out of reach of the rake when he waded in wearing Wellingtons. It looked thick, horrid, and even evil. What satisfaction to be in amongst it, clawing it out with the rake, three wheelbarrows full. Almost as pleasant as a succulent sneeze or heavy defaecation. Brown eggs, 3 mm across, were sacrificed too. Men prefer the destructive parts of gardening.

This time of the year, his hobby was dividing snowdrops. He lifted the corms, divided and replanted them.

The organisation represents the voice of bats in the UK. Well, more of a squeak, really.

She was a wire haired terrier: a ratter.
    "She's eight years old, getting an old lady now. Quite docile, friendly. But you should see her with a rat."

Now that is what you mean by ruffling feathers. The tail wind was so strong that it curved up his tail feathers, making it difficult to slowly strut along with a dignity matching his splendour.

She lifted up the whelk and peered inside, "Oh, there's someone at home," she said and put it back.

Biology

To your dying day, which will you remember? A nice bikini on a girl in Ibiza or the synchronised flashing of a million fire flies in the rain forest?

Sea turtles have a human life span. The smallest is the mass of a woman; the largest of four people.

He addressed the infernal scummy weed in the centre of the pond, "Your days are numbered. You wait till I get my chest waders."

After just two months, black mould (*Stachybotrys chartarum*) besmirched the blond varnished wooden nail brush around its bristles,

Glow worm and firefly are both beetles; using luciferic and the enzyme luciferase and ATP as in all life. The result: a splinter of the moon.

We like *Darwin* because he tells us who we are.

The ex-hunting lodge in Sherwood Forest had cow parsley sprouting from the chimney pots. From a perfectly round hole in the crumbling woodwork a clear plastic tube appeared to rise. But it was the fruiting body of a slime mould. Where was the fungus mycelium?

Gentle and therapeutic cooing of pigeons.

The religious relic collector thought it the skull of a dragon, not knowing of crocodiles.

"Shoo!" he shouted, banging the window and clapping his hands.
But the male and female pheasants continued to strut and peck at the gourmet breakfast of his expensive wildflower seeds.

The heavy branch of the gnarled carob tree had been supported so long by a post that it was cemented into the pavement.

Biology: the wet science. (Living organisms need water.)

Winning Words

Midges flow and twist together.

"I know you are beautiful but you should not be here," he told the ducks.

Combine harvester: great reaper; it kills baby ducklings.

Any dog eats any egg: crunchy, gooey.

After twenty generations, moorhens no longer fear man.

What was that strange haze by the wing mirror? It could not be a reflection. The physics did not fit. He lowered the wing mirror, stretched out his hand and felt ... nothing. But the strange play of light ceased. A cobweb!

The robin perched on a twig only two feet away and checked him out.

From the steering wheel, he gently brushed the little lacewing, expecting it to fly away. It did not; instead a wet smear that seconds later faded as if it had never been.

"Pupil" ("little human" from Old English) is so named because you see a little person, a reflection of you, in the curved eye ball.

Testosterone – that Puck of hormones.

Charismatic mega fauna: big animals that we love such as panda or leopard.

An eager pig, rooting for truffles, is like a four-wheel drive tractor.

Charred trees survived in the blackened Earth, smelling of soot; from each tree base, green shoots sprouted.

Farmers crushed the white insects, feeding on the cactus, and dried them, forming cochineal. But it was cheaper to crush them in their wine press, forming cochineal blood.

Biology

Notice taped above post box letter slot: "Please do not use. Bird nesting within."

As the killer whale approached, the salmon leapt from the water, not wanting to be dinner.

"We exert birth control over the Canada geese; they fertilise everywhere. We pay summer students to find their nests and addle the eggs." (Canadian)

Identify the sex of a fish by holding to the light. If a dark patch is inside, that means eggs so female.

I had seen more life in a tramp's vest.

Nature favours mongrels.

A bittern boomed.

The traps on the pine trees contained pheromone that attracted male moths. Once in the bag, they died. There would then be no caterpillars to devour the tender shoots.

The flowers of "ladies of the night" only open at night. Their scent is poisonous.

Do not approach an eagle owl. It can peck out your eyes, crush your arm and quite likes chasing pussy cats and eating them for dinner.

Removing bloom: billions of water fleas awaited their algal banquet.

Dung concentrates radioactivity.

Phosphorescent spoor of snails.

The rotting apples had fermented on the ground and the golden admiral butterflies, fieldfare birds and all of nature, were tipsy.

Human oestrus is the same length as the lunar cycle. Why?

Winning Words

The barred sandpiper waded in the (toxic) settlement pit of the sugar-beet factory, unconcerned about either its poisons or the dozens of twitchers.

The best place to find goldfinch eggs is Bramley apple trees. Goldfinches interbreed with canaries that have escaped from cages. Their mongrel issue flaunt beautiful colours.

A cousin of cabbage and a child of mustard.

The giant elephant seed, 1 ½ feet across, floated between islands.

About a German Shepherd (dog) co-inhabiting a nuclear bunker during peace-time:
"Do you like dogs or can you take or leave them?"

The turkey-sized bird consumed two kilograms of giant elephant dung beetles at one sitting: a lot.

A dissected earthworm is all guts and gonads.

The "camel spider" *(Solifugae)* was huge and hairy. A stick did not frighten it, but eventually it would run away with feelers in the air. It locally anaesthetises prey (including humans) so can then munch, undisturbed.

All life, whether branch or bone, splintered stick or splattered rabbit, is in the same web.

It is good to observe animals going about their business that is so completely different to human concerns and reflect that you are part of the same gargantuan web that will continue after your death.

Biology

The water lilies were two metres across.
"Do not throw coins on the leaves," said the notice.

In the sun lit car port, a swallow caught a moth on the wing and swallowed half of its body; the remaining half still wriggled. Then it ate some more including one wing. She paused and ate the other wing. She did not miss a scale.

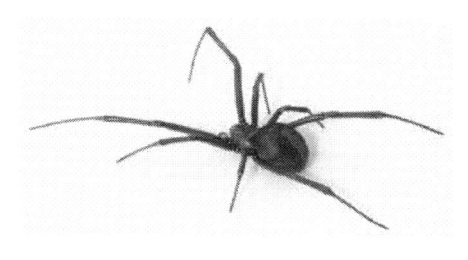

First a spider moved into the empty box and then a bird.

Diagnostic field mark of plover (a bird): walk, pause, listen, spear worm.

The tree explodes every spring.

The kittiwake looked down in the dumps and about to fall over backwards.

"... is ditch-water dull? Naturalists with microscopes have told me that it teems with quiet fun."
(G.K.Chesterton)

Gerbils love toilet roll cores.

The dodo is extinct but is remembered.

Inner city tower blocks with light only from glass skylights offering dingy views are the kingdom of the pigeon.

The chirping of crickets in the spruce, as soon as the sun rose, was 79 decibels on the cricket scale.

A dog will chew on bone dipped in blood until exhausted with frustration.

The swan had rubbery webbed feet. It looked cross and hissed. It was big. One flap of a wing was fabled to break an arm. Back off.

Winning Words

The jogger nearly swallowed a butterfly. What would be its next encounter? The beak of a thrush?

Instinct: he discovered a big black spider in his pullover. He instantly jerked away without conscious thought. Similarly, something crawled inside his jumper: a one inch-long furry insect. Adrenaline rush. Yanked jumper off over head. Then turned jumper inside out several times to ensure no friends remained within. Shook with irrational fear.

Of cat: "Little sabre tooth. Too fat. Never caught anything."

Under the gutter, ivy grew. It punched through the felt/tiles/plastic downpipe.

Logs loose much mass (water) during the first six months. Ideally, only burn after three years.

It does not take long for storm-uprooted trees to sprout shoots.

Some leaves are thin and brittle; other thick and succulent.

He viewed the heron through the brass telescope. It wobbled on its rickety pillar and claw tripod. That library boasted a stuffed bittern within a domed display case. Birds wheeled and screeched outside.

Chemistry

Preferred weevils to chemicals.

The builder, wearing ear protectors and sweating, was demolishing an enamelled cast iron bath with a sledge hammer.
"You must stop your ears," he said. "I've got to swear."
On cracking, the sharp break released the smell of soot (carbon used in the manufacture of brittle cast iron).

His inner chemist swelled with pride and applauded the priorities of a nation that engraved, in red and blue and gold, on the side of the building, *Mendeleev's* periodic table.

The two identical stereo-isomers of limonene smell of either orange or lemon; of carvone: spearmint or caraway.

White smile: calcium on parade.

On the salt flats, the water was coloured pink, "It's the biggest evaporating dish I have ever seen."

In some situations, putting out a fire with water is the worst possible action, for toxic fumes result. Better to pour on petrol and incinerate toxins until harmless.

When you apply lipstick or drink *Campari*, you absorb the blood of the insects that parasitized the cactus. The insect *(Dactylopius coccus)* produces carminic acid. This is mixed with aluminium or calcium salts to make carmine dye: cochineal.

From your still, collect the correct fraction of "fire water" or it will rot your guts. Discard the early and late fractions. Methanol, that may change to formaldehyde in the body and cause permanent blindness, distils off first (i.e. at a lower temperature). "Methylated spirits" is contaminated with methanol to discourage drinking. Hence "blind drunk." Next, ethanol distils. Finally, at higher boiling points, fusel oils, chiefly amyl alcohol, are produced. Only ethanol (ethyl alcohol) is used in spirits that are sold.

- *Such distillation, in inexperienced hands, risks fire or explosion and, unless licensed, is illegal in the UK and many other states.*

Spoil heaps from gold mines around *Johannesburg* are attractively light, not dark like those from British coal mines. But the spoil left after extracting gold contains cyanide used in that process. When the wind blows, all sorts of problems result.

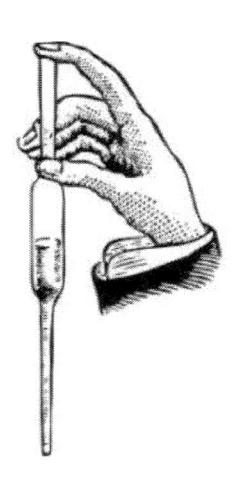

Soap in soft water foams into luxurious lather.

Black volcanic ash absorbs night dew and feeds grape roots. Red ash, containing iron, is useless.

Arsenic is inert. Arsenous oxide used to be called "inheritance powder" because so often used as poison. The Marsh test detected it. Green wallpaper containing copper arsenite may have killed *Napoleon*; in the damp, mould decomposed the pigment to arsine and methyl arsine gases. He breathed them.

Boil up horse chestnuts in water: foam results containing saponin, a splendid "soap."

Arsenic 5 is less mobile, less poisonous (by a factor of about 60), than arsenic 3 (arsenite). Some micro-organisms can convert between the two.

"They haven't been caring for their (swimming) pool. It has a high solid content; I can tell by the (high) viscosity of the

Chemistry

waves. They've just thrown in a handful of chemicals and ignored it all season."

Uluru has a red surface where exposed to the atmosphere because of rust: iron oxides such as Fe_2O_3.

During shopping for shoes or handbags, women's brains secrete the same chemicals as during making love.

In the yard of that German company, inspected by a British auditor, sat a cylinder of chlorine, carefully guarded. Yet both Germans and Britons had rolled that gas into each other's trenches to kill the other in agony, during World War 1.

To teach chemistry in the girls' boarding school, it was thought prudent to locate in the stables.

"We no longer use formaldehyde to pickle specimens; it is too toxic. We use methylated spirits or isopropanol instead."

On returning to his childhood home he checked out the garden shed. His laboratory had been there. He had produced phosgene and other poisonous gases. In that lawn, sodium thrown into boiling water had exploded causing a crater and streaks of caustic soda (like rays from a lunar crater). None had splattered his (unprotected) eyeballs; he could still see. There had been the vegetable patch with peas that tasted so sweet.

The long hot summer, in *New England*, had stored so many chemicals in the leaves that their colours were brilliant.

Many men and molecules synthesised the success of ... .

One "starting" material that the body uses to manufacture testosterone is cholesterol.

Copper has been mined in *Cyprus* for 8,000 years. (Cyprus = Cupris = Cu [abbreviation is the chemical symbol] = copper.) Around 1,000 BC, copper was exported as 4 cm thick fleece-shaped and sized pieces; each weighed about 30 kg. At the entrance to the copper mine, worked for centuries, were green deposits of copper sulphate or carbonate.

Winning Words

Two men, wearing Wellingtons, mopped the sloping ramp to a Mediterranean swimming pool in mid-summer. The air reeked of pear drops. He knew from the smell that the solvent was amyl acetate. The other man scattered sand. The concrete was so sealed with varnish. They wore no respirators. Had they no health and safety regulations? They were coughing but did not, surprisingly, stumble or lose consciousness.

Tourists find limestone country attractive: the carbonic acid in rainwater is weak but strong enough, over geological time, to widen the fissures under the rocks.

Nostalgia: lovely old 1960s laboratory with dark wood, drying cabinets, fume cupboards – plus modern state-of-the-art instrumentation.

Forty parts of sap from maple trees must evaporate to produce one of syrup. Density measured. If too low (dilute) it would ferment. If too high, it would be too concentrated and the sugar would crystallise out. If maple syrup drips onto snow, a chewy toffee results.

Sufficient fumes to sedate a horse.

"The waste collection tanker drivers are the best analysts. They could tell if waste had phenols. The most difficult waste to treat is curry sauce."

"Waste" is a subjective word: one person's waste is another's "gold."

Chemistry appeals to stamp collectors: all those elements - 118 and rising.

Chemistry is ancient, far older than Greek philosophy. Metallurgy, winning metals from ores, names ages (copper, bronze, iron).

Chemistry

Within the warehouse, once used to manufacture sulphuric acid, were piles of drums of liquid. He could not read the German, but the skulls and crossbones spoke.

Throwing potassium into hot water is more stimulating than watching iron rust.

The indigo wool was yellow in the vat but changed to blue and green when removed.

The alchemist *Paracelsus*, who tried to find the nine stages of converting lead into gold, was "nature's secretary."

Phosphorus burns with a yellow flame producing dense white smoke. A phosphorus burn is yellowish with a characteristic garlic odour.

The long-immersed object had "the scent of the sea": iodine.

Distillation of the hooves and antlers of deer made "Spirit of Hartshorn." It contained ammonia.

No hoods were resistant to the acid (nitric oxide fumes). The reaction was moved into the yard; there, process workers stood to windward.

Ether boils at 35°C. In the tropics especially, it was deemed "dangerous cargo." It had to be shipped in, on deck. Even so, it partially decomposed to (spontaneously) explosive peroxides. The answer was small metal cans stored in wooden chests with zinc sheet linings.

Speculation about the discovery of soap: pig roasted over fire. Rain leaching hot ash produced soap suds.

Teflon®. Rises again, shining. Some humans effortlessly shrug off mishaps.

A *Bakelite* (invented 1907) plug, overheated, smells of rotting fish.

Children

"Daddy wants a beer."
    The two-year old boy ran to fetch it from the fridge. Watches his dad drink it, longingly.
    "Want some!"
    Drinks, slaps lips, rubs tummy.

His latest trick was learning how to kiss. He kissed me. He kissed the stone lady statue, *Aphrodite*. He also fed her stones. Logical.

The big people each had a whistle with a different note and a number from Christmas crackers. The girl was amazed to hear the tune "Jingle Bells" played when each person was tapped.

"There is always one moment in childhood when a door opens and lets the future in."
(Graham Greene)

"Children are like sundials; they record the happy hours."
(Heidi Thomas)

At the boy's party, all the superstars (*Catwoman, Spiderman, Superboy, Supergirl* and *Superman),* plus one dinosaur chased around and around.

The girl's two new words were "adder" and "ibuprofen."

She only wanted a toy bike and was happy. The satsuma was a bonus. The mountain of parcels blew her mind. But best of all were the empty cardboard boxes.

When he was young there were only beginnings. He could not imagine any endings.

Children

We stopped the evening bottle of milk; the last trace of babyhood: cold turkey. No complaints.
  "No milk now," he said.

He loved hiding behind the curtains. Then he giggled. It was difficult to get out. He would repeat it, again and again.

He started to string words together, such as "car" plus "key" that became "car key."

Some of the food now went in with a spoon.

Now he was copying words such as "church" and "water."

"THE UNITARIANS HAVE SUCH NICE CHILDREN'S PARTIES"

He toddled into all the rooms, passing objects back and lifting tops off all the pans.

A doctor stitched up a 5-year old with a cut knee and then dabbed on tincture of iodine. The child screamed and punched the doctor in the face.

He walked across the room hanging on to furniture and clapping. He then looked back to check that people could see him and smiled.

When carried between two people, she squealed with delight.

She liked feeding grapes to her dad.

Winning Words

Everything with wheels, including a pushchair, became a "car." Boats became honorary cars.

He pointed and used a pincer movement to insert things into his mouth.

In a pacifist household where guns are banned, small boys make their own. Any forked twig is an excuse to point and shout, "Bang!"

Insanity runs in families. Parents catch it from their children.

The two one-year olds played side by side but not with each other. One liked cars; the other, balls.

The specimen jar contained four bloody wisdom teeth. The father looked at his blood-splattered son.
   As the father rattled the teeth in the jar, he thought, "How amazing that these came from something too small to see – and these teeth contain half of my genes."

He dragged *Pooh* bear around by the scruff of his neck, so squeezing out all the stuffing. *Pooh* looked rather floppy.

The toddler waddled backwards, shuffling with a serious expression and sat down on his chair.

When you are four, you cannot cut with scissors using your thumb and finger. But one hand in each hole does the job.

The boy was reading the children's book about flying. He went over to check that airport staff had placed a label on the suitcase. A scientific career ahead, maybe. Or a traffic warden.

In a marquee at the bird reserve, a large owl greeted each child with a "wing shake." It looked hot and bothered. You would if your talons were twisted backwards.

First day at secondary school:
"We kicked around a football. The older boys are so strong!"

Class and Status

Many of the 1960s pop artists, that "Sir" prefixes ennobled, were in the art gallery in a sort of ghetto.

Nigella Lawson's court appearance (2013):
"a masterclass in makeup as armour and weapon of mass destruction ... pastel-coloured frosting."
(India Knight)

You recognise the great and the good when you see them; public school and Oxbridge educated, firmly received accent, utterly confident, profuse with praise for their inferiors. It is prudent to let them have their strut, generally.

The royal carriage was on a sledge as in fairy tales.

Are they "us" or "them"?

"To have a long life you must have no watch upon your wrist and no boss over you."

"Life with ... was in the fast lane. Life with Malcolm was on the hard shoulder."

(Occupation) ... "are jettisoning one wodge of "dirty work" only to be lumbered with another."

For travellers: "Bragging rights? Landing on *St Kilda* is near the top."

Refined aristocrats of the enlightenment expected to possess pictures, library, and possibly a telescope, microscope and a cabinet of curiosities.

Gynocracy of pretty young female TV historians.

Winning Words

About boss of Savile Row tailor:
"I call him George but he always calls me Mr. Bloomberg."

Someone whose bones I would not grind down to use as cat litter.

Retired ... who had returned from two months' holiday in Australia: "I am now a poor man but rich in memories."

Of politicians:
"Ye sordid prostitutes, ye are grown intolerably odious to the whole nation."
(Oliver Cromwell)

People think politicians are grubby.

His hotel offered five acres of swimmable lagoons.

A limousine with attitude: a *Harvey Davidson* tricycle with a grey-bearded old-timer as cabbie.

"I've been admiring your car. It's the colour ('sea mist') that does it for me."
(Registration document description: "green.")

The ex-Hippies would no longer allow the church, or their politicians, to tell them what to do.

The young man spoke to Lord ... in a loud voice, "In my prep. school ...."

Queen Victoria only stocked her ice house with the most transparent ice. Through a sheet two feet thick, from a Canadian lake, you could read a newspaper.

About commerce and competition: as a(n) ... (occupation), he had been used to the cream. Skimmed milk had been my diet; bit of a semi-skimmed would be nice.

Class and Status

Landlubber commenting on a photograph, "He has four stripes on his arm. He must be a captain."
"No. He's a commodore – not any old person."

"The higher up the stairs (of the theatre), the less important you are. You should see the dressing rooms of the stars: white leather settees."

Less than one in a million of the diamonds extracted from the *Kimberley* mine are pink. Each is a national treasure. The best are intense and large.

Orange squash, orange juice from concentrate in long-life cardboard cartons and freshly squeezed orange juice form an ascending hierarchy.

"Champagne for breakfast? How decadent can you get!"

He was a member of the great and the good yet always had time to talk to people.
"He was a lamp lighter in a dark valley."

The notion of poverty is connected with *comparing* yourself with your neighbours. You do not feel poor unless your neighbours eat meat more frequently, have a second car while you have but one, and live in more rooms than you do.

In the playground, bigger boys push smaller boys off a model aeroplane. Smaller boys push yet smaller boys off. Little girls just watch.

A patient to others also well enough to sit to eat breakfast together at a table in a hospital ward, "We are the walking wounded."

The offending vehicle was big, black and with bull bars. Ouch!

Racing bicycle cost £3,500, a *Colnago*, first introduced 1954. 120 lbs/square inch pressure tyres. Flat streamlined tubes. Special forward-facing handle. Cycling porn.

"To me, a horse is an animal with four legs and a tail. Why is this a thoroughbred champion?"
   Look at her hindquarters, her apple, her bum, the size, the roundness. There's power there, a *BMW*."

The estate agent serving the upper-crust sounded so posh and identified himself with an aristocratic French name.

Road virus (RV): men hiring huge camper vans who have never driven a large vehicle before.

"Assistant curator", a deliciously archaic title.

The vilest vermin that hell ever vomited out.

Those waiters think that they probably should not be.

The goddess of getting on was dethroned.

Antique guns and membership of shooting parties.

Each cup sat on its little doilly.

Surgeons, plumbers and other possessors of arcane and privileged information.

"Her Britannic Majesty's Secretary of State Requests and requires in the Name of Her Majesty ..."
(Preamble to passport of United Kingdom citizen)

"He's as much use as the skin on a cold rice pudding."

A solemn stillness, the ambition of every prestigious hotel, reigned.

Lawnmowers lined the service truck. His walk-behind 22 inch seemed like a toy compared with ride-ons of assorted sizes.
   "That one costs as much to service as a car."

Class and Status

There are many good actors but few good plumbers so, on average, plumbers earn more.

The five-star hotel offered turrets, battlements and flunkies on the door.

Two men each carried large thin square black cases. Each contained neatly packed Masonic regalia: aprons in different patterns and colours.

For a marriage to be valid it must be officiated (e.g. by a vicar or registrar) and consummated: rather like the theory and practical driving test.

In her voice were thick carpet and velvet curtains.

When signing a treaty in London in 1960, *His Beatitude Archbishop Makarios* 111 used red ink. Emperor *Zeno* (around 500 AD) confirmed the right to use that royal colour.

Never argue with a man with a plank.

At Christmas the most senior butcher sported a garish bow tie.

The bride was blond and pretty. Her dress was size eight, tight at the hips and legs, flaring from the knees: a mermaid fish. Her shoulders were bare, breasts corseted upwards, like a cone offering ice-cream for licking.

Someone so dominant and expectant of respect that, when she smoked and exhaled, the smoke came out in little squares.

Rolls-Royce registration plate: "999 VET."

He taught *Gutenberg* the alphabet.

Lovely open-topped sports car; shame about the driver and passenger with matching bald patches.

His interviewers were not fit to sharpen his pencils.

Winning Words

The groom was solid, stocky, a bruiser - but rich.
Wife wore 22 carat gold in ears as insurance against problems.

It was the *Morgan 4* with its 1940s lines and ash frame, that required a check for woodworm on servicing, that the man and the boy went out to ogle.

They scrubbed up well in their morning suits.

The car park flaunted conspicuous consumption.

Humble yet unable to accept a yoke.

The old way: prestige was fame and antiquity of lineage.

The maître d' sported a white jacket.

Dark wooden panels, polished for five centuries.

The attentive young head waiter kept on using their names.
       She observed, "That young man is going up in the world."

3.9 Litre *Jeep* with its "*stonking* tyres that cost £400 each to replace" (2000) "was fully expensed".

It is not the words, but who says them: scriptwriter or President.

We have to remove the film of familiarity.

Emotional clout.

Stellar career.

The arm chair and dark leather and wood reeked of generations of money.

Neo-Palladian mansions were designed with enormous windows. They enabled the people within to better view their vast luscious acres.

Class and Status

Searching for restaurant in classified telephone directory in the USA:
"Just look for the one with the most dollar signs."
    Pointing with a finger, "We'll go there."

Criticise my philosophy, that's fine. But criticise my medicine and I get feisty.

As damaging to reputation as woodworm to a *Chippendale* chair.

The hotel was so expensive that he felt it necessary to confiscate his room's supply of headed notepaper and the ballpoint.

From around his neck, the large monkey snatched the garland and started to munch it; you do not argue with an animal that might carry rabies.

The *Audis, BMWs, Jaguars, Mercedes* and *Volvos* were there.

In the best jobs, you earn money while you sleep.

Trappings of power: stage props of little Bible with faded cover (on which to swear an oath) taken from drawer, row of venerable leather-bound tomes, Law Society certificate.

The Maharaja took his own Ganges water (in two silver pots weighing 390 kilos). Each held 900 litres; British water would be dangerously impure.

To press: "I'm going off to my farm house and five hundred acres. You lot can piss off to your council houses."

Observation of dinner lady:
"(The schoolchild) made her own packed lunch using mouldy bread and loose crisps, in a big ... *(superstore)* bag."

The rule of the road is simple. The biggest can do whatever it likes; there is a pecking order. *(India)*

A twittering of fancy gifts.

Winning Words

"Ooy! She be bitch woman."
(South African)

"I do not like broccoli. And I haven't liked it since I was a little kid and my mother made me eat it. And I'm President of the United States and I'm not going to eat any more broccoli."

(George H.W.Bush)

Politicians and journalists are at the bottom of the status table.

Shiny *Mercedes* parked beside the dull *Trabante*.

You just *have* to use *PowerPoint* or be labelled a dinosaur.

In the river at Norwich men dunked strumpets and common scolds (nagging wives).

More beautiful people, having symmetrical faces, compared with average people, earn about 10 – 20 % more.

"You can go a long way with British received speech."

The proclamation of a royal birth (that four doctors signed) was on headed paper within a *foolscap* sized frame. An ornate easel displayed. Its size was 343 x 216 mm, not 297 x 210 mm that is the more usual A4.

Apprentice angels.

The 50 year old business man arrived in a *Mercedes*; the 70 year old pensioner on a bicycle.

The apprentice was taught to call everyone "Sir" and did so to one man.
　　　That man pushed ahead of him and said, "Boy, you can call me Colonel."

The emperor had 3,000 concubines.

Lamborghini manufacture supercars – and tractors.

Class and Status

Shanty towns and mansions behind security fences.

The number one wife had a fence around her hut. All the other wives had to ask her permission before they could talk to her husband.

The more prestigious the café, the longer the waiters' white aprons.

In the centre of the cigar factory on a dais was, not a supervisor directing workers but, someone reading a newspaper to a microphone; all could enjoy the news content. (*Cuba*)

The desirability of your shoehorn depends on its length and stiffness. Her shoehorn was so long that it reached above her knee.

"I just compare the cars in the car park. Longer is dearer."

The washroom assistant turns the tap on and off and hands you a flannel towel.

Darwin inherited sufficient wealth to never have to work for money. *Cambridge* trained him to be a gentleman. At Down House, Kent, he accepted that being the local JP (Justice of the Peace) with the "right" to try a "lesser" person, was his self-evident entitlement.

A pair of complementary gas masks in the hotel cupboard illustrates exemplary customer care.

Those of high status were served drink with the evening meal until "wine rapt." *(China)*

The director was very proud of the burglar alarm on his *Škoda*. It barked.

"Your Highness."

Inscription on tombstone: "a grandee."

Eminent, that mausoleum word.

Winning Words

All those resplendent in chunky golden regalia, congregated, gossiping: a bigwig support group.

Lufthansa: "The pilot's hat must be immaculate, top off the status of the captain: always in control, in command."

Constable was only the son of a miller and so was in trade. His beloved's father was a clergyman and so of higher status. At first, he would not permit them to wed.

A Christmas hamper provides a prestigious larder.

Advice to aspiring consultant:
"A five-year old car lacks car park credibility; to overcome, get a personalised number plate."

To the man in the wheelchair, the man with a crutch is a threat.

"Downtown Abbey's" opening scene flaunted the great house, the grass expanse, the gaiters - but above all the swaggering hindquarters of the dog.

"Our wine is better than that of the French. They put everything in: leaves and stalks; we only use grapes."

When the official from the Office of National Statistics spoke of "data", he cupped his hand, as if describing something precious.

Cavernous volume of a mediaeval keep; great stones and flying royal pendants lined.

Consultant surgeons were a cut above the rest. They sported black mirror-polished dancing shoes (patent leather) and black bow tie.

Queen Elizabeth 11 appeared to be parachuting down with *James Bond* to open the 2012 Olympics. At one silken stroke, she had made the billions of pounds spent a good investment.

Class and Status

The opulent hardwood was merely veneer, given away by its "clack."

Of archbishop: wonderfully articulate words, crystal-clear pronunciation, the sound of class and authority reverberated in the sacred space.

His degree was in a mostly useless subject.

Fashion diktats.

The thousand acre farm had a druids' circle. *English Nature* came every so often to ensure that the farmer had not damaged it.

Label on Kilner jar: "Tea from the family plantation."

"They look down on her because she is quite flighty."

Graduating student and college footballer (USA):
"He had a *sackful* of job offers like this ...."

Vroom! A *Bugatti* sports car, with V-shaped boot, reminiscent of a track racing car roared up the Avenue des Champs-Élysées. And other ... . Seven parked outside *Fouquet*'s. An admiring crowd, all men, milled around, every one grinning. What was that parked at the roadside? He stepped forward, eyes bulging. He hoped for even more porn. He got it. A *Bugatti* Veyron, eight litres, 16 cylinders, 253 mph, costing a million pounds! So low and curvy. Such a long bonnet. Drool.

In the cathedral with beautiful mosaic walls, during 1917, they had stored cabbages.

Only one *Fabergé* egg was crafted each year for the Romanov family.

In the car park of the Inner Temple, London, headquarters of the professional body for barristers, prestigious cars predominated.

Winning Words

In Tudor times, planning permission was required to build castellations (e.g. battlements like a castle).

In exhibitions, the Europeans used to have glitzy double height stands while all the Indians and Chinese were in the Asian pavilion. Now the Europeans have given up attending or are cramped into the pavilion in little booths. The Indians now possess the glamorous stands. Their prices (2008) are 70% of the European; the quality is the same. Their factories are in bubbles, high tech with marble floors and computers amidst mud huts, hovels and streets running with sewage. The factory owners are the new maharajahs.

Wild American West: playground of desperate men and fallen angels. Heady dangerous ethnic brew swirled through as painted girls of the line advertised their charms and sang their siren songs.

The dust from the top of *Vesuvius* was grey on his white trainers. Maybe he should leave it on as a status symbol.

Rich businessmen build themselves great mausoleums.

When you are old enough as a teacher you can just say, "That behaviour is unacceptable."

"That's a girlie press-up." (back bent)

Harold Macmillan slept in pyjamas embellished with his family monogram.

"Dung ho," and "In your face."

Class and Status

The biggest, most brightly lit stands (career exhibition) advertised the most "dead end" jobs such as at a poultry processing factory where you stand in water in Wellingtons, surrounded by gore and stench. The Law Society stand had a yellowing card stating "No-one available."

The Worshipful Company of Scientific Instrument Makers or *Glaziers* or *Launderers*.

After lunch he could not help but snooze. But he awoke when the clapping occurred and joined in.

Mahogany, marine-varnished, sun-warmed, encircled the liner.

The most splendid singers are, to some extent, born (heredity), benefitting from large lungs and high cheekbones.

In *Pompeii*, pearls set into the pavement outside prestigious villas were a conspicuous show of wealth, like parking a red *Ferrari* outside.

Present given in Belgium:
"These chocolates are made by my daughter. They are not for you but for your children and grandchildren."

A monarch's palace may crush the self-esteem of visiting subjects by the sheer mass of gold, velvet and silk. Pointed spikes, overhanging fences, barbed wire and flunkies preventing access to certain areas also contribute.

The couple suddenly realised that everyone else on their table were millionaires.

The baby sat on a cushion in a wheelbarrow.

A four-star general gets an escort with blue flashing lights.

Symbols of monarch: rare and precious fly whisk, hat, leopard or even whole lion skin vestment.

She felt like a very small sardine in a very large can.

Winning Words

A white shirt lasted for two days. It looked dirty on the inside collar but tolerable on the outside.

Tomes of double elephant size (26½ x 40 inches) in the library. One, of American birds, hand painted, was the most splendid then produced.

A single screw did its best to do the work of two, to support the toilet paper holder, but it hung crookedly and swung. The towel rail was similarly afflicted.

The metal of the spoon was so thin that he feared it would cut his tongue.

He respected people who had earned their status; not those born into it.

The intelligence of a flip-flop.

The doctors' parking space was slick with *Jaguars*.

"Scientists should be on tap, not on top."
(Winston Churchill)

In the sunshine she flashed like another sun. She held out her fingers dripping with big diamonds; a *Cartier* watch encircled her wrist.

Honours system: a dash of enamel and a splash of ribbon.

Actors experience more glory in an evening than the rest of us do in a lifetime.

Of those boys, who will be kings and who kings' messengers?

About British NHS patients:
"... stop acting like grateful patients ... start to see ourselves as savvy consumers ..."
(Anna Bradley)

Class and Status

Biology departments at British universities have a pecking order. It depends on where they send students on their field (ecology) placements. Australia, South America, continental Europe and the UK are in descending order of prestige.

The villagers were no longer a two-car family. But they were a five barrow family: three one-wheeled wheelbarrows, one two-wheeled sack barrow (collapsible) and a four-wheeled garden barrow. That was the flagship of their fleet.

A succession of phone calls from old girls complained that the present pupils were not wearing their boaters.

(Company), purveyors of paint to the National Trust: a satin sheen than you can feel.

Within a prestigious magazine, the UK (2008) advertised itself to the Chinese using *Prince William*, the household cavalry and *Bentley* (German company owned) cars.

Gaggle of 16 year-old schoolgirls:
    "Nice car," shouted one and they all giggled.
    He blushed and did not know how to react but it made his day.

The *TVR* (British Sports car) matched the woman: late 40s, very slim, facelift, pampered, designer clothes including leather trousers.

Czech intellectuals really did wear all black.

(Company) were proud of being founded in .... . It was embroidered on all their lab. coats.

From the neighbouring table came loud corporate power-talk.

I don't know a single woman of my age who doesn't look at other women of the same age and physically measure herself against them.

The big plasma screen cost £6,000 (2001)

Winning Words

The wife whose hand most drips with diamonds has the worst marriage.

Conspicuous opulence.

Deprived in Britain (1993) was not having tasted supermarket freshly-squeezed orange juice.

Only men of the cloth, men rich enough to keep horses (and so could supply the king with soldiers on horseback) and prostitutes were allowed to wear silk.

The municipal baths were dingy with flickering lights. The left lane boiled as be-goggled men churned up and down. Goggled girls populated the next lane but even that was too choppy for him. He plodded along in the comparatively calm water outside.

Londoners think Norfolk folk are "carrot crunchers."

Mandarinate.

Products of homes of great diligence and a little prosperity.

What we all crave, whether we admit it or not, is the approbation of our peers.

Parachuted onto the board.

The power dresser wore a green suit and a green bow in long auburn hair.

If the droppings are left unburied in the garden, the tomcat has left them as scent markers because he is dominant; cats of lower status bury their droppings.

He faxed an image of his hand to his goldsmith who fabricated a golden replica, fingernails and all, for a chain on his beloved's neck; his hand would be near her heart.

Class and Status

Fish wives were of higher status than pudding wives, who made fish offal into pies (puddings).

Mrs Archbishop was hanging out the laundry on the line at Lambeth (*London*): purple surplices.

Two hundred muscular motorbikes parked at the hospital. As he entered, he raised an eyebrow towards security staff.
     They said, "It's all right. You'd visit a friend in hospital, wouldn't you?"

Ugly over-ornate teapots.

I will never soar with the eagles while I am tending turkeys.

He loved that car; it showed he had made it.

The (music-loving) Chinese emperor had tonnes of bronze buried with him to make bells and 22 musicians (beheaded) to play for him during his afterlife.

Soup kitchens at Christmas in the crypt of the church "St Martins in The Field", *London*.

The tadpole won the show; the only other entrant was a stuffed owl. That was disqualified because it was dead.

About selection of an NHS chairman:
"I am *de facto* kingmaker. But then they are invited to the …'s mansion in … and the political process starts."

He's past his "Sell by" date.

The only child thinks that the present under the Christmas tree must be for her/him.

"Non-one takes any notice of me. I'm like a little puppy dog, yapping in the corner."

The mentally ill homeless are litter.

Winning Words

After *Yuri Gagarin* landed, the local villagers, expecting spies, thought that he was one.
    "Hello guys, I'm Russian," he said.
    They did not believe him for surely foreigners could be trained to say that.
    He thought again. Out came a succession of strong vile swear words. They were music to their ears. Only then did they believe him.

They fawn and flatter him.

"Could I have a receipt?"
    "Sorry. Haven't got one. Have to buy them."
    "Write on the back of this."
    "Haven't got a pen."
    "Try this."
    "Sorry Guv. Can't write. Write what you like."

The senior surgeon was as stiff as a ramrod, white coat fully buttoned and "Call me Mr ..., not John."

Private affluence and public squalor.

Whale scrotum leather covered the bar stools.

He thought that he had made it when they fitted a carpet in his office but was deflated when they told him that it was cheaper than repairing the lino.

It is good to tell glad tidings to rich women.

Some accents can rot your chances in life.

The primitive man in the wolf pelt was saying, "Look what I have killed! Aren't I the best!"

Of *Land rover*:
Drivers of ordinary cars seem to be cowering beneath.

The secretary taking the minutes asked, "Is that one L or two?"
    The consultant also had a stamp saying "BULLSHIT."

Class and Status

Contrast between a hundred gold statues in *Vienna* monastery and deprived children.

Toilet paper was grey and disintegrated into pulp in the hand.

Squirearchy.

At *Harrods*, he nearly bought a double collared shirt by the royal shirt maker, by appointment to the *Prince of Wales*, thinking it had been reduced in the sale to £39 (2007). But it was still £110 so he refrained.

The Victorian gentleman, with a waxed moustache, that he wished to keep dry, had a special tea-cup with a porcelain ledge.

Victorian conservatory with coloured glass.

Human relations manager, "Is he for real or winding me up?"
    "He speaks to everyone like that."
    "*No-one* speaks like that."
    "*He* does." (ultra posh).

They used nothing so tawdry as an advertisement but twelve leather-bound albums made and mailed to a dozen handpicked men, each worth more than £100 million. They were intrigued and flattered.

I like parking by her car because it makes mine look immaculate.

The *Bishop of Norwich*'s official signature is "Norvic."

In the restaurant at ... the tramp walked around drinking the dregs from every used cup until chased out.

On autobahns, 150 mph *Mercedes* did not see little East German cars.

Winning Words

Sotheby's broke the imperial seal on a crate of honeyed wine, fit for a Czar, bottled in 1830.

Aristocrats may ignore a member of the lower classes like a discarded paper cup.

The top five accountancy companies keep chomping each other so that they can be in the top five. So do pharmaceutical companies.

One-up-man-ship overheard at *Harrods:*
  "Do you have swans on your lake?"
  "Only on the small one."

Inside her jacket were designer labels; inside his jacket were ink stains.

Landowner, patrician (affected, firmly received) accent, was getting out of *Land rover*, "My father gave it to the *National Trust* and we have a lease-back over 100 years."

What is the difference between a Rottweiler and a poodle urinating on your leg? You would let the Rottweiler finish.

Class and Status

"Could I have the keys?"
    The estate agent laughed. There was no roof.

GPs wear casual clothes; consultants (and pharmaceutical sales representatives), expensive suits.

The moral flabbiness born of the bitch goddess, success.

Fame is a powerful aphrodisiac.

He gave the impression that very many cities had rubbed him smooth.

The hotel had slipped downmarket. Real flowers to plastic. Classical background music to advertisers' muzak. Real open fire to radiators. Credit card accepted to rejected. Younger to older waitresses.

In the Yuppie restaurant (1989), on each table, sat a telephone.

A spotlight bathed the priest in his church, "We have used candlelight for ages and have long been media conscious."

Every interviewee was female. Each wore a uniform of grey suit and black tights.

Top management took time out on a jolly in a posh hotel to massage each other's insecurities and carve up the future service.

Living in the countryside, you are cursed with outbuildings. You fill them with junk, in the hope that one day you will sell it for a fiver.

Nurse, attending patient on drip, "I felt ever so important, going up in a helicopter."

The nickname of the "Starfighter" was "The Widow Maker."

The grandfather said, "You don't see many of those around."
    The metal whistle was marked "ARP" (<u>A</u>ir <u>R</u>aid <u>P</u>recautions).

Winning Words

The starving crowd could not eat the culled swans for they were royal birds. The police watched them burn the pile.

Avuncular

In the Middle Ages, a hermit was a tourist attraction.

The 12th century church boosted numerous individual knitted pew cushions (air force, army, village scenes)

Olivier's voice cut through like acid through metal.

No one person can expect to capture all the good things of life.

Posh woman in a car stopped, "How do you grow things? I can't."
People often stopped to take photos of his cottage garden.

Graves varied. The massive stone mausoleum of a 1840s JP; its slab heavy enough to deter snatchers of the fresh body (so it could not be sent by night train for a London teaching hospital to buy it) *v.s.* simple softwood cross with white paint saying "Ami – we miss you."

By the end of a day, the pressure on your backbone results is your shrinking by ¾ inch.

"Take a tip from me. Give them a photo. of you ten years ago."

At large contentious meeting behind closed doors:
"We are all professionals. Let us behave with decorum."

He had a special, louder, "telephone" voice.

Blood spilt – mainly mine.

Pushchair with eight wheels looked like a jumbo jet.

The most junior reporter, the "lowest form of life", attends the presentation of charity cheques.

Class and Status

Overnight, a press changes cylindrical trousers into trousers with razor-sharp creases.

He looked upon himself as a piece of porcelain that has been through the furnace and had become glazed, armoured against adversity.

When drunk, a local accent increases.

On entering the windowless WC the extraction fan deafened.

"Never go back. Those you respected are boring old farts."

His study bulged with mementoes of occupation.

They drank from 18th century champagne flutes.

The television hid within an antique cabinet surrounded by other antiques.

A pretty girl turns a cheek to deflect a kiss. A plainer girl seeks it with enthusiasm, full lipped and moist. God bless the latter.

"If you are a (surname) and live in (city) you have to be an undertaker. (Name)s have been since the nineteenth century."

The wife of the groundsman to a cemetery boasted, "My husband has 5,000 men under him."

"The ruling classes are sent away to school at the age of eight. They don't know what life is like for the rest of us."

He wore his "Invigilator" badge with pride.

Killer question to overbearing bureaucrat who will not do as you want, "Have you authority for your own budget, to pay my extra expenses?"

"She's all right. I couldn't care a toss about the others."

"Not a pretty sight with his cauliflower ear and without his plate," he said, distorting his mouth to one side.

Winning Words

"Which side of the (hospital bed) screen does the visiting pharmacist go to when the patient is undressed?"

He was a mountain of a man, so large that he blocked out the light.

She was well-dressed but went around the train carriage collecting all the newspapers to take home and read.

To jogger: "Don't leave the grounds or the local farmer will take a pot shot at you!"

Military personnel were exempt from writing their car registration or room numbers as a precaution against bombs.

When the police woman arrived at his 18th birthday party his heart sank: his motorbike tax disk had expired. But then she started to undress: a kissogram from his mates.

A batman served early morning tea to your bedside.

British train: cold, no buffet; dirty, late.

Self-satisfied affluence.

Managers are like tea-bags. You only know how strong they are after you have put them in hot water.

Candles lit the oak-lined room. Solid silver napkin rings. Many obsequious servants. Heavy velvet curtains. Port passed around, anti-clockwise, in a decanter.
    "The Queen."
    "God bless her."

Harrods: "Enter a different world". Green liveried footmen, multi-millionaires disgorged from taxis.

Padded lift.

Packet of bath salts as a gift displayed; the house had no bath.

Class and Status

The private roads usually have more potholes.

Home swimming pools look less opulent when covered with bubble wrap to retain heat.

Being a JP is often something to do for leisured affluent women.

"Where is my mother's wedding ring?"
    Child had sold to buy drugs.

Of black eye:
    "Is it bad?"
    "Eye like an egg!"
    "Put some steak on it if you have some," said the doctor.
    "I felt like saying, show me some, so that I can recognise it!"

Gold rings, cut with a bolt cutter, melted and reset.

Class and status (non-human)

BMW made bubble cars; the company and cars have grown.

"Bottom feeder" (as *Tubifex* worms in mud bottom of pond): low status (animal) person who gets by doing whatever he can such as by eating the scraps that those above discard.

The lion was controlling the situation now and bending the future to his will.

"You cannot outrun an ostrich. They will respect you if you carry a thorn bush because they are concerned about their eyes. If they attack you, play dead. They may jump up and down on you and break your ribs. But they will soon lose interest. It cannot be much fun eating their parents' dung while a baby and having your throat slit. No wonder they get cross."

The country mouse has poverty but security; the town mouse wealth but uncertainty.

A huge ocean liner has a big horn that shouts, "Look at me. Get out of the way!"

Virologist who kept the last few hundred samples of smallpox in the world:
"They are not friends or foes but inanimate collaborators."

Communication

'... we had good talk,' Johnson said.
    Boswell replied, 'Yes, Sir, you tossed and gored several persons."
(James Boswell)

Even though he did not understand the words, the diva had a crisp vibrant energy-pumped voice; she zapped straight into his brain and tinged emotions.

There was a ritual for meeting a stranger. Three warriors stepped forward with their shields and challenged. Three white men did the same. Bang, bang, bang. The whites won for they had the stronger weapons.

He counted his blessings. He lacked ultra-fast broadband but could quickly walk to his vegetable patch.

Cooking

A single goose egg makes the very best sponges.

Turkey bewitched to a golden brown.

"There were too many grapes and I saw this recipe for grape jam so I made some. A few pots are going off (mouldy) on the top, but this one looks all right so here you are – but I'd eat it soon if I were you."

"We used to find a little 'ole' nest on the mardle (small pond surrounded by scrub in Norfolk), take a duck egg and cook it there, in a tin lid."

Kettle of hob boiling for tea ejaculated its top at the height of its whistle.
Perfect parabola.

"Great restaurants are, of course nothing but mouth-brothels. There is no point in going to them if one intends to keep one's belt buckled."
(Frederic Raphael)

About dirty plates:
"Let them apricate." (bask in the sun)

I cannot cook spaghetti; I have no pan long enough.

When the kettle is on the way to boiling and you turn it off, it gives a great sigh, as if exasperated with the change of plan, and subsides.

Cooking

The burnt caramel coated with velvety *ganache* was so luscious that he could only weep.

The cute pink piglets swayed from side to side in the trailer. Presumably it was training for being turned on the spit.

The cook wiped sweat from her cheek. The dough, liquid as diarrhoea, sploshed into the boiling fat. There it spread into a perfect ring and solidified. The moving grill flipped the ring over and over. One minute later that grill disgorged the ring onto a bed of sugar.
   "One doughnut. That'll be 25p."

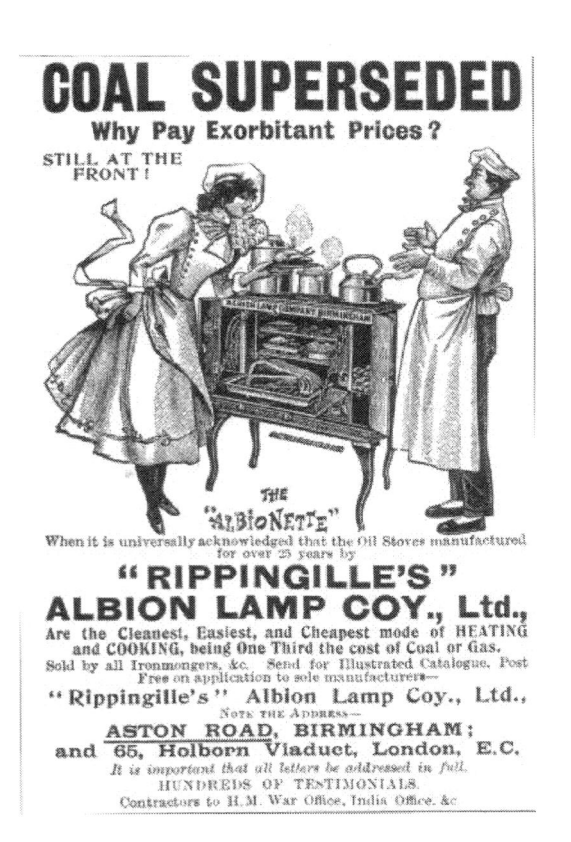

Courage

Some sad people looped their exhausts into their cars to commit suicide. It would not work now.

"I had never been more scared than as a deck hand on the Bering Sea.
    The captain opened a window in the cigarette-fogged cabin and shouted, 'Chip harder, lads, or we'll tip over'.
    I was chipping the ice off at − 30 degrees. I never resent paying money for cod. I know the effort that went into catching it."

The men could urinate in a dark corner of the field, unseen; the starlight TV camera was pointing elsewhere. The night was moonless.
    "More tea?"
    "No. I want the opposite. I'm bursting."
    How did the women (including the filming team) survive for five hours without toilet facilities? All heroes.

Some conscientious objectors during Word War 1 volunteered to act as human guinea pigs in experiments. Some individuals where infected with diseases (e.g. jaundice, influenza) to see if treatments worked.

Decay and despair

Time warp.

Same style of spectacles as in youth.

Veins bulged on head.

Little fish *(Garra rufa)* tickled: they nibbled off (hopefully) only dead skin from feet.

The waist thickens and jowls form.

Disappeared into the undifferentiated sludge of time.

All your parts, once firm and pert, are heading south (in northern hemisphere).

"When I went into the baths at *Roturua* I wore pink toe nail polish. When I came out it was silver. It took three days for me to stop smelling of bad eggs. But wonderful for the skin."

Life is so fragile.

The 18th century landscape of an aristocratic house may seem forever, but the great trees (for example beech at 250 years) will all die together.
(After Diana Athill)

The house foundations had sunk by a foot. The builder told her that all the plants growing up the walls must come down. She cried.

During storms into narrow streets, loose tiles fall, killing people.

Winning Words

"He was at the medical school teaching the best ... and needed this instant recall, what bone is joined to what, and he found that he had lost it, so he retired. As you get older you loose the speed and you forget."

Of the snowman, only the buttons and carrot remained, scattered on the concrete.

Internet has left our ability to concentrate in tatters.

Christmas tree: object of fervent desire to problem for disposal in two weeks.

Of organisation: behind the veneer the wood was rotten and powdery.

The tree root ferreted into the salt-glazed drain pipe, and eagerly expanded, cramming it so full that it shattered into a myriad fragments.

After the flood of 1938, Horsey (Wind) Mill temporally became an island. A bold merry and contented crow feasted on the bodies as they floated along the dyke.

On the train in the morning, the train is clean, fresh, and uncrowded. Returning home in the evening the train is overcrowded, its toilets blocked and you are exhausted.

"Life is what happens while you are busy making other plans." *(John Lennon)*

There used to be a war memorial and a village hall in a Nissen hut on the Main Road. Gone without trace. Only memories remain, for a little while.

She was in love with a kind of life that had gone. The National Trust now owned Castle Howard, used to film "Brideshead Revisited."

They fought for a life slightly longer than the one destined. They protected themselves with fashionable electric toothbrushes, hair dye and any detail that would enable them

Decay and despair

to last a little longer before they – and we – are engulfed by the black background.

The magnificent pearl is the result of injury to the oyster.

They brought in the food (to a great wooden building) from a mile away because fire so scared them.

You should keep your old things: valve radios, sepia photographs. They are you.

Vertical plasma screen displayed cat-walking models thinner than size zero.

"That was the week that was," (an early 1960's TV series), introduced wit so sarcastic, so acid, that it burned holes in all the cherished institutions.

"Rage, rage, against the dying of the light."
(Dylan Thomas)

The purpose of dogs is to die before us so that, from the death of a little loved one, we can understand the deaths of larger human loved ones who will follow.

"I am now but a veneer and not solid oak."

"Bury the dead, sire, and look after the living."

You are lucky if the straps on your goggles or the knicker elastic on your swimming trunks last a year. It is the chlorine. Fortunately, your skin is made of tougher stuff.

Time tends to creep up on you like the windscreen on a fly.

We all have bumps and bends in life.

The pond water poured over the top of his Wellingtons. Then, with each step, muddy water slurped and bubbled within the pistons of his thick socks.

All of art, nature and human relationships are in flux. For example, *nothing* is permanent in the landscape. The very tectonic plates move. The very soil had flowed around the substantial Second World War pillbox and floated it from cliff to beach. Since *Einstein*, matter can *disappear* and become energy and the reverse.

> Everything fails, everything breaks, everything passes.

> "You cannot step twice into the same rivers ..."
> *(Heraclitus of Ephesus)*

Everything in the hotel was refurbished except the electricity switches. They were angular, chunky and yellowish, displaying their 1960s vintage.

Overnight, a jug full of milk curdled into wobbly cheese.

The voluptuous curving bonnet with its sexy air scoops, thrusting forward with its 3 litre engine, degenerated into a spade as it dug into the verge.

The park he had played in, swung on its swings, drank at its water fountain: all gone. He had jogged around it, picnicked within it, enjoyed a funfair and painted it. He had embellished his painting using a specially-purchased pot of glittering gold paint and taken his picture to school. He had won a cut glass bowl and a goldfish. In a nearby church he had christened a son, buried two fathers and one mother. Goodbye park.

He carried his mother's death with him. It was like having, in his pocket, a knife. If he reached in, it could cut him.

Rust grows.

The key failed to open the door, even when encouraged by oil and a hammer.

Burned thumb on grill wire: immediately plunged thumb into cold water. Line seared. Flesh mortally wounded. Liquefied into a valley but kept breaking down. Rebuilt, wonderfully, in two weeks but only using generalist connective tissue.

Decay and despair

Daughter died before her sixth birthday in form and intellect most exquisite. "The unfortunate parents ventured all on this frail bark and the wreck was total."
(Inscription on tomb of Penelope Boothby, Ashbourne)

The murky day deposited a trail of filth along the bonnet.

Curmudgeonly.

His body had its own intelligence, emotion after reading the obituary. The first of his cohort, had died. Of its own accord, as if not directed by his brain, his shoulders slumped, back bowed and he breathed a noisy "Oh." He looked diminished, was diminished, shrunken. He wanted to hide.

Candle watcher to King Alfred: "(Sire) Oh lord, another hour has fled."

"It's knocked the stuffing out of me."

"You young people, get on", said the bus guide, aged seventy with black-dyed hair. "You do not know tiredness as I do."

The leather-bound books had whitened. Leave them to the corruption of dust and the munching of bookworms.

I have all these balls to juggle and will drop some.

He has a shrivelled heart.

Broken pallets, empty bottles and black bin liners besmirched the hedgerows in the chalky field.

When your mother dies, you become less solid. Your connections, achievements dissolve at the centre of you. You are made of dust.

You are never truly alone in this world until both your parents are dead.

Life is a risky business and something gets you in the end.

Winning Words

How dated, yellowed, unevenly typed, the memorandum from 1968, the year he registered, looked. Was he that old?

"The rest is silence."
(William Shakespeare)

Squirt-tailed (diarrhoea)

On opening the suitcase with clothes from the rainforest, all were mouldy, rotten; all had to be destroyed.

Miasma of gloom.

They will use you up, just as you or I use dental floss.

The drone exploded his sperm within the queen bee. Leaving his penis inside her, he fell away to the ground, dead.

About death: You have been a visitor in a very great city and should not complain when you are asked to leave.

One month you attract and swat flies; the next, you attract and feed them.

Commentary on videogame: "You, oldest maggot, are you not dead yet?"

He saw his contact lens flip from his eye in the (British) train toilet. He scrambled down onto the bouncing floor. His lens had gone. But he picked up two other lenses, brittle, jagged – and old. The floor had not have been cleaned for years.

The stranger's skirt was short, hair blonde, tights and hat, black. She strode from the bar of the pub and sat next to him. His heart fluttered.
    "Do you mind?" she said. "I want to be next to my mother. We've just buried my father."

The concrete delusion of the city: no soil seen, while in the countryside the houses were transient pimples floating on the soil. Both constructions are fleeting; man cannot tame nature.

Decay and despair

He had squirted window cleaner containing vinegar onto the car windscreen and polished it off until it shone. But the next morning, a sticky grey line besmirched it. The neighbourhood tom cat had curled asleep on the roof and anointed the window with piss.

You must always find a place by the fireside for sister grief.

Photograph: time had routed the red in the roses and washed all in blue.

The heart has rusted to dust, surrounded by irony and loathing.

Men and women were buried in separate pits, but covered with the same quicklime. Even birds migrated high over the town.

Grandpa was less solid, voice thinner, hair so sparse that you could see age spots underneath.

Beneficial as boils.

In the chapel was a volume with copperplate appreciations of babies who had only lived for days.

Carefully prepared food: so much ephemeral beauty disappearing down lavender-scented lavatories.

They gathered all their eggs into one basket and they were scrambled.

God played a cruel trick giving us just three score years and ten.

Thirty five is my favourite age. After that, your bits start falling off.

The oscicle (ear bone) from a fish, examined microscopically, tells its age: one ring every year; up to fifty for the cod.

Send your cremated ashes to a firework manufacturer to mix with rocket shells. There goes ...

Winning Words

"Visited by the terminator of delights and the separator of companions, the devastator of palaces and houses and the replenisher of graves."
(From the Arabian Nights)

Viking cosmology: everything started with the sea and will end with the sea.

Only dirt kept his squalid skin together.

"Hospital for decayed fishermen," founded by the corporation
(Great Yarmouth 1704)

Voice like ash.

Hope had grown grey hairs.

The cod, 3 ½ feet long was perfect on one side. But the other had an ulcer as big as your hand. Could it be the untreated sewage?

The newspaper from 1945 had lost its spine. Only a jagged edge remained. The paper was frail and yellowing. Advertisements were in guineas. The Japanese were warned to evacuate cities.

The driver doing 80 mph on a road with black ice is overtaking to the undertaker.

"We look before and after and pine for what is not."
(Percy Shelley)

A society under tension can detonate.

About transience of human intervention:
"There is a poignant beauty in the process of decay. ... As stones crack and mosses creep, as roots pry into fissures and insects digest, Venice will return to real life."
(Rachel Campbell-Johnston)

The village is dying. The young have left for the excitement of the cities.

Decay and despair

After the coffin was lowered into the grave, first the relatives threw down long-necked roses and then, everyone, handfuls of petals.

If you hit a moose, you break its legs but 1,400 lbs of body falls, smashes the windscreen and you die.

You look at life differently after you have felt on your cheek the butterfly wings of mortality.

What was this lump clogging his pocket after dry cleaning? His handkerchief and the shrunken remains of a comb.

Gravestone inscription:
"Here lies Fred who once was alive and now is dead."

To someone with dimming eyesight, the sun is like the moon.

"Man wants but little here below,
Nor wants that little long."
(Oliver Goldsmith)

"We think caged birds sing, but indeed they cry."
(John Webster)

"Totter towards the tomb."
(Dorothy Sayers)

Pick today's fruits.

"They are not long, the days of wine and roses."
(Ernest Dowson)

Salty water rusts razor blades, scissors, everything.

Leathery brown paunch at the front. Sweaty shirt clinging to back.

Daughters are tauter versions of their mothers.

Winning Words

The chimney smoke from the sugar beet refinery rose and then, on meeting the atmospheric inversion layer, stopped and levelled out. He hoped not to inhale what came down.

The museum curator thought that the exhibit looked tatty. He threw it on the bonfire. The office boy saved it. But only the head and feet remained of that dodo.

Vera effigies huius auis WALGH-VOGEL *(quæ & à nautis* DODAERS *propter foedam posterioris partis crassitiem nuncupatur) qualis viua Amsterodamum perlata est ex Insula* MAVRITII. ANNO M.DC.XXVI.

Mans Adriani Venny Pictoris

He walked home from the party because he was drunk. The car of another drunken party-goer hit him.

Now rubble, graffiti embellished the remaining, partial wall. Pipes stuck out. Shelves smashed. It had been his office.

Apple orchard, established for a century, uprooted. It disappeared without trace in one day.

Sunburnt to a pinker shade of white.

The medieval houses with bleached timber frames were all at different angles.

Plastic bags sheathed the padlocks to beach huts against salt spray.

Decay and despair

The 18 inch deep garden pond had 12 inches of mud. Excavating that was archaeology: golf balls, plastic bendy man toy.

Inner demon.

A man cannot confront two things directly. One is the face of the sun; the other is his own death.

Drugs of addiction

Drug addicts are poor copers.

Silver cigarette paper littered the bird hide/roadside café WC. Drug snorters?

Pushers smuggled (in their knickers) the designer drugs (E) into the hanger boiling with rap and five thousand teenagers. It was safer than alcohol. Who cared who had cut it – and with what – to increase profit? Or whether, within its manufacturing garage, the temperature had been too hot, so that its toxic impurities would mutilate livers, kidneys and lives?

Cabinet of poisons.

Given ergot-infected grain, it is so easy to obtain the ingredients to manufacture LSD.

During a pub crawl, drinkers become less and less coherent and alert. During a coffee shop crawl (such as of attendees at the Royal Society, London, in the 17th century) drinkers become progressively more awake and wakeful. Indeed, they may not be able to go to sleep.

Tip: when eating your mushrooms from the garden, always leave one uncooked, to take to the hospital.

A "god shot": *espresso* coffee at 7 atmospheres, double tamped (caffeine).

Business person in coffee, said, "I'm in the vice business. I sell the last acceptable vice. Top-shelf porn is the biggest profit. But

Drugs of addiction

if you're reading it on the park bench, sitting next to a little old lady, you'll upset her. There's nicotine in tobacco but that's now so anti-social that you have to go outside to enjoy your smoke. There's alcohol but if you're drunk when driving you might get sleepy, crash and hurt someone. All that's left is coffee. That has the opposite effect. Its caffeine keeps you alert. Drink enough and you'll get high. It's still socially acceptable."

In the 1960s, LSD made the very letters swell like balloons.

The girl lay down by the side of the brook. She rested on one elbow; her heel dangled into the water. She clutched a cylinder of lighter fuel.

Security guard who searched bags at festival entrance: "You gents (aged 30s and 60s) have not got any illegal substances?"

Silver birch tree sap produces excellent wine.

Assorted local fermentations.

"We hang drug dealers. Hanging day is Friday. Better one death than a thousand." *(Singapore)*

The hot water bottles thrown over the prison walls contained spirits (alcohol); tennis balls, heroin.

(18th century) A lavender tincture was popular "very commodious for those who wish to indulge in a dram under the appearance of an elegant medicine."

Cannabis pressed down with camel piss; you could see the salt crystals.

Alcohol has zero order kinetics. That means that, no matter how much alcohol is in the body, it metabolises the same amount: 10 mL, every hour. This contrasts with other drugs such as gentamycin (an antibiotic) that have first order kinetics, with half-lives ($\frac{1}{2}$, $\frac{1}{4}$, $\frac{1}{8}$, $\frac{1}{16}$ and so on) like radioactive fallout. *(Figure 1 illustrates first order kinetics)*

He hoped the heroin bought on the street was not "cut" (diluted) with brick dust or *Vim*.

"Gentlemen, I am a *Hedonist*; and, if you *must* know why I take opium, that's the reason why."
(Thomas De Quincey)

Smoking nutmeg is fabled to have the same effect as magic mushrooms.

Laboratory alcohol was potent booze.

The first opium war between Great Britain and China ended in 1842.

Several 19th century literary figures were addicted to drugs. *Coleridge* is one example.

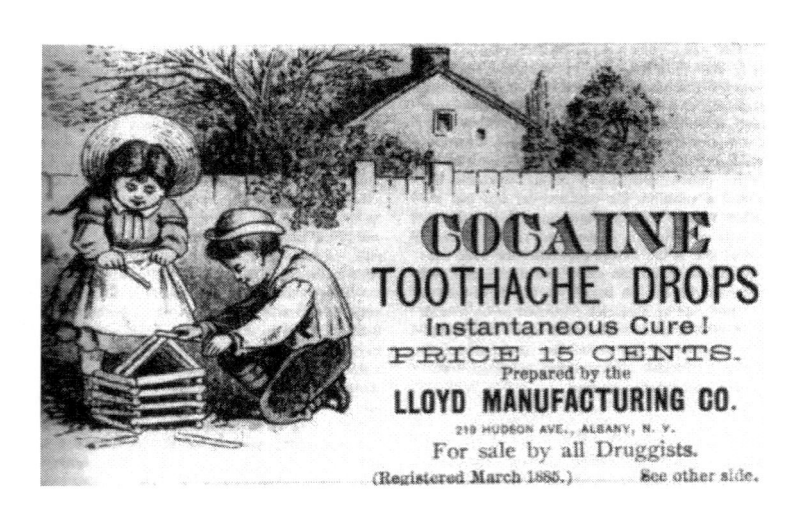

Food and drink

The Arabs roasted the whole sheep and served on a plate. The eyes were separate but the tastiest part was the unborn lamb within.

"There is nothing local on this menu. Where is the rabbit?"
"This hotel (five star) would not serve it. It is thought of as a peasant dish."

Poachers' relish with lemon zest.

Popcorn: bloating agent.

Edwardian desiccate soup.

Beef in aspic.

Food rationing.

Village cricket: cucumber sandwiches, ale.

The slender lager glass wore a frilly skirt.

Two rosettes looked like a classy plate including light crisp chips in starvation portions as a work of art.

Blue tits (birds) learned, by watching each other, to peck holes in the aluminium tops of glass milk bottles. Birds drank the energy-rich cream floating on the top. Then, humans homogenised milk: its top fat layer disappeared. Birds initially confused but soon stopped pecking. "Triangular" holes ceased to irritate humans.

Food may change character on grinding. For example, mustard seeds become "hot" and more exciting. The particle size of certain drugs also matters. As size reduces, the effect of a particular amount may increase from inactive to a normal dose to dangerously poisonous.

Now matter how fancy the meal containing asparagus, the smell in the lavatory is identical.

The first green vegetable grown was watercress.

Wine given as a gift / consumed on holiday always tastes better.

Tarry long enough for goulash and doughnuts.

He could not stop scoffing handfuls of the fat dry cashew nuts coated with sea-salt and cracked black pepper. He was addicted. He reassured himself they contained the right sort of cholesterol.

From clammy cold parsnip roots dug from frozen soil, numb fingers removing mud, to cubes sizzling in herb-flavoured fat.

During the cold spell in his houseboat, the water froze and the propane gas would not vaporise, so he could not even brew a cup of tea.

Stressed parched tomatoes are tastier.

"I'll have that one."
      She'd take it home to cook. That crayfish had climbed to the top of the pile of its friends at the bottom of the hazy aquarium.

He expected the Chinese wine in the hourglass-shaped bottle to be chilled but its bucket steamed. Dry ice? (Solid carbon dioxide that sublimates at −79 °C and then looks misty.) He felt it. No: hot warm sherry like *glühwein*.

"When *McDonalds* opened in Moscow we could not believe it. It was clean. They asked you how much you wanted, rather than telling you. When you left, some people with five burgers under their arm, servers said, 'See you soon.' That gave some

Food and drink

men heart attacks so they had to stop saying it. Those men thought that the *KGB* would be told."

In sporting celebrations, raw-edged association between the explosion of the cork, expulsion of frothing wine and the very essence of champagne.

The honeycomb chunk was flavoursome and chewy like candle wax.

A boy dug out and put a honey pot ant into his mouth (to eat: a delicacy) in the Australian outback. You have never seen such coughing and spluttering.
    "Wrong end," he said.

Pumpkin oil appears purple in the bowl but a thin layer on the side of a plate is green. It smells nuttier than it tastes. It completely coats the tongue.

Waiter removed two metal domes covering plates simultaneously: theatre.

Country people bring many roots to the table in triumph.

Fragrance of silkily sliced parsnips, glazed in acacia honey.

Balsamic vinegar four years old is viscous, hauntingly sweet yet piquant with a rich nutty intensity.

To the lobster *paella*, that required special opening pliers, they threw in, for contrast, a little rubbery octopus.

The lobster in the tank had its jaws clamped together with tape. It had obviously been a naughty crustacean.

In the leek and chicken soup, the chicken tasted like a stringy, rather depressed, bird.

Teeth cut into medium rare elk like butter.
   The hunter said, "I get my butcher to cut it up into steaks, burgers and it goes in the freezer. It keeps for 2 ½ years.

Salmon, compared with sardine, soufflé tastes better.

Mother to child, "Eat your meat. A cow has died to give you that."

At Flagstaff, Arizona on route 66 was a diner where the servers sometimes danced on the tables to the juke box playing *Elvis Presley* and *The Beatles*. On offer were burgers with cheese and fries, hot fruit and toffee fudge cake, cream and root beer to die for.
   "I've taken my simvastatin (a cholesterol-reducing medicine)," he re-assured himself.

Grapes dripping down a wall.

Big fat flavoured whisky.

Wild boar crackling is black, which some people find off-putting, so butchers cut it off.

Restaurants have white noise, an atmosphere that is not entirely unpleasant. Generally the half-overheard babble of conversations is meaningless. We pay for it dearly. What it is all about is that it drowns out that we are a long time dead and a long time quiet.

Only sweet strong (15% alcohol) wine could be transported in antiquity. One reminded *Antony* of *Cleopatra*'s lips.

Old-fashioned *Lyons* tearoom: uniform of waitresses was black dress and white apron.

"How do you know that wheat is ready to harvest?"

Food and drink

"Two weeks before it's a little too brownish. Then, on rubbing between the fingers and palm, it's first like milk, then flour paste. Then it becomes so hard that only your teeth can crack it and you hear its field crackling on a hot day. That is the time."

Today, inexpensive hand-held digital moisture content meters are the norm.

Cheese so old it remained untouched in the mousetrap all winter.

"Take this pudding away. It has no theme."
(Winston Churchill)

The pale pasta had to be eaten first. It melted in the mouth. Only then the yellow parcels, creamed with mushrooms, picked from the forest that morning. Then tiramisu. Wash down with nut liquor.

Mushroom bean sprouts taste of the Earth.

The preacher men sat down to their "lumberjack breakfasts." They all had large bellies; perhaps that helped their presence.

He ate the meal on the house boat and the mosquitoes ate him.

They drank the wine, fizzy and strawberry flavoured, by the Venetian canal.

"We've some other news for you," he said, patting her tummy.

In the street hung sides of meat, crawling with flies, splattered with bird droppings.

Cooked on hot rocks, turgid green prawns turn brown.

Great chefs don't like to view food through glass. They are very physical. They like to poke it.

The monk who invented champagne shouted, "Come quickly! There are stars in the wine!"

Winning Words

"Grits" (type of porridge USA).

"You must try our speciality of the *Nuremburg* region. We call it 'the living cake'." (pork medallions in Christmas pudding sauce, with piped potato encircling).

The Art Deco restaurant on *San Francesco* bay with stained glass windows claimed to be the number one for seafood, globally.

"Have some more beef. Of course, in Britain, all your cows are mad."
(Germany)

There is something untrustworthy in the person who does not like apple dumplings.

Her capacity for alcohol was considerable and, as the evening passed, her head tossed more and more.

Friars and pilgrims travelled spreading cheese lore, such as of *Roquefort*: blue-veined, gritty, and soapy. It made you want to push to all corners of your mouth for every taste bud to deliver its verdict.

Cheese is milk's leap for posterity.

"Plant four seeds.
One for the rook.
One for the crow.
One to rot.
One to grow."
(Farmers' proverb)

Baby slapped its lips on gulping gripe water. She knew how to show that she liked it.

Leave the bits in punch. Like the quality of mercy, it should not be strained.

Dogfish still dripping from the sea, expertly cooked with the owner's smile and *raki*.

Food and drink

"To EAT is human
To eat well is DIVINE."
(modified from Mark Twain)

"I'm cherried out."

No cheese board is complete without "The Stinking Bishop", a soft and smelly UK cheese. Tooth and beard-washing recommended afterwards.

Soay sheep *(Ovis aries)*, small because unchanged in size from the Neolithic age.

You could almost stand up your spoon in a hot *cioccolata calda*; when cold it nearly set solid.

Tweet from ornithologist at Christmas:
"Moribund turkey found stuffed in kitchen this morning."

The market stall offered huge misshapen porcini mushrooms, freshly gathered from the forest.

She loved the strong Lancashire cheese. It seemed to cool her forehead. The same place on her scalp always itched.

Wine from the greenhouse vine was feral, farmyard and funky: drinkable but unlikely to be popular in the wine trade.

To add extra zing to beer brewed in shanty towns, fabled to add old car batteries.

Oxymels (acid and honey) include balsamic, cranberry and raspberry vinegars. Example of oxymoronic mixture: palm syrup and brown sauce. Oxymels such as of squill were used as medicines. That contained sulphuric acid and glycerine (sweeter than honey). The literary "oxymoron" (e.g. serious vanity, wet drought, malevolent cherub, female man) is related. Some are physical such as sweet and sour sauce or bricked-up windows. Some are so popular that they have become cliché's e.g. deafening silence.

Winning Words

They sat in the sunshine, relishing their ice-creams, lapping around them with their tongues.

A French cook first made mayonnaise in Mahon *(Menorca)*.

She tasted the Kiwi juice, "It's ... gloopy." (mucilaginous)

Notice on an allotment site:
"The leeks you thieved were sprayed. Do not eat for a week."

Yummy buckwheat crepe with goats' cheese and honey. Why are the nicest things so unhealthy?

Apfelstrudel pastry must be so thin that you can read a newspaper through it.

One of his five a day of fruit and veg. was cranberry vodka.

A piece of *naan* bread, heated, is like a pair of bellows. Bite off the top, squeeze together and apart: steam puffs out: party trick.

He carried back two pints of ale, one in each hand. He sneezed succulently. He contorted violently like a gyroscope but did not spill a drop. Mind you, you probably would not want to drink the beer.

One criterion of whether something is a "cake" or "biscuit" is that, over time, cakes get harder while biscuits get softer. In the UK, VAT is paid on chocolate covered cakes but not biscuits (e.g. *Jaffa*).

The home made beef burgers contained chocolate.

A "bombard" was a leather beer vessel of over 1 ½ gallons.

Maoris were cannibals; sailors were best because free range.

Sherbet powder, the taste of 1950's childhood in the UK, sugar and sodium bicarbonate, citric or tartaric acids, These liberate carbon dioxide: the fizz. Citric acid and syrup are used to make the cough medicine: "Simple Linctus." Sherbet power sported a

Food and drink

liquorice dip; it got thinner and thinner on sucking. That foam in the mouth could give you a sore throat.

Carrot and raspberry juice.

The Romans thought thunder and lightning made cucumbers grow curved. The EC does not like them because they require more packaging.

About *canapés*: what pervert had put fish *with scales* in the sandwiches?

I like a big bird, well stuffed.

After drinking eight coffees that day, sleep eluded him.

What a disreputable collection of drunks, loud 60 year old men wearing pin-striped suits, from ... (company) on the train. They were like overwintering Brussels sprouts.

Drink coffee (even without the dregs) in *Cyprus* and the stomach fights back. Presumably that is why their coffee arrives with a glass of water.

The goulash was within the loaf; the top was a lid.

"There's plenty of grapes," he said, plucking two bunches, each as big as his head.
    Their juice was sweet and sun-warmed.

He had only known of tamarind as an ingredient of *HP* sauce. Across his hand lay a tamarind pod, brown, sausage sized. He snapped it like a Christmas cracker. Within were big seeds between a chewy pith of sweet sharpness. He slipped the broken pod on his finger, a long thimble. Afterwards, that finger smelt musty.

No self-respecting dead fish would like to be seen wrapped in that newspaper.

Her son had rapidly gained weight:

"When you are breast feeding, you do not know how much of the contents have gone in."

While cleaning out the inside of the car, he found under the front seat, a chip. He asked his wife about it.
    "It couldn't have been me," she said. "I would have eaten it."

A curry so hot that it made his fillings sizzle. Curiously, the sauce made his scalp itch in exactly the same spot every time.

About strongest medicinal sulphur water in Europe: "Just pour yourself enough for one swallow, and knock it back in one gulp," said the jug minder.
    The water in the jug covered with a cloth with weighted tassels looked yellowish.
    "Danger! Poison!" screamed his eyes.
    He recoiled and pulled a face.
    "It wears off after about ten minutes," soothed the minder.

What glorious nuts in honey. But afterwards, his teeth ached.

"The Scoville Scale" assesses and communicates the heat of chillies. Heat units range from zero for green pepper to 300,000 for the *Habanero* and Scotch bonnet.

"Cider vinegar, night and morning: that's what keeps me going."
(Well-preserved vigorous regular swimmer, ex-pig farmer, 68 years old).

Diner advertisement: "Eat heavy."

The ancient stone horn of plenty dripped with overflowing food from its top; on the base was a teat; around it, children crawled.

The cellar dwellers ate grass, dandelions and pigeons.

The fingerbowl contained nuts like rocks.

Food and drink

You really know that you are a carnivore when, staring up at you from the plate, fins and all, is one whole sea hake.

The "Yuk!" reaction is what, generally, stops us putting disease into our mouths. But occasionally we can be misled such as rejecting autoclaved (presumably sterile) cockroaches or apple juice from brand new bedpans or chocolate shaped like faeces.

Of oil seed rape: the executive puffing his *PulmoTurbohaler*, the child tossing sleepless in the night, reduced to snivelling bags of juices by the bright yellow fields and the farmers' greed.
    "It's harmless. The pollen is too heavy to blow anywhere."

The Hungarians tenderised their meat by riding on it under their saddles.

Wine so rough it kicks your shoulders back and your belly in.

He had never eaten blue vegetables before. The cabbage, before boiling, had been red.

Of ugly, but tasty, deep sea fish: "Eat the fish before you see it."

"Me rabbit's died," after feeding with too many dandelions and lush grass.

Good meat has a silky texture: fatty, buttery and yellow, from β-carotene in spring grass. Fat gives the flavour. Food terrorists preach of lean meat. Instead, buy meat with fat; then cut it off.

Pineapple contains a ferociously strong enzyme (bromelain) that digests protein. Jelly-setting workers in canning factories wear protective gloves.

Rather than steak flavour, would not puss prefer sparrow favour?

The soil, under straggling oaks, was so chalky and impoverished, that truffles struggled to grow. Those that do concentrate the essence of the soil and they are tortured; it shows in their taste.

"Look what I've done," they boast to the diner.

"They had the real old faggots there: those covered with a veil." (1967).

"We have produced wine here for five thousand years."

Such was the munifence of the ... during the announcement that, when the embargoed document was presented, they offered a sandwich in a plastic case. He chose one labelled "Tuna." It was not. It was ham; he hated ham.

The little waiter tried to make himself as big as possible so that we could not see the people at the next table complaining.

The tiny potato left on the surface turns green and poisonous in one afternoon. (Not harmless chlorophyll but toxic glycoalkaloid solanine.)

The friendly cow, wide of girth, turgid of udder, craned forward over the water to chew the choicest willow leaves.

Drink was a killer, especially fiery "arrack".

Hell brew.

Coffee loaded with grit, slag and incinerated.

The little pig squealed when kicked away, having found the only truffle that day. It was perfumed and tasted of the bowels of the earth.

For storks, about to take off on an eight thousand mile journey, the cornfield served a good breakfast of lizards and crickets.

The sow with the rings through her nose and the number 568 stabled to her huge pink floppy ear was rooting in the soil,

Food and drink

dribbling foamy saliva and generally thoroughly enjoying herself.

To drink a wine too soon is infanticide.

The grub bored inside the bean, curled up and was roasted with the bean. Europeans loved the coffee's taste: it had that special something.

Free-range, compared with battery, hens, have freedom. They also have pecking, cannibalism and parasites. Man can ingest raw flesh, muscle, skin, gristle and even small bones.

The durian fruit is indescribably smelly. Aircraft will not allow it on board ... capable of inflicting serious injury on the eater.

Each huge pig had a big square label stapled to an ear.

Châteauneuf-du-Pape was grown in big stones in the furnace of the sun by day; the stones still radiated heat all night.

The cheaper the white plonk, the lower the alcohol content and the colder it must be to be drinkable.

Mass food is designed to appeal to everyone; it needs to be personalised. For example, add tarragon to the tomato soup.

The "angels' share" is the 2% of whisky lost by evaporation every year. That is a lot for an 18 year old malt. Some are so peaty that they taste medicinal.

Deep-frozen vodka has the viscosity of oil. Swallow in one gulp. In your stomach, ice becomes fire.

When spirit "warms the cockles of your heart" it does so, literally, because it passes near to your heart valves.

Memories of 1950s childhood: tomato sauce on fried bread, sweetened condensed milk in a tin or, if judged "under the weather", force fed flowers of sulphur beaten into black treacle.

Port is smooth, soft and tangy.

Winning Words

Mists held the fungal spores vital for Southern grapes. They look horrid: dirty, speckled and shrivelled. In the press, grapes only yield their juice reluctantly. When a liquid does finally emerge, it resembles dark brown toffee. It drips rather than flows, like old engine oil draining from a sump.

When sweet corn is ripe enough to harvest it turns brown. When prodded with a fingernail, clear sap means it is too early, if no sap, too late. However, milky sap means it is just right: the Goldilocks test. Earwigs often crawl out.

It was a quarter cake and three quarters honeyed cream. The result: one quarter gratification (afterglow); three quarters remorse (guilt). Five hundred calories, all the wrong sort.

Meal of the forest: rich venison, wild truffles, redcurrants and herbs.

Froth on the top; a weak brew beneath.

Mum sipped at her tea while little Angus sipped at her.

He would only drink absolutely fresh milk. Perhaps a bad childhood experience with a wrinkled breast?

Little tooth marks! A mouse had eaten ...'s chocolate Easter egg!

It is more brutal to be a vegetarian than a meat-eater. Meat is dead while vegetables remain alive. Look at potatoes: they sprout.

He tucked into the stilton and biscuits with gusto.

Some varieties of coffee bean have been through the gut of a wolf and were collected from faeces.

Fried pit pony tastes succulent.

Was it onion rings? No: rubbery squid. Mushrooms? No: granular liver.

Food and drink

Confected.

He took a good gulp of the communion wine. He hoped he would not catch the colds spreading through the neighbourhood. The vicar had wiped the rim with a cloth.

The bottle fell into the strawberry flan, crushing it.

The seamen took a sack full of mussels, six bottles of red wine, a chunk of cheese and some bread rolls into the dockside restaurant. Each threw some coins on the table.
"Impress us. Show us what you can do."

The lorry full of sugar burned on the motorway. Brown caramel rained down.

Drink sufficient olive oil and you can scrape it off your skin - like this (demonstrated with a fingernail).

Termites have a rich oily taste like pork scratchings.

A 250 mL wine glass holds about half a bottle.

De-alcoholised wine tastes abominable.

The chunk of chop nestled in its dollop of fat repulsed him. He wished he had ordered the vegetarian meal.

"Must have a leak."

About 18th birthday party: "I cleared up their puke when they were five – and I am still doing it!"

Red wine looks like *Coke..,*

Humans confuse saccharin with sugar; a butterfly, tasting with pads on its feet, can distinguish instantly.

Gardening

The middle finger of his right hand was stiff, swollen and aching. He had tugged out groundsel. They were bullies but he was a bigger bully.

Heaving ghetto of the flower show.

Water trickled in many places. A spirit of the druids had animated the gardener.

He dabbed the weed killer onto the impudent millet: the touch of death.

Horseradish grown in a small pot sprouts copious leaves. However, the taproot is intertwined, constipated, almost impossible to grate to make sauce.

The crackling of fir branches is the gardener's equivalent of bursting bubble-wrap.

A successful seat requires a prospect (view) from a refuge where a wild animal cannot creep up on you, unnoticed.

Tunnellers make the best gardeners because they want to spend their leisure in the fresh air.

A lawnmower will not prevent a cheeky lawn overflowing two inches onto concrete. He sliced down deep, hearing and feeling the spade grate against the concrete. He amputated the sliver of impudent turf and banished it to the compost heap. The operation reminded him of a tooth rescale leaving a trace of blood. How satisfying!

He hacked off the branches of the woody thistle and splattered the oozing stump with glyphosphate.

Gardening

Japanese knotweed *(Fallopia japonica)* is a thug that only understands glyphosphate when fully grown.

Yucca secretes poison from its roots that say to other plants, "This is Yucca territory: do not grow here."

Slay thistles or they will slay you.

The bus driver's enthusiasm was his allotment. His garden triumphs irradiated through his daily work. He had got the spirit of the earth in his bones.

The segment of the bonfire that glows red at night remembers from where the wind blows. (E.g. if the wind is from the West, the West-facing side glows.)

After just two weeks without mowing, the lawn sprouted a carpet of flowers. After four weeks its border offered a specimen thistle of architectural dimensions.

He assumed the bottle contained kerosene. He bent to light the damp bonfire with a match.
 "Whoosh!"
 His eyebrows remained but he now understood why petrol was not advised.

The fruit of the elderly apple tree were so tart, so flavoursome. He was sad that it would not offer its treasure for much longer for it was dying. The storm had split it into two but fruit still grew: its last grasp at posterity. Apples might fall and rot but their pips grow into its children.

Bonfire smoke's signature persists indoors, a lingering sugar-rush.
 "Love that smell," she said, nose in his pullover.

New potatoes eaten within a couple of hours of lifting have not, yet, had time to convert (polymerise) their sugar into starch. Eating that astonishingly sweet tuber is one thing that you must do before you die.

The Elizabethan garden was formal, ordered, everything in its place: it proclaimed, we command nature.

Mr *Middleton*'s "Digging for Victory" (1945) was merciless in his battle against pests. Slugs were spiked with a long hat pin and dumped in strong brine; osmotic pressure plasmolised them. His armament included: arsenic, copper, cyanide, derris, formaldehyde, hydrochloric acid, mercury and sulphur. Many have long been banned.

Rhubarb forcing pots were his fetish. He lusted after a line of gargantuan terracotta ones with lids that made a solid clunk and resisted frost, but had to make do with an old black plastic dustbin.

Gardening

Marsh dock was hard to uproot but tougher-looking thistles were surprisingly easy. He almost felt sorry for them as they slid from the earth. But wind had already floated their thistledown seeds beyond his reach. It was too late. The thistles had already won.

Thistledown is beautiful, insubstantial; thistles are hard, prickly bullies.

The armfuls of stinging nettles had seized upon the gap between glove and sleeve; a ring of numbness as if touched by ice, resulted. That skin felt tight as after surgery. The gardener learned that lesson and wore long pullover and gauntlets.
"I fear not the toughest thistle, so armoured am I."

Of a heavy-duty lawnmower: "It's a brute."

In mist, the Victorian stumpery was a magical place; stark uprooted trees, feathery ferns, moss, fungi and dew.

You need to get your eye in, to see the shape of the marsh dock and young thistle, when they hide within desirable foliage. Only then will you uproot foe and not friend.

A stagnant garden encourages rhubarb mildew.

At Hampton Court, nature was ruthlessly controlled (e.g. clipping elms).

At the advertising stands of the flower show, quirky inventors bubbled forth and clamoured for attention.

A garden is "culture": the gardener nurtures the wanted and destroys the unwanted. So do other cultures. Examples are art, science, nations, occupations and technologies.

The royal rhubarb was enormous

Generations

A baby might be a designer accessory; an eighteen-year old is not.

Do not blame the garden pool manufacturers for children drowning.
    Midwives should attach labels to all babies, "May be damaged by almost anything."

Adolescent impulses: angst, confusion, embarrassment, greed, instant gratification and rapid change.

"There is a lot of Peter Pan in us lot."

Toddler rocked to music and came over to rub his head against her.

Father about his son to son's grandfather.
    "What kind of a world will it be for ...?"
    "It will be his world. He will be at home in it."

We are the past and the present and together we face the future.
(Maori proverb)

"Children are the living message we send to a time we will not see."
(Neil Postman)

"You can have two yogurts," said mum.
    "Connected!" whined the girl.

Half of the riotous young dinosaurs, but few of their minders, at the natural history museum, were male.

Generations

The family party posted on *Facebook* risks gatecrashers, gangs, police and ambulances.

Phone call at 7 a.m. from a fourteen-year old, "Grandma, the dog's been sick. What do I do?"

"It takes a village to raise a child."
(African proverb)

Perhaps there can be no better time than watching your children grow up around you.

Grandparenthood: a special and fleeting time when there is no past and no future.

Within the first minute of the school play, tears flow. King Herod, with his sunglasses, would go far.

She tapped her head through grey hair.
"I only feel twenty in here," she said.

She made a small incision and stuffed his teddy bear *"Pooh"* with kapok. It made him feel queasy. But he was a big boy now.

People could relax at the post-conference networking sessions. Interaction was intense. It was wonderful to be a part of it. The group was difficult to categorise: young, old, students, grandfathers – but all talked animatedly with much waving of arms.

Having your own child is the biggest narcissistic trip on the planet.

A father held his baby. He looked backwards over his dad's shoulder while visiting a room crammed with rare objects in a stately home.
Nodding at the baby, an elderly lady visitor said, "This, to me, is the greatest treasure."

Winning Words

The actress played the essence of a teenager (even though she was not): confident, enthusiastic, unwrinkled and vulnerable.

"My daughter has returned and we are negotiating terms for the bathroom."

One son had become a Buddhist monk, one daughter was about to be divorced and another thought that she was a horse.

When she tackled her mother about spoiling her son, her mother drew herself to her full height and said, "The purpose of grandparents is to spoil grandchildren."

A new baby, leaving the birth canal, is born face first to the rectum, so benefits from a liberal helping of faecal micro-organisms. They help to colonise the baby's gut: crucial for survival. (Many such microbiota are ancient friends rather than foes.)

"... makes jelly with Gumpa."

"I knew I had to be home by 11.30 or my dad would kill me. I had on this pencil skirt and stilettos so after I had left the bus stop I would kick them off and run. I ran for the county once. I could in those days."

"The jam does not go all the way through the doughnut!" complained the son.
    "How true of much of life," said the father.

You start to say things that you remembered your parents saying such as, "Take off your coat or you won't feel the benefit when you go outside," or "We've had the best of the day."

He pored over the contents of the deed box. It was not the important documents such as birth, marriage and death certificates that made him sigh. It was the little faded photograph in the cracked cellophane wallet, of his mother, nana and himself, aged ten. It proclaimed that he was a part. It was a chain; he lived while they were dead.

Generations

The young mother said, "I am excreting my brain cells with my milk."

The eight year old girl in the aisle of the plane had a pony tail, tied with a ribbon and a luggage tag.

The bus lurched. 17-year-old girls sat while the 80-year-old man, with his pork pie hat and slight smile, stood.

After the death of both parents, the creators have gone.

At naming ceremony:
"We are the bow and you are the arrow that we fire into the future. We give you our love and our support but your thoughts must be your own."

We think, in a family gathering of four generations, that it is the baby who needs looking after. But really it's the great-grandparent who needs the baby – as a reason for living.

A 16-year-old daughter was picked up from the disco at 1.00 am.
    "Dad, can you help me with my maths project now? I've got to hand it in tomorrow."
    "No."
    "I'll have to bunk off then."

The knighted landowner, fallen upon hard times and concerned to avoid death duties by taking a wife who would inherit said, "I'll advertise: old cock seeks new hen."

The grandsons scampered down the springy heap of hay with such perfect balance.

"You cannot drive the car behind you."
(Children ignore parental advice.)

Teenage truculence.

The last generation to make the grand tour from teenage sweethearts to doting grandparents.

Winning Words

In your fifties you become somewhat baggy and saggy but the late flowers are the best.

Everything, all the body and mental parts of the 17 year old, worked accurately, precisely and predictably as if newly machined and just run in.

Babies under the age of six months, when submerged in water, do swimming movements as if in the womb.

Most people have done all their striving by the time they are thirty. They spend the rest of their lives trying to hang onto their achievements.

A 15-year-old son had dropped his *Walkman* down the W.C. and howled with despair.
"I did the same thing to a radio twenty-five years ago, and it still worked," said dad.
"Is that supposed to cheer me up, to know that it is inherited?"

Children need rules, chores and discipline.

In a shower, three–year-old boy said to his dad, "I like weeing."

Elderly man's observation of a teenager wearing scanty clothes, "She doesn't have much washing."

Six-year-old girl looked at her wrinkled fingers after her soak in the bath and said, "I'm dissolving!"

The father dies a little when he discovers that his son can runner faster.

Girl who did not wash: "I'll buy you a sand-blasting for your 16th birthday."

The tractor hit the car, "That will teach you, you young road hog!"

Generations

In order to read the leaving card signed by all the girls on their grandson's art course, "Love from ... ," Grandma borrowed Grandpa's glasses. He became impatient to read and went to find his other pair.

"Conspiracy, cunning, deceit, dogma and old age will always overcome ability, creativity, enthusiasm and youth."

Full of "last chancers" in their fifties and sixties.

"Mummy, I've got lemonade legs. They are all fizzy (pins and needles)."

We watch teenagers. We watch over them and we watch out for them.

"There are two things we should give our children: one is roots and the other is wings."
(Hodding Carter)

No matter how you bring up your children: by aloof distance, Dr Spock or religious rigidity, you will be wrong.

Winning Words

Of grandson swimming like a tadpole: "I think they learned him real good."

"When I am old and manky I shall live in Morocco and do disreputable things."

The boy brought in from the garden, and arranged on the sunlit table, a perfect apple, plum, blackberry and damson.

    He took his three-year old son out to a country field on a clear night with no moon. They lay down looking upwards at he Milky Way.
    "Behold, the stars, my son," he said.
    "What's that light, moves?"
    "An aeroplane," he sighed.

    I hope you have a little playtime, a good "poo" and a long nap.

"Yours is the Earth and everything that's in it,
And — which is more — you'll be a Man, my son!"
(Rudyard Kipling)

Arab street trader: "A knife for the mother-in-law?"

God

The church has plenty of time. It thinks in decades and centuries, not a four-year presidential term.

All male octogenarians are friends.

Young children are the stimulus to know local people. Once, he would have known all the people at the party; now he knew a handful.

It is poignant when you live for so long that the values of the society around you have changed, such as towards authority-figures.

A nineteen year old boy cannot match a pair of socks, let alone rule a kingdom.

A new vicar can do no wrong in his first year, in his second year no right; in his third year non-one cares.

Have you any objection to swearing on the Bible?" asked the solicitor.

Humans are just two metre high sacks of impure water under slight pressure with sense organs mainly on the top front. But in every culture, some people think that we are more than this and so exist after death.

"I am digging myself deeper into a hole here," said the lecturer, "I did not expect to see a dog collar on the front row."

"I don't believe in God but I miss him."
(Julian Barnes)

Winning Words

"Religion? (Shiver) It's poison," said the man from Beijing.

"I see no need for that hypothesis."
(Pierre-Simon Laplace)

Graveyards were short of space. What is the minimum sort and size of bone required for the resurrection, at the last trump? ("Trump" is an abbreviation of *trump*et call.) A 3rd century ecclesiastical conference answered that. The skull, because that was where we were, and the two long bones so we could rise on our legs. Hence the popularity of the skull and crossbones icon.

Cromwell chose to stable his horses in churches to make them less sacred. During the Soviet era in Russia, magnificent churches became cabbage stores. Long term, sanctity and reverence are difficult to maintain.

Freud wrote widely about religion including dismissal as a thought disorder, mass hysteria and infantile.

A powerful creator and a force for good are not necessarily connected.

One day the great systems programmer in the sky shall uninstall my software.

A statue of St Barbara, patron saint of tunnelling, is erected at the entrance to the excavation. Tunnellers will not enter until the tunnels have been blessed.

"We are an atheistic people. Our god did not save us for 500 years so why should he now?" *(Bulgarian)*

God

The Church of England saw itself lying deep and steady beneath the nation, the ballast that kept the ship of state on an even keel.

In the cathedral, the bishop presided, towering in his mitre holding his shepherds' crook, for us, his flock. Singing was angelic. They processed around and around in the candlelight to show every soul in that congregation their splendid robes and magnificent banners thrust aloft. That was the Church of England at full bore, full fat, high octane, in their gigantic building: a cathedral one thousand years old with two thousand of the faithful a-praying: such power!

The Devil, vexed, spat and stamped.

In the Egyptian "Book of the Dead", hearts are weighed at the entrance to the afterlife. The "Book of Spells" helped to prepare for the Egyptian afterlife. It was a sort of "Hitchhiker's Guide to the Galaxy." The book offered spells for every eventuality, including avoiding agricultural labour.

The British have no religion but they do believe in their welfare state.

Nuraghic communal burial mounds always faced the rising sun: East.

It is normal in many religions to contemplate death. A symbol such as a skull may help. The entire building comprised human skulls.
    The notice within said, "We bones that are here, we are waiting for you."

In those days (*Alexander*) Gods walked with men.
Religion is philosophy with pictures.

Winning Words

When people get on their knees they expect something in return so they put God on a kind of "performance related pay."

Everyone must have a God in their life; someone to care about and to do things for.

The aborigines are frightened to go on walkabout trips now. It is because they have not looked after the land well, lately. The spirits, the monsters, grow strong and dangerous. If the aborigines do go, they want a hot shower at the other end.

At least one of the seven Christian virtues will fell you with guilt: faith, hope, charity (love), justice, fortitude, prudence and temperance.

Take time in your fleeting itty-bitty life to close the battered door behind you and contemplate the inside of a church eight centuries years old.

The abstract trinity has an embodied human equivalent: those who pray, fight and work.

As Hindus, there is a little piece of divinity in all of us.

King *Olaf* of Norway crusaded with the message, "Baptism or death!"

The Abrahamic religions can't have it both ways. Either their God is all-powerful and worth praying to for intervention or He isn't.

"All shall be well, and all shall be well and all manner of thing shall be well."
(Julian of Norwich)

"My genius? But a talent borrowed from God."

Colours that no man knows.

You don't need a modem to be connected with God.
You're not here to fill a pew.
You are here to fulfil your purpose.

God

"Atheists are my brothers and sisters of a different faith... Like me they go as far as the legs of reason will carry them – and then leap."
(Yann Martel)

Religions, like any organisational structure, may excuse man being evil to man.

Do your notions flow up from you or does a god whisper in your ear?

In 1965, the pope and the orthodox patriarch lifted mutual excommunication orders dating from 1054.

He was brought up to believe that to do anything less than his best was a crime against God.

In the little shrine were an icon, two seats, three syrup containers, lemonade bottle, cleaning materials and a hundred dead flies.

Why were paper towels around the bases of the icons? To collect the tears and blood that they wept. They kept it for the soldiers. It was good to cure battle wounds. A communist, indoctrinated to be an atheist, reported that they analysed in military laboratories and found 16 proteins not previously discovered.

A bishop is consecrated; a vicar is ordained.

Nepalese airlines fly with a song and a prayer.

The king collected religious relics as, today, a man might collect postage stamps.

My god is not a god of the gaps who dashes around fixing problems but a god who gave humans free will to do well or make a mess of things.
"See, the problem is that God gives men a brain and a penis, and only enough blood to run one at a time."

(Robin Williams)

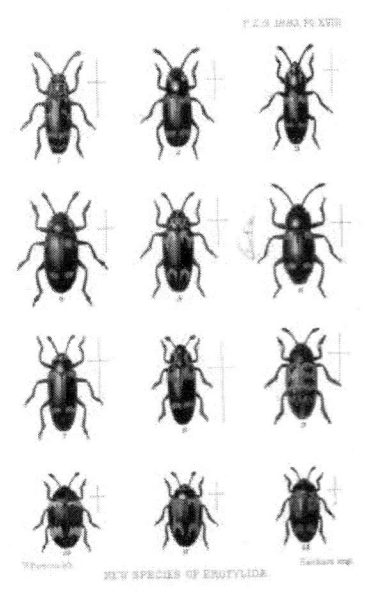

God, judging by their variety, has "an inordinate fondness for beetles."
(J.B.S. Haldane)

We can bring nothing into this world but when we leave we can have influenced others, written a book, constructed a building, donated a gift.

Once a year they get out their ancestors (ashes in urn), place them on the table and have a happy meal with them.

"*Namaste,*" means I salute the God within you.

"If I must bow my head it would be to a mountain."
(Maori)

The priest prepared for the christening party. Into the font, he poured boiling water from a kettle.

"The God Delusion."

God

(Richard Dawkins)

In the Middle Ages, hedgehogs were considered Devil's spawn because they presumed to raise their spines towards heaven.

Man planned and God laughed.

Blue protects from the evil eye; white means purity; green means paradise.

Dr ... (archbishop) had "a crippling capacity to see both sides of every question."

The living god, a pre-pubescent girl, peered shyly from the beautifully carved temple, which was also her prison, until she bled. *(Nepal)*

Rationalisation of the theological colleges in today's heathen Britain is like re-arranging the chairs in the *Titanic*.

Do not touch idols lightly; you may disturb them.

The purpose of the word "sacred" is to prevent us from thinking.

Trinities popular e.g. Christianity: Father, Son and Holy Ghost; Hinduism: The Creator, Destroyer and Preserver and Taoism: man, earth, heaven.

Do you worship the deity of the sun, lotus blossom or red bottom of a monkey?

Notice on church door: "In charity, pray, close this door upon the latch, lest a bird fly within and die of thirst."

When, after four hours, the electricity returned, the waiter stared at the light and crossed himself.

Full metaphor mode: the soul symbolises permanence; the body crumbles but the soul lives forever.

A family's ceremony to the sun god: take an attractive twig, decorate it, and saw off a piece to keep until the next year, Burn the log on a bonfire. The oldest drinks the *aquavit*; the youngest throws some on the bonfire. Homage to the sun god ensures the fertility of crops, animals and men.

Onlooker, "It's a wonder you are not wearing woad!"

If a year was bad, the farmers used to march in a procession to their blessed saint; now they ask for compensation from the government.

Today, supermarkets are built to look like churches with their towers and they open on Sunday for the god *Mammon*.

To nomads, the winds are the souls of the dead.

Outside the church was crumbling unpainted squalor, disintegration and beggars; inside was fresh-painted, immaculate, pristine, pampered with polish and scented with incense.

The Victorian age lies between us and the religiosity of the 18th century like a mountain range.

Most astronomers, in my experience, are atheists.

The devil took the form of an ass, goat, raven, dog, fox, frog or weevil.

Animal blessing puts bums on pews.

Excommunication: The officiating cleric closes his book, quenches the candle by throwing it to the ground and tolls the bell for one who has died.

"I don't hold with these churches. There is only one reason why they bury or burn you. That's because you smell like a rat. The bigger you are, the more the smell."

Before we start, let us say a little prayer, "Thank you, Lord, for letting Mr Brown come here this evening."

An Act of God is defined as something that no reasonable man could have expected.

God

Chanting, bowing, kissing of icons and signs of the cross.

"God is subtle but he is not malicious."
"(God) does not play dice."
(Albert Einstein)

"The Earth hath a skin and the skin hath diseases. One of those diseases, for example, is called man. The Earth is a mass of white hot chrome nickel steel. The surface of that liquid mass has long cooled into dross. That dross corroded into hills and valleys of earth, minerals, water and gases. Those have recombined into plants, insects, mammals, humans, all conforming to physical laws like gravity. Most wonderful combination is man. Now add your personal genius to this groundwork."
(Friedrich Nietzche)

"Be respectful to strangers. You never know when you will meet an angel."
(A Hindu)

"A Being who hears me tapping,
The five-sensed cane of mind,
Amidst such greater glories,
That I am worse than blind."
(After Harry Kemp)

Note by prone statue of statement by king at Ely cathedral, "Most sermons by fat priests are lean. His were not but larded with much good teaching."

"If I met God I would ask for my money back."

Goodbyes

Style and prestige: some things change quickly, subtly, or crudely. Images in glossy advertising booklets included a girl reclining in a bubble bath but smoking a jaunty fat *cigar* and an opulent (conference/seminar) theatre flaunting an *obsolescent overhead* projector for A4 acetates (2007)

In 1950's films/novels: *medical practitioners* (who, presumably, set an example for good health) *smoke*.

The leaving present was niggardly. Waspish comment: "We only asked in the department. After all, she's only been here for two years."

About change: "This is Harold, the stuffed Stegosaurus. I do not want to be like Harold."

Arthur C. Clarke, science fiction writer and stimulus for many future scientists and technologists, inventor of the notion of the geostationary orbit, died today.

Of unpopular staff member about to leave:
"Should we send him a thank you note?"
    "What? For leaving?"

The final event that stimulated evacuation of St Kilda (island) was the pregnant girl with (easily operable) appendicitis; she died because she could not get to hospital in time.

The "Log Age" only finished in 1960. (From the 17th century, logarithm tables were a tool to speed calculations.)

Goodbyes

Retired consultant surgeon, once so dextrous, could not even bend down to pick up his "puffer."

Near the Falklands, the lecturer said, "You will not see any blue whales."
    The *Tannoy* announced, "Blue whale spotted."
    The ship stopped. Everyone rushed to the deck.
    One old man remained in the bar.
    "Don't you want to come out and see them?"
    "No."
    "Can we help you?" noticing he was crying.
    "I used to be a whaler. Once they were everywhere. I killed them."

"Goodbye cashmere pullover. You were so expensive. But you have shrunk. Despite hanging heavy G clamps on you for a week, you remain shrunken. You also have holes at the elbows next to your lovely leather patches that made me feel like a lumberjack."

People hate changing a habit, generally.

Italians do not give chrysanthemums, symbols of death, except at funerals.

"She came back from her singles holiday with this Bulgarian gorgon but soon got rid of him."

When people had made things, the view had pulsed, oozed, smoked with satanic fervour.

Dentistry was agony before anaesthetics in the mid 19th century.

Reach down into folk history.

He had only just learned to find his way around, but soon, so soon, it would be time to go (from life).

Tenderness of the deathbed.

Winning Words

It was -2°C outside.
"Your beard has snow on it," the widow said as he kissed her. "Nice ... memories."
Her husband had had a beard.

He posted off his retirement letter to the General Pharmaceutical Council: a kind of death.

The second-hand bookshop owner rejected a heavy bagful of books, saying, "Obsolescent text books have no value."
The disappointed, seller lugged them away and wondered if he still had any value.

The necropolis offered a spectrum of graves, from monumental pillar to pedestrian, carved and plain, telephone boxes, photographs, polished black to cheerful multicoloured mosaic, flower-strewn to overgrown, beds for contented moggies and a solitary praying nun. The mayor provided convenient conveniences.

He heaped his printed notes onto the bonfire. They were heavy.
They were obsolete. If he needed to know anything he would look on the web. But as the notes smoked, he felt their loss; he felt diminished: part of him had departed.

Anguish of loss because of UK government car scrappage scheme (2010): he washed her. He positioned, on the passenger seat, the leather-bound instruction folder so that the salesman (his co-conspirator in murder) might feel a little of the owner's pain, when she was scrapped. From gorgeous 3 litre, six cylinder *Jaguar* to "stand up and beg" 1.2 litre, three cylinder *Škoda* in one sickening, lurching fall.

Goodbyes

Once so strong and solid, the man, who had guided bulls by the rings through the end of their noses, was dead.

"Today is my last day of work as a pharmacist in direct contact with the public. I wore my red tie with silver pestles and mortars. It is the end of forty years of trust from patients. I had not expected to feel quite so tearful. I will miss the caring staff too."

Gravestone for a still birth: "*Home without a journey.*"

Radioactive face cream will make your face glow with health. Put radioactive bubbles in your bath. Drink radioactive water from this little shiny urn. The *Curie* museum. *Paris*, displays a price list of various radium salts, all expensive.

The nostalgia of visiting a museum with real artefacts and 3D dioramas instead of the shadows of computer simulations and twitchy buttons.

"Fond of this spinner?" said the big boy.

Tom nodded, suddenly fearful, but 6 ¾ year old boys did not show it.

His mind flashed back. He had rubbed, coaxed, the film lid that the opening of the milk bottle supported, so carefully. He was an expert. His spittle-moistened fingers had massaged, burnished, in tight firm circles. He had manufactured a smooth sunken hemisphere and rubbed until it refused to deepen. It had shone in the sunlight. It was aluminium, like the champion *Comet* airliner. Tongue protruding, he had prised off his construction. There were no dents: his best flying saucer ever. No-one could have made it better. Nobody could fly it better. He had practised and practised. His eyes had shone with pride as he safely cupped it in his hand. He polished it some more.

He had spun the feather-light disk between trigger and middle fingers while jerking his hand forward. His saucer launched into a long soaring curved flight. It landed gently, safely: no dent, near a big boy; too near.

"This the *champion* lid?" said the mean-looking boy.

Tom nodded, again and bent.

"I'll just colle ..."

"Not now," said the boy, stamping on it.

Winning Words

Health

To dislodge the deer tick, hold as near as possible to the head and twist; otherwise the mouthparts will decay and the wound go septic.

"my mind is full of scorpions"
(William Shakespeare)

A green cross meant a pharmacy; a red cross, open all night.

Retirement: When you stop flapping your wings you tend to fall off your perch.

The cut required many stitches and "Get well" cards.

He coughed repeatedly. Atmosphere clogged with oxides of every hue and complex carbon rings and chains yet to be classified. Chimneys belched. Silos oozed. *(China)*

Merry at breakfast, dead by noon (commonplace in the Middle Ages).

The outpatient clinic seethed with continuous and continual emotional uproar: a clamour of hope, despair and resignation.

Exercise harvests happy hormones.

Bang. "Is your nose normally that shape?"

Darwin, famous hypochondriac.

Paramedics attended with stretcher and oxygen. The blood darkened on the bottom step of the outside stairs where she had fallen and banged her nose.

Health

Surgeries and pharmacies were full of the worried well.

During the (medical) exams) he had a protozoan infection caught from a pathology slide.

Jogging backwards exercises different muscles.

Long mental hospital corridors smelling of floor polish with turpentine (1973).

Exercise (e.g. at gym.):
"It takes six months to get into shape and two weeks to get out of shape. Once you know this you can stop being angry about other things in life and only be angry about this."
(Rita Rudner)

His uncle diagnosed his condition; his GP had not because it was so rare.

The loud old man no longer swam. He kept on getting ear infections.
>Maybe that was why he shouted, "Wear a bathing cap."
>"Use ear plugs and *Vaseline,*" another counselled.

My old man rode the cage. He worked in the "Widow Maker" shaft. He died from siliconosis. Most did.

"An apple a day, if well aimed, keeps the doctor away."
(P.G. Wodehouse)

"The air (tugs at shirt collar) it is so bad. The smog is always bad this time of the day (evening)."

Most symptoms are not diseases and most diseases are not serious.

Medicine chests on remote stations in the Australian outback contained medicines numbered 1 to 200. To help diagnosis over the radio, they also had a body diagram with numbers.

Winning Words

The smog made him screw up his eyes. They itched and were crusted the next morning.

"When your CPAP (continuous positive airway pressure) machine fails and they bring another one out by van in three hours and when that one also does not work and they bring another in another van in three hours, *then* you realise how ill you ..."

"*And* when the electricity company put you on a special register, and bring you your own generator if the electric fails," another user interrupted.

He had to urinate a lot.
"I've got an old man's disease," he said (prostrate).

A bone, broken and healed, becomes strongest at the break.

It was a wake up call following falling asleep at the wheel.

Wear a bathing costume to dry in the sun and the parts remaining wet evaporate to a wet bandage soaked in concentrated brine; that may irritate delicate parts.

"Oh!" said the boy. "It hurts."
He had not been for two days. Bananas fixed it.

A neurotic is someone who knows a little about what is going on.

About keeping awake while driving:
"Whale music? You can't play that! It's birthing music. You need a gallop!"

They lined up the children for tonsillectomy in the back room, and operated quickly, like fishwives gulleting fish.

Flat lining.

Obese? That's when you have to haul aside flaps of fat to expose your belly button.

Health

"You won't pass their fitness assessment if they decide you are a fat heifer."

"Good swim?" asked the vigorous swimmer.
    The fit pensioner replied, "Just a good stretch really."

Every time you suffer depression, the pattern cuts deeper into your brain and becomes easier to enter again.

He benefited from her kissing him full on the lips and the resulting mild and persistent gum infection.

At 1 ½ miles height, 30% less oxygen, you may suffer headache or dizziness. Drink two litres of water daily - or more if your nose bleeds.

Exercise to consciously lengthen your spine. Broaden your shoulder girdle and hips to provide the largest possible internal volume for your organs to work and blood to flow. Your machinery will work more efficiently if it is not cramped by poor crumpled posture.

With age, your body may require longer for PPM (planned preventative maintenance) such as 2 ½ hours weekly (olive oil, very hot bath, shower spray into ears) to avoid impacted earwax.

When your hands are leathery and insensitive, and you cannot see, you push a button on the remote control with your thumb.

The NHS is not caring but coping.

"I am a friendly yeast infection and I get everywhere."

Laughing massages your internal organs.

It was no wonder he got indigestion after a week like that, with heaps to audit, culminating in a day with the Vice President.

After chewing a wasp:
"It's starting to swell" she said, sticking out her tongue. "I'm not able to talk so well."

Looking after their garden kept them fascinated and fit well into their eighties.

Man unable to bend foot outwards after his hip replacement operation said to consultant, "If I'd sent a car for repair and it came back like this, I'll send it back to the garage."

Medieval notion: "My pulse is a soft drum heralding my death."

"TATT": "the always totally tired."

His mother used to say, "Here, have a cigarette. It will calm you down and keep you slim."

He sneezed suddenly. The couple at the next table said something in German meaning "Bless you."
    Memory of the plague lingered across the sea.

"Nobody likes working for the NHS any more. It is a monoculture: only money."

When the dentist de-scaled his teeth, he did not mind. He welcomed his mouth rinse being bloody. It was as if all his teeth suffered an itch, continuous but just too faint to detect, that the probe, hard, sharp and cunning, banished.

In the ex-USSR, diphtheria was increasing; herd immunity was becoming flaky.

"I used to be able to write the Lord's Prayer on a postage stamp: a test of hand steadiness and eyesight. I can't now. For close work I have to wear two pairs of reading glasses, like this."

Robin Hood died because an evil abbess indiscriminately applied leaches.

It is surprising how a little pain in the third toe of your left foot, or grit in the eye, can displace the pain in your heart.

Health

Seals have bacteria in their mouths. Before antibiotics, if a seal bit a mariner, he would slice off his fingers, knowing that otherwise his joints would ache and swell so badly he would wish for death.

Kidney stones: he had this concrete factory within.

The only certainty of the British NHS was queues.

To live long, eat 40% less food and avoid stress (humans and roundworms). If you do not live long, it will seem is if you do.

Crystals are important. Do silicon chips not run our lives? One crystal may resonate with something in one person at one time and heal.

The birch tree reduced the hay fever sufferer to a snivelling bag of segregations. The only place he could feel well was the desert.

She felt ripe.

Pannacotta: wonderful food, but full of fat.
    "What about my cholesterol?"
    "Doesn't matter. You are on holiday."

A spiteful bristle had wormed its way between molar teeth and gum. Nothing would dislodge that bristle. Neither toothbrush nor floss, bread, chewing gum nor forceps clumsily self-applied.
    "I can see it," she said and plucked it out effortlessly with her eyebrow tweezers.
    Bliss. Bless her! But where had it come from?

How toxic is the metallic paint covering the stationary human statues?

The Minister of Health (1991): "The NHS (British National Health Service) is an administrative slum."

Until you are thirty, your body just works; diets and so on are just fads.

Winning Words

"How is Sam?"
    "Pardon?"
    "Your latest great-grandchild."
    "Spell it."
    "S ... A ... M."
    "What fan?"

The drink that the poor parents in ... pack in their child's lunch box is cold milky tea. The tannins mop up the little iron they have; they are often anaemic.

Behold the little spike in heart attacks at the start of the manual lawn mowing season.

Young boys sent up chimneys suffered Chimney sweep's cancer or Soot wart (of scrotum skin).

When a leg is lost, that part of the brain withers; the phantom limb diminishes.

Fair-skinned, fat, fecund females over forty are more likely to get gall stones.

"... is not a poultice to cure all ills."

Undoubtedly, they were expert horticulturalists. But did they check for Legionnaires' disease in the shower sprays of the water-fogged Victorian conservatory?

It felt as if there were a red-hot rod through her gum; the dentist, on the patient's insistence, and after she had signed a disclaimer, reluctantly extracted the tooth. The pain then moved to the next tooth.

He smashed his knee into four pieces. Three were wired together. The fourth remained a mosaic so he could not run well.

She was a little unbalanced. Repeatedly, if life was not going as she wished, she would try to drop a lighted match into a gallon can of petrol.

Health

Patent "life enhancer" contained 36 needles and a book. That explained where to prick for different diseases. The wound was then rubbed with oil to encourage to fester (as a "counter irritant; so unpleasant that you forgot about your presenting disease).

The patent smoke ball slippery elm and phenols. Sniff in one puff for influenza and six for cholera.

"The crippled boy had never been able to walk more than two steps. The look on his face when he saw the walking frame – he would not let it go - made it all worthwhile."

A nuclear power station released beryllium oxide. 100,000 people were affected. Public buildings hosed down; sand in children's sandpits replaced.

He could not get enough Thai curry; he binged, burning a hole (ulcer) in his gullet.

Revenge of the game meal: straining stubborn constipation.

Twice as many women as men survived on the waiting list for hip replacement. Indeed, at every life stage, including in the womb, more women than men survive, as if men were the trial version and women the definitive product.

"A woman in a car suffered an accident. The scaffolding went straight through here ... They took her, the scaffolding and her seat, to the hospital. They did not know what to do. Was it a job for the orthopaedic surgeon or the gynaecologist? Fortunately, the anaesthetist used to be a scaffolder. Miraculously, scaffolding missed all the vital organs, blood vessels, nerves and bones. Twelve units of blood were prepared but none were needed."

To smuggle out to the oil rig, they put his methadone into a shampoo bottle.

During the operation the surgeon threw the used swabs into a theatre corner.

Winning Words

Husband went round with a photograph of his wife asking shops not to sell lighter (butane) fuel. She inhaled eight canisters a day. Small shops agreed; supermarkets would not.

'Flu produced fever. He really participated in the Romanian revolution.

Jogging down into the cold misty valley was a cold balm for the lungs – unless it contained chimney smoke.

"Do you think that it is too early for a gin?"

About 16-year-old girl in a coma:
"She looks dreadful covered in spots. I suppose they will clear up once they stop tube-feeding her (intravenously) by TPN (total parenteral nutrition) and the dieticians can get at her."

The anxious mother had nothing to do except to look at the drip. Should that bubble be moving along the tube?

The diarrhoea was explosive. The tummy was bloated and bubbling. Skin and faeces were a similar brown.

"Who is that smoking like a chimney?
　　"The occupational health nurse."

The woman, with silvery curls in disarray collapsed (in supermarket). Soon concerned people clustered around her. But it took five minutes to place her in the recovery position.

Reason to wake: full bladder.

A tractor hauling nine tonnes of slurry or a fire engine with 400 gallons of sloshing water can be harmful to your health. They cannot, easily, stop.

Loose top teeth result in characteristic speech. Remember *Churchill* and his dentures

His neck swelled slightly on one side; maybe not a good sign.

Health

Anxious representative, about to plunge in for the hard sell has the urge to urinate. Is that your prostrate calling? You are the right age.

Stone-age diet: lamb, pears, spring water.

Some human worms are thirty feet long. They burrow in a gruesome path through the lungs, liver and heart. You spew out their eggs in your faeces. Hand-washing advised.

That dose of warfarin was only safe with a particular number of units of alcohol every week. Continued boozing was essential.

Dentist: "Let me know if it hurts."
    Patient's mouth was too full of gadgets to reply.

How could a dentist be so nasty as to root fill without anaesthetic? The ironware (motorised reamer) seemed to expand, explode, inside the bone.
    "The decaying smell is just bits of bone and pulp."

The 13-year old avoided wearing the brace whenever possible; he whiffed a bit.

She was barred from the job because overweight.

Bin of hot tar at the road side: women used to take "chesty" babies to smell it; now condemned as carcinogenic.

Jargon

Ornithologists:

"Got your bins and scopes?"

"Bird!"

"LBJs" means little brown jobs (jargon shared by birdwatchers, often using binoculars, and mushroom hunters, who require microscopes).

"FIT" means "foreign independent traveller."

"BC" also means before children.

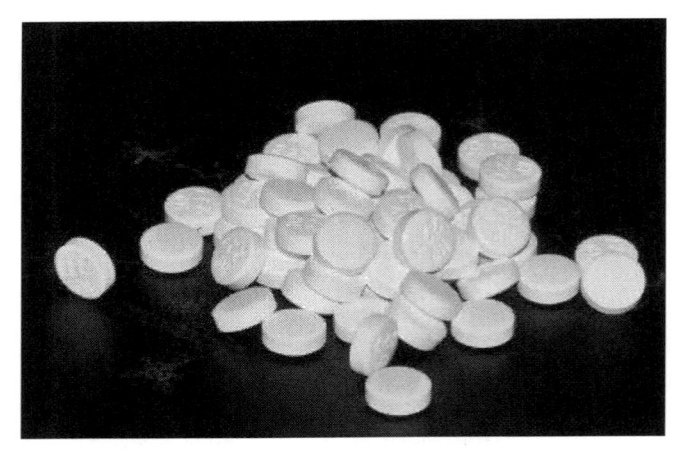

"Script" for pharmacists means "prescription".

His language had changed but his friend used the same jargon as 22 years previously.

Joy

May your life be full of love, interest and wonder.

He had passed his "Advanced levels" and had the sense of doors to an unknowable future opening. He relished a brand-new hardback (extravagant) fresh-smelling book by his favourite author.

Ring out wild bells.

Zest.

"Jazz – difficult to describe but you know it when it comes through the door."

Seeds of their becoming.

"Laughing like drains".

Oceanic feeling.

Happiness is leaving the M25.

He sat low in the sports car, deeply inhaling the smell of the leather, in a well of yellow carpet, relishing the attitude of the long bonnet and stubby windscreen wipers.

Afternoon tea at the *Ritz:*
Flunkies in red jackets. Korean, French *Maitre D'hôtel*. High-backed hall porter's chair in the male cloakroom. Soap squirted onto his hand. Towel handed out. A choice of aftershave perfumes offered but none taken for they gave him a rash.
"People come here from all over the world. They book on the internet. There is a three-month wait for this sitting. You

know, the women love it so much. They are so happy when they go home."

A golf ball floated in the WC. Washing that ball with their streams of urine to make it spin provided fun for the boys aged 3, 6 and 64.

He stood astride the truck of a great tree uprooted, pointing 45° upwards. He squirted a solid stream of urine, not dribbled and sprinkled, into the wind stream; that further increased urine speed. Years slipped away.

Overall, the business part of the WI (Women's Institute) meeting was comforting, routine. Committee members made the tea, clanked out chairs, discussed international support. It felt comfortable like eating bread and butter pudding smothered in steaming custard. It was reassuring. There could

Joy

not be too much amiss in the kingdom while such WI branches survived.

"...a man who could sit under the shade of his own vine, with his wife and his children about him and the ripe clusters hanging within their reach, in such a climate as this and not feel the highest enjoyment, is incapable of happiness and does not know what the word means."
(James Busby) New Zealand's first recorded wine maker (1830).

Blank paper, pencil, sharpener and rubber. Stencilling abstract thought into the corporeal world of things.

"It felt like morning and the freshness of the world-to-be intoxicated us."
(T.E. Laurence)

Bliss, rapture, awe, reverence, wonder.

Jonah complex: fear of achievement of potential.

Which was the best part of the meal to tell them about his little triumph (very first publication)? When the plates of food arrived? When their glasses were half full?

Football to fans: 2 ½ hours of unscripted drama.

A bonfire satisfies a basic human need.

Sheer power uprooted the red onions. They nestled in neat rows. The brute power of the harvester, burning diesel: sunlight captured from when dinosaurs ruled the Earth. The thud of the bulbs, high-piled into attentive trailers. Fine design and organisation of military precision. In the autumnal sunshine, just one lonely onion remained – and their smell. Harvest home.

Location inside

Pantry: thick marble shelf that helped to keep food cool, fashionable in 1935.

His mother was going around the Chinese takeaway shop that she had just sold. She was pressing surfaces with a charm and her forehead - and distant.
 "She was thanking the door, the counter for being such a good provider, all those years, for her, for her husband, her children. I felt chocked up," said her son.

The door closing accidentally, locking you inside a walk-in refrigerator or autoclave, may be fatal.

Squeaky clean.

Oak beams improve with age.

How does the hospital deal with a naff donated picture?

As persistent as the streak of cochineal, spilled onto the white plaster, that, despite rubbing, always bled back.

They cleaned and polished and titivated as best they could before the party/house sale.

He stood centre-stage at the lectern in the cosy red lecture theatre of the Royal Institution (*London*) and dreamed his vainglorious dreams.

During the gale, fluff floated down from the ceiling.

Book-lined room: scholar's retreat.

Location inside

Scandinavian high stove finished in glazed brick.

Rumble! Woodlot collapsed onto concrete in the heat.

The Christmas tree looked sad; leaves were yellow. He had planed the bottom four inches of bark to fit a stand: the water in its bucket had evaporated.
    "Don't touch it or more needles will fall off!"
    Its smell had vanished, too. Rather like the last miserable year.

The wood-burning stove made her house so warm and cosy.

Open fire lore: rotten field posts crack malevolently, rocketing incandescent cinders towards his eyes, their mission to blind. Their stink made him splutter. Wet wood wastes most of its heat drying off its water as steam; only then can it spare heat for you. Willow spits and provides little heat. Instead, burn hardwood dried for at least three years. Apple wood burns smoothly with soothing plops and fragrant smoke. He shielded his eyes from the hot spray. A youthful branch, fresh cut, hisses and foams. Its sap drips on the open fire grate, complaining with explosive "Splats."

The narrow spiral staircase twisted to the toilet with an aspidistra in the anteroom and a view over steep gables to the river *Seine*.

In laboratories, a favourite technique of pharmaceutics examiners was to require students to weigh a dye into many capsules. Measuring messily, leaving nearby any volume measure uncovered and upright, or not washing hands regularly, resulted in any colourless liquid then compounded assuming that colour. Fiends!

An ancient low-wattage bulb, nearly invisible beneath dirt, cast a reddish glow over venerable bottles of port.

Yellow textured wallpaper was everywhere, even on doors.

Roads, conversations and ideas intersected in that famed café.

Winning words

"*Artex?* Applied before 1990?" asked the decorator.
"1977"
He grew in breath, expensively, "Contains asbestos. Removing it is a *specialist* job."

Compacted dung floor keeps flies away and is warm at night and cold during the day.

"Come to our autism-friendly film screening! Lights left on, sound turned down, make a noise and take a break anytime!"

The star was the huge scrubbed deal table.

The huge iron bath, the bulbous hot tap and heavy drapes, the lashings of chrome and mirrors, the height of opulence.

After water is added (hiss...) to the heater in a sauna at 50ºC and 50% relative humidity, it feels hotter. Opening the door into falling snowflakes is not unpleasant, but insufficiently pleasant to cool off by rolling in the snow.

Visiting *Woolies* (affectionate name for *Woolworths* [1909 – 1998]: retail department store) on its closing-down day was sad. Most shelves had gone; those remaining were almost empty. Staff wearing jaunty Christmas hats looked sad; the manager, sombre. No-body spoke to them, as if suffering from a contagious disease. *Woolies* had been the film set to our lives. As children we had bought our sweeties there for a treat. The loose sweeties section remained but its trays were bare. He stood before it, stuck his nose inside a tray and smelled; the smell of sweeties remained: a ghost. He shook his head slightly, compressed his lips, and gulped a manly gulp. Perhaps dentists would rejoice – or miss the trade.

In the rural fuel filling station at 6.30 am the atmosphere was blokeish and polite.

"I was happy as a child on the landings of those crumbling flats. Family were around, and neighbours, and we could play safely. It was warm. We had combined heat and power stations with hot water in pipes."

Location inside

Backstage, the famous London theatre was decrepit, blackened and grimy. A gargantuan Victorian water main dominated. In the dressing room with its single bunk and sink, only half the lights worked.

In the studio, the broadcasters were acutely conscious of noise. Examples were turned pages rustling or porcelain cups clinking saucers; they used plastic disposables.

Host at party:
"Is everybody talking?"
"They've all gathered in the kitchen around the *Rayburn / (Aga)*. They won't go anywhere else."

"Big cruise ships terrify me: such a danger of fire."

The billiard table weighed 2 ½ tonnes. Its legs were slate, carved and painted to look like marble. In India, termites attacked the usual wooden legs

Advice on Aboriginal story line on wall painting: "Here are honey ants."

Winning words

A place of ceremony, reflection, food and shelter.

Notice on public WC: "To flush, waggle knob and hold."

Up three flights of narrow stairs, a poky, congested attic room with a sloping roof.

In the baths it was rush hour.

The *BMW* showroom glass was so spotlessly clean that it appeared absent. A pretty blonde wearing high heels offered smiles and, on request, free coffee and big biscuits.

Within the hardware store, go left and then down into the basement. Behold an Aladdin's cave.

A real wooden floor goes click-clack; laminate makes a sharper, more annoying sound. Carpets are silent but harbour dirt and crawl with living creatures.

He entered the hogan by its east-facing door. Inside smelt aromatic with wood smoke from a central stove. The hogan's juniper wood dovetailed together; packed sod surrounded it, sun baked.

I believe, but cannot prove, that the coat hangers that cling to each other in the bottom of my wardrobe are lazy. They hide there to prevent giving service.

In that adapted 16th century building, he found it quite impossible to navigate between lecture and bedroom. Many junctions led left and right, up and down multiple stairs, to his tower. Corridors were astoundingly windy.

*Denve*r airport was so new that its marble was unscratched, lined with images of natives and filled with their music.

Boutique 5 star hotel had just a door between staid banks in the City of London. Within were spacious marble lobby, domed stained glass ceiling, trays of stones and wet soft moss, a *Beretta* scooter and iconic picture book. Toilets had cloth towels, not blowers or paper and waste bin.

Location inside

He loved the in-between times, the evening half light, the afternoons with murk and half-drawn curtains.

He wished that flies were not so black and had less guts and blood when squashed but he splattered them anyway.

You must say "Goodbye" to the house, the sound of the key in the lock, of gates closing.

Dark ambience of old railway carriages.

The sound of the front door closing shut behind you: a muffled clunk, the feel of the big sheet of leaded glass with a yachting scene that bowed slightly.

At dawn in the night shift, the plastic panels on the zigzag roof lit up, glowed, ticked as they expanded. He could see the crows' feet and hear their patter. The strong acrid smell remained in the cavernous space.

The house fashion (e.g. white walls and bare wood) that is *de rigueur* changes about once every seven years, despite efforts by interior decorating merchants to accelerate the change.

Specks of warm cat food, moistly decaying, were scattered over the warm conservatory floor.

Nightmares persisted during the thunderstorm; the air prickled with electric tension that permeated his brain.

This (modern) box-like public building has no soul.

Open air baths: "In *Tokyo*, you cannot open your windows; it's lovely to have all these trees."

The dispensary area with curved glass, clock and carousel (circular space-saving shelves rotate commonly prescribed medicines to your fingertips) with "commandments" on how to use was breathtaking, like the Star Ship *Enterprise*. The

Winning words

surrounding area seemed so solid and smooth; it cost £60,000. (2000)
"You could buy a house for that!"

The manor had ancient plumbing; water flow challenged, reduced to a trickle if another tap on that floor opened. Taps labelled using cracked porcelain.

The copse belongs to a neighbouring estate so is a borrowed pleasure.

Sea of green glass light shades in a public library.

Peals of bells over ancient houses.

The sea of bluebells around the door made the entrance sing.

Puddle of a party.

A proper general store offered: snow-clearing spade, ovens, beans, dog food, sacks of grain and brooms. A little lathe stood. You could hire it and immediately cut your own groove in your special nut.

Long arched library with two storeys of books, tall ladder to reach and a double row of busts.

The workhouse with its "master" (who used to have a whip) became a tatty neglected NHS hospital. Its master remained as its first "secretary." That post was renamed "administrator", "general manager" and finally, "chief executive". Refurbished with a bright clean interior, the hospital was transmogrified – again - into expensive executive flats.

Leaving the family home is a wrench but moving between flats is an administrative operation.

Moving into (smaller) retirement home: "I'm condensing (furniture, ornaments)."

"Is it a 'Wow'?"

Location inside

In bench alcove:
"Sit ye here and see,
No enemy,
Save winter and rough weather."
(After William Shakespeare)

Earthquake instructions: stand below the door jam.

... (store) built over old plague pit.

The time-share salesmen were six deep.

Live in a finger of countryside in a city. Guaranteed neighbours are teachers, graphic designers and other professionals.

The theatre fire exit opened directly into a graveyard.
    Granddad said, "I've picked my plot."

From the unsealed bathroom, they often picked slugs.

Two faces, overlapping, stared back from the double glazing.

The fisherman's reading room contained seven volumes of shipping registers.

The artist's house had a studio with a huge north-facing window. The light was always even for the sun never shone in. The golden naked toddler was crying because he wanted to watch the TV.

An eight-second acoustic at mid-frequency defines a cathedral's resonance.

"The place had itched and squirmed with life."
(Sherwood Anderson)

He walked on planks over the marsh. There, one man had built his shed of corrugated iron covered in reed. Within was a bench upon a plastic drum.

Winning words

What is the mystery of the haunted house? We get no answer from the crawling things that inhabit the place.

In the capital of *Bulgaria*, only six types of food were in the shops; the people never smiled.

No wonder the buildings fall down in earthquakes: almost no mortar joins the bricks.

He felt isolated: none of thirty television channels spoke English. But conflict was occurring between nations. All he could suss out was the financial news, Shares fell, except those in arms companies and gold.

The body builder and his girl sauntered back to their room. Would the earth move for them in this city built on 17 volcanoes, awaiting their next eruption?

Tired: peeling wallpaper edges, dirty carpet, tile holes filled with mastic, sink draining slowly.

He rattled the door of the WC. It wouldn't open! Even worse, he was caught in the ladies toilet; in his haste, he had misread the door!

The drowsiness of a summer afternoon in the conservatory. The sun baked the walls and the whole house seemed stultified in this flaming air and dead silence.

The tailors with their big scissors worked in the basement. There was no natural light but it was a good big room in central *London*.

A brown bear peered through the window of the Russian log cabin.

Location outside

Location outside

It was a bad weather day. At the open air baths, where sunbeams half-blinded through misted goggles, the sun shone when he wanted clouds while on his walk without a coat, the thunderstorm poured down.

He found what looked like the rind of a tree in the deep coal seam.

Sand as white as cocaine.

Breeze like hand drier above blood heat.

Police kept an eye on the Jewish ceremony in a hotel with a *Rolls* and three stretched limousines outside by the red carpet; the other side of the road, in the central park, a pro-Palestinian demonstration offered loud reggae music.

Mountains like haemorrhoids.

A pile of rubbish surrounded each native settlement. It was not in their culture to dispose of biodegradable material such as bones. Disposing of other material cost them money so they did not.

The bonfire in the rainy industrial wasteland burned with sudden brilliance; unknown toxins belched out.

A loo with a view (no roof).

The Romanian Factory chimneys emitted black, grey, white and orange smoke. A cauldron poured a splodge; it glowed at the roadside.

Winning Words

Soft marsh sounds.

"Hope and the future for me are not in lawns and cultivated fields, not in towns and cities, but in the impervious and quaking swamps."
(Henry Thoreau)

Rich berry colours of sunset.

Charring Cross Hospital, *London*, was approached by walking through cemeteries studded with subsiding gravestones. Transportation of cadavers had presumably been cheap. The hospital was a plush glittering castle towering sixteen stories above crumbling shops. Their window frames were unpainted and rotting away.
"What's 'cosmopolitan?'" asked the hopeful future medical student from the country.

If you have a white stork nest on your house it weighs up to two tonnes and is six feet across. It makes a mess, but you feel honoured.

The boy was sick into the sea around the barrier reef. Two minutes later, the sea swarmed with fish 1 ½ to 3 feet long. They had no teeth but the boy could feel them rubbing the hairs on his legs.

"poverty and debauchery lie festering in the dark alleys"
(Charles Dickens)

Hedged with thorn.

There was a one mile long drive across 350 acres to "The Hawkhills", the Civil Defence College at *Easingwold*. First used in 1931 for training against gas attacks, staff could let off their stinks without the neighbours complaining.

Mountains like up-turned udders.

Vines, clung, marched in regimented rows, up every south-facing hill that man could climb, on the banks of the river.

Location outside

Putting out garden rubbish on a non garden rubbish day or splashing in the swimming pool was *"Verboten."* (Germany)

She lived in a little cabin at the edge of a bog.

The field, that needed lime, was acid and unkind to metal relics.

London was so quiet after the congestion charge. You could imagine the ghosts of horses and carriages in the grand crescents.

The rise and fall of the insistent shout of the melon seller on the beach like that of the rag-and-bone man, cruising the neighbourhood, in his youth.

Melancholy marsh; gargling ditch.

Next stop Antarctica.

In rain or snow, the pedestrian traipsed through a faecal mud. From October, the mists over the river trapped the smoke from thousands of chimneys, creating a brown miasmic fog tainted with the odour of the open sewers.

Undertow of ozone-fresh breakers.

In a season, seeds grow into shrubs the size of hedgehogs.

..., that one (railway) line town.

City: noisy seething feeding frenzy, spawning ubiquitous threats to clamp.

"You think you have problems with aphids eating your roses. How about hippopotami eating your begonias?"

The *sirocco* was Sahara hot.

Colossal cranes, painted yellow and red and grey, portentous against heavy grey flickering thunderclouds.

Winning Words

In Africa, no-one asks about the weather. It is always hot and dry.

In the mist, the sky wept.

Noise so loud that his back teeth became numb.

The 1930s city hall, unlike the mediaeval building next door, was "best seen in fog."

Dank mucky city morning; windscreen cleaned with tissue: filth blackened it.

Lidos opened in the late 1930s in the heyday of the fresh air health movement and people learning to swim. Now (2002) each swim in *London* costs £37; lidos closing amongst gentle decay.

Constipated traffic.

Village lolled on the landscape.

Mowing the lawn of a centuries-old house is intimate. You push within foliage and do not know what you will discover.

Mass of seaweed six inches deep, squelchy, buzzing with gnats.

At the funeral was a forest of black umbrellas. Just one was brightly coloured, proclaiming an advertiser's slogan.

Villagers alone built the commanding dome, making landscape look magical.

He walked around the hotel grounds searching for any trace of the Nissen hut hospital of his birth.

Underneath the lambs, cowslips and surveillance cameras on the limestone hill were three storeys of tunnels tall enough to drive double-decker buses.

Location outside

The full moon shone through still stratocumulus clouds with intense regular grains. The great sky was sharp, monochrome, expectant.

He felt dizzy and feared that the emptiness of the canyon might suck him in. He had never before witnessed on a plain, such an awesome chasm.
    "If someone falls over the edge, they don't bother looking for them."

"Could you direct me to Pall Mall, please?"
    "I believe it is over there," pointed the American, with a grin.

He stood at the law stone before the high cliff that acted as an acoustic sounding board. *(Iceland)*

Fair is the field where I cannot ride.

To stubborn brown growth on gravel drive:
"Die, weed, die."

Storm. Foam blown like soap suds.

Slime and hair clogged the drain grill.

The griffins, and other clawed stone beasts, looked proud and smug in the Victorian palm house. They were tilting back on their pelvises, contentedly confidently casual. Either that, or they were pregnant.

Public house sign. The owners were hedging their bets. On one side was the Greek god *Apollo*; on the other, the moon rocket

Only a gargantuan sucking machine could vacuum out the fat congealed in the drain and overflowing onto the pavement outside the Chinese takeaway.

In *Scotland*, you have mini-hurricanes. You cannot see them except when they lift twigs or stones just a few inches.

Marsh gas (methane) bubbled from the stagnant water.

Winning Words

"Brecks": "broken landscape."

The golf balls at *Fylingdales* (early warning radar "domes", Yorkshire, UK) had disappeared; a concrete monolith replaced them. The purple blaze of heather remained.

Rotting piles and slimy wood.

Row of rails (for horses) outside *Newmarket* terraces.

The porch was a silly place to build a nest. The pigeon's egg lay broken on the tiles. Its yolk remained hard-boiled by sunshine, congealed in cracks. His mouth pursed in distaste while scrubbing away that unborn life.

A diphtheria epidemic (1937) closed the bathing pool on the river bend with its flat-roofed changing room. Chestnut saplings of 1900 had grown by 2013 into gnarled giants. All trace of the changing room had vanished.

Ultima Thule, on medieval maps, is a place beyond the borders of the known world such as the desolate Northern land of dreams.

Outside the wedding venue, cars were decorated. Cheerful festive white shiny ribbons festooned windscreens, wipers and wing mirrors. *(Italy)*

Laser pointer in fog: "That really is a light sabre."

Water on the bridge so high that you could stretch your hand out of the car window and splash. Police pleaded with "flood tourists" to leave.

The sinister wail of sirens was urgent in the storm-driven rain. The wind had backed up two thirds of the water from the last high tide. Could this be the next big flood, the mass killer, the orphan-maker?

Rumour before flood: "Haven Bridge is closing at 4 pm."

Location outside

Cleaning gutters confers unique knowledge of their geography and botany.

On walking with Wellingtons with a swinging stride through dewy grass, toes flung droplets of clear water forwards.

London, last bastion of black patent-leather shoes.

The city had gridlock and sufficient anxiety to give indigestion when eventually able to budge on roads frozen like glass.

Thatch so compacted, sodden and mossy that it resembled turf.

Scurrying, sweeping and sucking. Could not the imposing golden leaves be left to rustle? The posh suited gent., wearing black shiny shoes, was at it too, moving leaves about with his hand blower.

Low-lying sun gilded the apples.

He closed all the windows. The pond boiled with hail. Wind buffeted so violently that he thought a few minutes with the most central dining room prudent. The moorhens scurried around on big feet, not knowing where to go.

Long flakes of rime crackled off the branches.

Forget big harbours with towering arrogant walls. Celebrate small harbours and their give-and-take with the sea. They catch sea-creature food, provide income and identity remote towns.

Land of pumice.

"Here be dragons."
(Ancient maps)

Drying rice covered every footpath in the village.

The media and their satellite dishes set up their own temporary camp at the roadside. *(Paris)*

Unappreciated but ubiquitous feature (mosquitoes).

Winning Words

What a fearful, hardened locality with high grills on the footpath over the railway track and many television cameras and recordings played back on screens so rub noses in that surveillance.

Liquid mud a foot deep surrounded the concrete apron of the dairy farm.
   "Terrible working conditions," thought the walker.
   He felt sorry for the farmer. The walker frowned, suddenly feeling less sorry. Parked in the drive was, not a disintegrating *LandRover*, but, a showroom-fresh muscular, top-of-the-range, off-road *BMW*.

Cloud-to-cloud lightning zigzags utterly unpredictably.

Reassuringly near the centre of things: trams shook the ground floor.

Crick and *Watson*, DNA investigators, had enjoyed a pint at this *Cambridge* pub. The other two hundred people wanted to soak up the atmosphere, too. He sat outside, by the RAF bar, drain and tiny heater. He projected its tiny red image, through a wine glass, onto his trousers.

"I have been to *Hades* and returned."

Sunlight sparkled off a wet bracket fungus while a fly supped its juice.

"There is some interesting wild life outside at 2 am," said the first floor urban flat tenant.

Through that paradise serpents slithered and hissed.

A crucible of ...

Bungaloid.

"City life: millions of people being lonesome together."
(Henry David Thoreau)

You walked up steps to a more ethereal plane.

Location outside

"A map of the world without utopia would not be worth looking at."
(*Oscar Wilde*)

A newspaper left outside in the rainforest, by morning, becomes *papier-mâché*; within its tub, powdered salt consolidates into a solid cake.

The *UK* is cold, dull, wan, pastel shades, green and moist; ample grass for cows.

It was the city's spinal chord.

Within the cathedral courtyard lived thirteen white geese.

"Stonehenge ... is the roofless past"
(*Siegfried Sassoon*)

A desert only has seven inches of rainfall a year; nine inches is merely arid.

They traced out the location of the main street with a horse and plough. The odd kink remains.

In the harbour and estuary, sharks swam.

Beach of legend tatty around the edges.

Deep hidden valleys, barren wastelands, remote mystical mountains and lush low valleys.

Hissing fumaroles.

The signs urged "Jogging" but sad sods no longer struggled around the track.

The air was warm and perfumed.

The train pounded into the West. From the dining car, the view astounded: desert without people, snow-topped mountains and full moon.

Winning Words

The back entry to the famous *London* theatre was through a tatty single door. Its neighbour had an opulent double smoked glass door. It was a strip club.

Outdoor café life means sitting in the sunshine, chatting to passing friends.

The branches were restful to behold; crusted with matt green lichen and *Pleurococcus*. But the bonfire burned fitfully; branches were spread too thinly.

If you suffer mountain sickness, leaving water inside your bottle is useless. Water needs to be inside you.

Along the valley they pulverised rock; it was gritty in his eyes Bubbling mud of brown kaolin is gloopy.

The urgent clucking of the zebra crossing was like a kiwi laying her egg that was 80% of her body weight.

Some volcanic pools were periodically as acidic as battery acid. Birds and humans avoided them.

Water hyacinths floated down the canal. Each tin shack lining it was different. Lack of planning permission resulted in an explosion of organic reactivity.

At the gate, the wind did blow, heavy with sand from the beginning of time. (More factually, sand aggregating into sandstone and powdering back into sand has occurred six times over geological time: about 5 billion years, around 36% of the universe's life.)

The sun came out and the landscape blazed yellow, brown, and green. It was so vibrant that he sucked in his breath in delight.

The mud looked beautiful from above, but below it was ugly: black, sticky and stinking.

Location outside

"When the mangoes were ripe, the black monkeys came. The males were nearly as big as a man, fierce, and would bite. They would jump from roof to roof and afterwards we had to go out and look at the tiles and repair any that were cracked." *(India)*

After nurturing the wildflower meadow for a year he expected, as reward, at least a badger and a deer. He only got two large bunnies; one was squashed on the road nearby the next day.

It never really got dark.

People and things pass on but the place remains.

Ash/sand/soil/pebbles raked into pleasing patterns.

A spiritual place with four wooden staircases in the thin mountain air.

Love other

Beautiful car; lousy driver.

Although the *Jaguar* was five years old she was still glamorous. Fingering the remote control, he loved making her flash her headlamps at him across the car park. Then everyone knew she was his. So he must get her repaired even though she was so expensive. She winked at him with her big round eyes.
"Come to me," she said.

I love this place with a passion.

Alcohol is the love of my life: an abusive lover.

Love other

Hovering over the display case, he licked his lips at the sheer mass of the telephoto lens, the bottomless black of its enormous lenses coated with exotic materials, the reflections in their blooming flaunting colours he could not describe. He salivated so much that he dribbled onto the glass case, wiped it off with his handkerchief and looked around, embarrassed.

He loved leathering and polishing his car because it gave an excuse to feel her voluptuous curves.

"...'s dog has died ... now just sits around all day, glum."

"But Ope, why did you develop the atom bomb and then not want to work on the hydrogen bomb?"
"Because the mathematics were so sweet." (I.e. he loved them)
(J. Robert Oppenheimer)

In the corner of the office in his factory was a settee. On it lived two Labrador bitches. They licked each others genitals, enthusiastically.

"Why is my husband being so nice?
What does he want?
What is he hiding?"

Love people

He was in love in the springtime, all the leaves were in bud and all the birds were in song.

Romance is gaudy and perishable as petrol station carnations, but women miss it when it is gone.

The island of love arose from the foam of the testicles of a god, thrown into the sea. *Aphrodite* came ashore in a seashell. Did *Freud* know that? Origin of the romantic heart symbol was the ancient Greek temple of the (ideally shaped, female) buttocks that the goddess *Aphrodite* typified. That may be the only religious building dedicated to the worship of buttocks.

The groom turned around and his eyes filled with tears. The vision was a corset with veils at different levels.

The days of love are few.

Love and laughter can dissolve darkness.

Love people

Marriages are like concrete, strong in compression, the stretches of tedium, but not in tension, when people can get hurt.

When you think that you glimpse a beloved person who is dead, it is not a trick of the light; it is an ache of the heart.

When you kiss, you exchange 4,000 parasites, 100,000 bacteria and up to 0.5 gram of fat.

The sewing kit contained a needle with a head so minute that it had to be designed by a masochist.
"Cut it so it has a clean edge. Wrap it around and around like this. Push it through a loop and tie a knot - like this," she told the mere man.
"If you die first, I shall remember that you taught me to do this and cry. If I die first, don't forget to blow up the tyres on the car."

Husband to wife:
"You complete me."

"She'll only change him and his ways if he really falls for her."

She loved her son, knowing that he could go where she could not.

"Love is an irresistible desire to be irresistibly loved."
(Robert Frost).

"Man wants not only to be loved but to be lovely."
(Francis Bacon).
Woman too.

"Do you want love (honours) or money?"
(Margaret Thatcher)

The unemotional doctor saw his son at university at the end of the first term, a big impressive figure with a group of other lads. The father felt a lump in his throat.
His son had left home still a child, "and, you know, now he is a man."

Had the luxuriant bunch of pink roses and top-of-the-range chocolates come from the ... who had invited her out for a superb meal?

"If he's spent that sort of money, he will make himself known to you," said her male colleague.

"I've got to find out who it is," she said.
"You're married."
"Yes. But it's gone flat."

To find, late in life, the love of your life, bowls you over.

"To love in secret. There is longing in it and a gentle envy; a touch of contempt and no little innocent bliss."
(after *Thomas Mann*)

Maybe we expect too much of "love." We have used it too much, worn it out. Maybe it just means caring for someone, someone that matters and being on their side.

"What is it like to be in love when you are 23?"
"I am so happy. I laugh. We laugh together at the silliest things like walking along with hands in each other's pockets. We don't care what anyone else thinks."

There is a kind of love called maintenance. It restores my crumbling edifice, does the grouting and knows where the money goes.

Cupid's poisoned arrows.

A kiss is like a marshmallow, soft pink, chewy and sweet.

The little, but expensive, restaurant on the left bank of the *Seine* served salmon in a pancake and veal with truffles and sour cheese cake and cream with just the right amount of sugar and fine wine and served it very well. It seemed to him the centre of things, the very heart of civilisation on the planet. It was for him a cusp of his life; it was their silver wedding anniversary and there was love in his eyes as he looked at his wife.

Love people

He, like all of us, was searching for true love.

A love too fierce to be satisfied with a kiss.

Love may be very selfish, destructive and corrosive.

"He took me in his arms and gave me a great big hug and said, '... , I do love you.' I think he had a sort of premonition. They put an electrode in his throat but could not restart him."

"I saw my father sack the man who later became my wife's lover."

"physically warm love, that seemed to make the corpuscles of his blood glow."
(D.H. Lawrence)

"the fire in your stomach, the howl in your head, the ache in your heart, were all caused by longing"
(Miranda Sawyer)

"My Nana has died," she said, in tears. "Can I go home please?"

Love will do what it can.

Heart warmed and wrenched.

She looked like a frumpy old bag - but when she opened her mouth and sang she became a beautiful siren.

"I want to be me and I want to be loved."
> Sobs raked the normally assured person.
> "You silly sod."
> There was not a dry eye in the house.

By the alcove on the bridge facing ancient floodlit buildings on the *Isle de Paris*, a kiss can never fail.

"Takes a girl to make him clean his shoes."

Winning Words

In 12th century Britain, child marriage was common such as eight year old boy to ten year old girl: a matter of property; romantic love did not enter into it.

In the early Wild West (USA) there was only one woman to a hundred men. She kept the bar and was a whore. She became wealthy and chose the best man. She really did.

"Wore" is, etymologically, from a "lover."

"She entwined her creamy arms around his neck."
(Lynn Stark)

Macabre

- *Warning: this section may upset. It is not for the squeamish. It might not be your cup of tea or just might spoil your day.*

In the rear mirror was a cloud of feathers and a heap that flapped.

Check bonfires before light: "Bake potatoes, not hedgehogs."

From the bonfire ashes crawled a featureless heap on short stumps. Was it a rat or a hedgehog? He was very fond of hedgehogs but poisoned rats with warfarin.

It takes 7.5 seconds, 2,400 volts and 8 amps to heat the brain for long enough to be fatal.

Long wobbly strand of snot that the wind caught.

George IV's body, embalmed carelessly, swelled greatly in his coffin. Attendants feared an explosion. They hastily drilled holes in the lined casket; rotten air escaped so the pressure was reduced.

After a post-mortem the brain (and other removed parts) were sewn into the emptied abdomen.

The Browns Lane *Jaguar* plant in Coventry was closing. *Jaguar* was in the city's DNA.

The reference sample to determine whether the exploded body fragment is yours is in your toothbrush.

Report on moles trapped for three weeks: "One was stinky; the other soggy."

Winning Words

Elephant shot with a bullet laced with acid. It took three days to die. It had trampled their crops.

Russian blog speak: "Man, what a bitch."

Pigeons were trained to peck at a screen projecting an image of a ship in a free-falling bomb, to alter its fins, to guide it to the target. Goodbye, ship and pigeon. Project aborted after electronic guidance became cheaper and more accurate.

A basket case: a soldier, still living, fabled to have lost all arms and legs; carriage to the medical facility was in a basket.

Catholics are told that they are sinners. Even nuns are sinners. So in that Aragonese castle in *Ischia*, when each sister died, they did not bury her. In a small room on a stone chair, they put her lifeless body. They let it decay and the liquid run out down a groove. The body decomposed, slowly. Body fluids collected in special vases.
    Those left were taken to see it and told, "You are nothing. You will die, too, and be like this. So *know* you are nothing."
    This custom highlighted the utter uselessness of the body since it was merely a container for the spirit. The nuns spent several hours a day in such an unhealthy environment. They often contacted serious diseases. Some proved fatal. Eventually, dried skeleton heaped in an ossuary.

"What would I have if I had one green ball in my left hand and one green ball in my right?"
Answers own question: "The undivided attention of 'Kermit' the Frog."
    "Now, can I please have your undivided attention?" said the teacher.

Cadavers' blood and guts decay. Male corpses get erections ("angel lust").

Escaping air makes copses emit foul-smelling gases and they defaecate. "Vapours" include $NH_2(CH_2)_5NH_2$, a poisonous

Macabre

syrupy liquid: "cadaverine." Its similar cousin, "putresine", a poisonous solid, is also found. The pair also contributes to the smell of living animals and comprises some components of the smell of semen. They contribute to "bad breath." Nylon garments have some similar building blocks, but the small odorous (amine) molecules cannot reach our nose, so we cannot smell them. Neighbouring molecules anchor those amines.

During the flood he grabbed hold of a cactus ball. The thorns went straight through his hand. On the second day, his hand had swollen as large as a ham.

At night, the basement with the gargantuan pickling tanks including giant squid was, perhaps, a little ghoulish.

Robin Hood gelded monks because they distributed their seed into maidens.

The doctor said, "Madam, you have fungus growing under your bosoms."
"Oh? Have I? I haven't had much use for them lately."

If you put a frog into boiling water it will jump out immediately. But if you place it in cold water and gradually heat it up, the frog would not realise that the water was too hot until it is too late and would be boiled to death.

"After the Second World War, my (Dutch) parents, who had nearly starved to death and were yellow from only eating tulips, were served this meal of meat. It was rabbit and it was delicious. They discovered three days afterwards that it had been cat."

"Every year we hire a man who tells us how to keep the unions out." *(USA)*

Tears flowed before the cleaner, the girl from *Age Concern* and the undertaker: "Thank you for giving me birth, mother. Thank you for suckling me. Thank you for feeding me cakes. Thank you for feeding me encouragement. Thank you for letting me go."

Winning Words

They sacrificed their children to the gods. They burned their toddlers and scattered the ash. We know because we have found milk teeth.

The big arthritic dog limped from the front door into the snowdrift. His legs sank into it. He stuck, immobile, in his own wetness

One washerwoman to another, "I win agreements with my ass, like you do."

It's like chopping off your testicles and then inviting you to join them in an evening of fun at the brothel.

"(I wish) I had your balls in my hand ... ; ... I'd (put them) inside a hog's fat turd."
(Geoffrey Chaucer)

Faeces roasted, aromatic, in the sunshine.

To quieten and break elephants, use fireworks.

Time has flit. Oh shit!

"She was a nice old bird, but eccentric. She would not hurt a fly but smelt a bit and would take her knickers down and go in front of you.
    Once, she got onto the mound of her husband's grave and danced, saying, 'I'm glad you are dead because you gave me hell!'"

Using your lawnmower at night converts it into a kitchen blender; its grist is slugs. Jelly will line its insides.

Chop out the voice box from a duck's neck. Blow: a chicken squawk.

Macabre

For the tenderest goose, eat alive. Tie a goose on a table between many candles. Cook slowly; baste periodically. Slice off as required.

Better an Ivan on the tum than a bullet in the bum.

When his mother was making him, for his brain she used dung.

Sam's digits (sliced off by wayward machinery) hit the deck like half a pound of live prawns.

The lobster clattered and tried to climb from the basin. Its screams in boiling water provoke more anger amongst animal activists than the fate of millions of shrimps and prawns dispatched in the same way.

Germans in WW2 used 312 calibre *Mauser* bullets. Each contained 3.2 g phosphorus. Result included necrosis, destruction of the liver and "smoking stool syndrome." Death occurred after six days.

They do not smell the dunghill at their end.

The kind of person who sees an elephant's footprint in the mud, full of water and thinks, I could carry water in an elephant's foot.

The twenty Roman centurions sat in a row in their communal lavatory and passed around the sponge stick in salt water; it was their toilet paper.

Used needles flung into a bucket of water for re-use (without sterilisation).

"They hit the cow on her head with a blunt axe until dead. It squealed. They took her with them lashed to a pole. On the mountain it was tenderised by flies, sputum and faeces. Some laid eggs within. It turned me vegetarian."

The seaman's body lacked fingerprints or face. From a batch number identifying his surviving jeans, they were bought in *Holland*.

Winning Words

"We have had a leg for two years. It is not murder for you can live without a leg. We are still looking for the rest."

At the (medicinal) baths they proudly keep a collection of "skin balls", removed by the rough scraping during the *annual* baths of the (cleanest) aristocratic Georgians.

A ride-on lawnmower, driven by a twelve year old, ran over a two year old. Could not "restart" him. The PC was upset. He went off duty and crashed out with a bottle of red wine.

Have underpants been washed? Check them out for brown tramlines.

In the Knackers' Yard, body chunks were boiled. Fat floated to the top. It was skimmed off and set in barrels.

"Do not identify burned bodies with paper labels. The rendered fat makes the labels unidentifiable."

Treat every family as if they were the only ones to have lost a loved one.

After burial at sea, small arthropods enter by the mouth. "Wild life" infests all the internal organs, especially the kidneys. They seem to be moving.

During an air crash, your body suffers 50,000 gravities. No wonder it is not easy to recognise.

They stored the 200 bodies (mass fifteen tonnes) on a (ground floor) ice rink. Many building floors will collapse with that weight.

Ultimate humiliation for a defeated enemy: victor slices off body parts and eats, with smacking lips, until so little of enemy's body left that dies.

Macabre

A paper bag is better than a plastic "bin liner" to allow the matured volatiles from cadavers to escape.

In death, because relaxed, a spouse looks different.

The brain is like a lump of cold porridge.

"We always leave them (cadavers) with a smile by stitching internally."

The vacuum pump for erectile dysfunction had a bulb to suck out the air and a pressure gauge. To fill the plastic expansion chamber he would have to be a very big boy. His wife came in to collect it. Apparently, he was very pleased with the results and much preferred it to *Muse* self-injection directly into his member (entry before sildenafil *[Viagra]* tablets available).

In a fire, as no exit, mercury from dental fillings explodes in the skull.

After the propeller hit, the body was an unusual shape.

The locals had knitted the specific national flag for each copse. On each lay a posy.

The psychiatrist, scheduled to counsel the morticians, had domestic trouble, so did not turn up.

He thought a shoe lace had dug into his foot. No. Six months before, an insect had laid its egg. The grub was just hatching; it wriggled. A dollop of *Vaseline* would asphyxiate it, eventually.

The ancients were more relaxed about excrement. Their cosmology said that the Earth was the centre of the universe so it was rational for filth to centre there too.

Big cats (e.g. lion) eat the liver and spleen first. "Tiddles" does too.

Mathematics

Imaginary numbers are amphibians between being and non-being.

To weigh up his personal calculus of risk of 1 in 1,000, to understand it, he thought of one boy in an assembly of a thousand boys in the great hall at school. He might know that boy.

Tormented mathematicians.

Behold the golden mean:

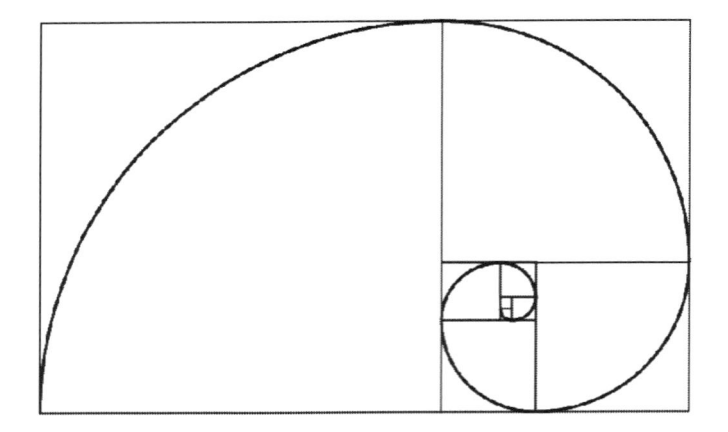

Zero is dangerous, an infidel idea. It is the devil: annihilation.

Mathematics is the catalogue of all patterns.

Statisticians' quip: "Once is an event, twice is a coincidence, three times is a trend, four times is a whole load of trouble."

Mathematics

Which switch positions are off and on? Answer 0 and 1 respectively: the universal digital language.

The Queen of the sciences.

Even mathematics may not allow us to communicate with aliens. We try to become ever less anthropocentric (human centred) but struggle. We seem hard-wired to view numbers to the base of ten: we have ten digits (ten fingers and thumbs)

A statistician gave birth to identical twins but only had one baptised. She kept the other as a control.

"Mathematics, rightly viewed, possesses not only truth, but supreme beauty - a beauty cold and austere, like that of sculpture."
(Bertrand Russell)

The most popular A - level subject in the UK is mathematics; English overtaken (2014).

"Why did the chicken cross the Möbius strip?"
   "To get to the other ... er ..."

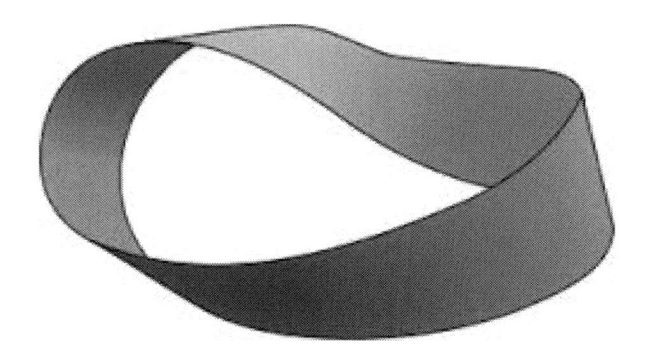

Medicines

The headache returned like an alarm clock, six hours after taking the last dose of two paracetamol tablets.

Fungi in yew bark synthesise chemicals initially used to make the anti-cancer drug Paclitaxel *(Taxol)*.

The venom of the *fer de lance* pit viper was used to develop the ACE-inhibitor Captopril (reduces blood pressure).

Tall sea squill, bulk roasted on a fire, centre mixed with olive oil to make a hair restorer.

Penicillium chrysogenum mould (1943) exudes "magic juice" but in pitifully small quantities.

White bark rubbed off aspen trees makes a natural sunscreen.

The original source of *FSH,* (Follicle Stimulating Hormone) now used in hormone therapies, was the urine of post-menopausal Italian nuns. The nephew of Pope Pius XII suggested that source.

Dose is crucial; increasing changes ineffective to effective to poison.

The medication habit (remembering to take your prescribed medicine and at the correct time and so on) starts as a cobweb but should become a cable as soon as possible.

Medicines

"Purchase our patent conservatory with sphagnum moss," for leeches (akin to a glass aquarium – but, within, medicinal leeches awaited between meals of human blood).

Ground-up cinchona bark killed many patients because of the large volume required.

Time to get a drug to market is 15 years.

Mixture containing less than 0.2% morphine has no legal control.

That dose of diamorphine would not treat a mouse.

The archaic instructions on the prescription for sulphur presented by The Rev. W. H. Rowland were, "Put in a gallipot and tie over with parchment. Sig. (Latin abbreviation for 'Label') The confection. Take a teaspoonful three times a day."

Boy and girl in their twenties, "Is this where you can come and stay, they test drugs on you and you get paid?"
"Yes, but wrong door. Please go to the next one. They give you an information pack and talk to you."
The sleeping accommodation was six beds to a dormitory. They passed time playing board games until they saw what happened to them.
£250 a night; £2,000 a fortnight. Not bad to save up for Christmas presents. They offered even more where your heart might stop. (But only for seconds; they would immediately restart it).
At least, that's what the taxi driver said.

After flunitrazepam (*Rohypnol*) injection: "It's amnesiac. He's with the *Woolwich*. You're in charge for the next twelve hours." (*Woolwich* sentence copied from TV advertisements for a British Building Society in the 1980s)

164,000 tonnes of paracetamol (acetaminophen) are produced every year (2013); about the weight of a very large cruise ship.

The installation artist used *Pepto-Bismol*. It was really strange stuff. Its colour was unnatural. It is used to treat diarrhoea.

Winning Words

Because of its pinkness and its texture it has a kind of very sexual quality.

Chemical crutch of *Prozac*.

300 Damask roses yield 1,000 g of petals. They produce 2 litres of rose water. That produces just 5 mL of volatile (rose) oil.

From that manicured Kentish garden 4 ½ tonnes a year of yew clippings were used to make an anti-cancer drug.

The heavy, gritty speckled human ashes in the funeral urn were labelled meticulously. But on the top and not the body of the container. Tops could be swapped. He bridled. To a pharmacist, labelling medicines on a transferable closure, *that could be muddled up*, was a heinous crime.

"That stirrer is like a *Silverson*. It's got some grunt. Best to keep your fingers out."

"... ... is accepting new patients. Locally owned by a pharmacist. Not an out-of-state corporation."

In the language of pharmaceutical glassware and ceramics, ribbed denoted poison. (Blind person or sighted in dark can feel.)

Erythropoietin is "go-juice" for healthy people and athletes may misuse. But it so thickens their blood that in the resting early morning hours the heart may be unable to pump it.

Drug use is ancient: witness Stone Age healing herbs.

The doctor observed that all his men had a peculiar condition. The French Legionnaires had been ready for action (non-military) for two days. They had eaten frogs that had eaten insects: Spanish flies (*Lytta vesicatoria* often incorrectly named *Cantharides*) containing cantharidin.

"The *Pfizer* riser (*Viagra*)?" said the GP. "It won't do anything that an aggressive woman in red underwear cannot do."

Medicines

Pharmacognosy: the study of drugs (plants and animals) of natural origin. Archaic term: *materia medica*. One modern term covering part is "ethnobotany."

Tigers are icons of strength. One fifth of the world's population take tiger body parts, reduced to pills and powders.

In that factory, "elephant trunk" dust extractors hung down to extract powder-laden air from near its sources. Banging the trunks, watching a pile of toxic powder fall onto the floor, was a favourite party trick for medicines inspectors.
    "Can I see your SOP for cleaning these?"
(*S*tanding *O*perating *P*rocedures *are crucial to occupations requiring "Good Practice."*)

Costoreum is a musky secretion from the beaver's anal gland. It was one ingredient of the 65 in mithridate, a remedy used as an antidote for poisoning. It is an ingredient of some perfumes including those to give "leather" its expected smell, instead of its natural smell: of a decaying corpse.

A society tends to claim that locally occurring material (such as *Mānuka* honey in *New Zealand* or *Aloe Vera* in the *Canary Islands*) is a "cure all."

"Medicine ... it's brutalised me."

The company's quest was to cherry-pick, from their library of 60 million samples, the good from the bad and ugly molecules (2004).

Advice to inspector: do not "squash the ants and miss the elephant."

Instead of prison, *Alan Turing* chose judicial chemical castration using stilboestrol tablets dispensed in a glass bottle with a metal screw top. They turned him into a bloated monster. It is fabled that he chose suicide by eating a cyanide-laced apple.

Citizens within that smog required heavy-duty eye lotion. A best seller contained local anaesthetic and vasodilator: so sore were their eyes.

Star anise *(Illicium verum)* is one source of shikimic acid, a starting point in the synthesis of the anti-influenza drug oseltamivir *(Tamiflu)*

Mistranslations

A man carried a big marrow.
    "What is that?
    "A radish," said the Portuguese.

"What was the brown powder?"
    "Powdered mice." (rice)

"Bio data" (*India*) for "CV" (*UK*).

"Drink the rum and it will warm you down."

"Omelette of erbs."

He thought that he had ordered a cup of hot coffee. They laughed. He had mispronounced, changing the meaning to "hot diarrhoea."

"The exploiting entity shall not be responsible for the loss of any jewels."

"This used to be a dog track. Now it is for the fatty people."

"They had an earthquake and the town was completely equalised."

"This wine is elaborated from several fine vine varieties."

"The accident department is at the backside of the hospital."

"What is in the soup?"
    "There is sheepies."

British fish and chip shops attract all classes.
    "Can I have some batter?" said a woman.

Winning Words

The assistant gave a bag of batter pieces.
"No, no. I mean batter that you spread on bread."
("Butter" pronounced with an ultra-posh accent.)

Menu: "Venison and smaller wide forest creatures."

"Butter bread pudding."

The "Hello" vendors were offering good deals on *"Lolex"* watches for they could not pronounce the Western "R."

"Windymills."

Money

"Brigands only demand your money *or* your life; women demand both."

Stamp: dirty little scrap of paper spat upon by someone (before self-adhesive).

A "cub" is a "cashed up bogan" (Australian "bogan" has some similarities to British "chav": council housed and violent)

Name of luxury yacht: "Sheer profit."

Barley barons.

Oil wealth: donkeys to *Mercedes* in one generation.

Kayapo natives of the Brazilian rain forest call banknotes, "sad leaves."

A fresh kidney (for transplant) has become a commodity that the poor world sells to the rich.

"On Friday we burned £3,000 of diesel," said the farmer (2008).

A country cannot pay its way by its citizens only cutting one another's hair.

Christmas is the consumer society's orgasm.

"Greed is good. Inequality is inevitable. Envy is a valuable spur to economic activity."
(Boris Johnson)

Business opportunity: "Do you want a slice of that?"

Winning Words

In the Middle Ages, there was no economics, only greed, avarice and the ultimate sin of usury (lending money at exorbitant rates).

Money is "frozen desire."
(James Buchan)

Famously, in family businesses, the first generation creates, the second develops and the third squanders.

Filipino workers in Saudi Arabia call the money that they send home, "Saudi juice."

A thick grass roof with overhanging tufts once sheltered only the poor. In 2013, Icelanders smelled the money underneath.

In the Neolithic Age, obsidian was traded far afield: black gold.

All of money is an act of faith and might suddenly lose its value. Puff! Got any gold?

"The bride price of twelve cows was hard to meet; usually the families arranged a lower amount."

"I am hungry. Feed me," said the note by the beggar – who was fat: not the best sales proposition, even in France.

"Pensions are so small and health care has disappeared."

"Nothing is forever"
(Ukrainian proverb)

Chocolate, coffee, men; some things are better rich.

In the 1960s, *New Zealand* marketers rebranded the non-indigenous "Chinese gooseberry" as the "kiwi fruit".

Money

The self-service shelves of the pharmacy were almost bare.

Supermarket shelves were sparsely laden, the refrigerator was off. Featured items were cans of fruit containing mainly juice and poor cuts of meat.

The hot crowded conference would be uncomfortable, dehydrating, and even dangerous, without water. Fortunately, he had money to buy water to drink. In fact, by law, establishments that serve alcohol in England, Wales and Scotland must provide free drinking water. The toe-rags might charge for use of a drinking container or service, though.

City: machine for extracting your money, minute by minute, hour by hour.

The beautiful trophy wives merited a lingering glance. The men must be the famed Russian oligarchs. They had their cheque books out and were buying pictures.

One koi fish, transported in a plastic bag in a polystyrene case in the ship hold, floated belly up, dead. That fish was worth one million pounds.

There is a difference between going up to claim your parking expenses and someone coming to give them to you (that you could, if you wished, decline).

Instead of cement, they used sticky rice and alum.

High maintenance wives.

Special offer: hip replacements, three for two.

"I don't want to do business with those who don't make a profit, because they can't give the best service."
(Lee Bristol)

Winning Words

After the bursting of the South Sea bubble had stung him:
"I can calculate the movements of stars but not the madness of men."
(Isaac Newton)

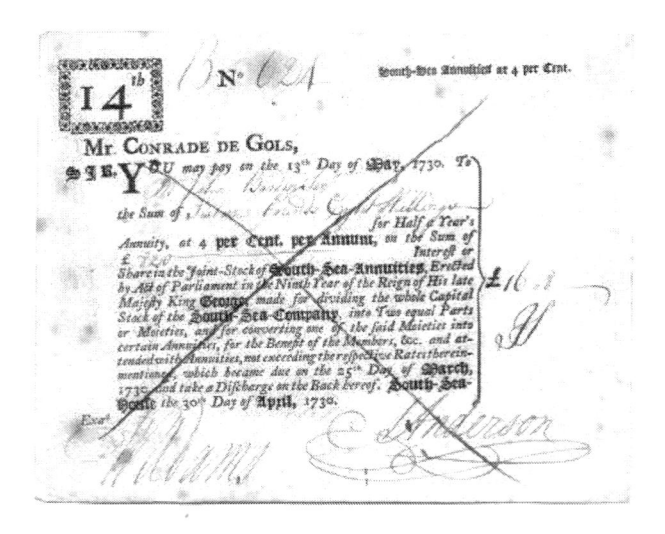

"We can't afford our own house or car but do come on one *SAGA* holiday a year."

During the economic collapse of 1988, some Russians, believing banks safe, retained their life savings there. They queued for days trying to get savings out. But they had all gone. Some people never got over it. Some people are still committing suicide because of it. (2007)

"It's the economy, stupid."
(James Carville, slightly modified)

In a company's annual report, the auditors used to just say it was correct. Now, four pages disclaim responsibility, including that numbers may have been added incorrectly.

Money

He sighed with pleasure. Here, the *Darwin* family had lived in style. The acolyte witnessed the mixture of science, *Darwin's* study, recreation room, the billiard table where he laid out bones; his butler aided. Outside, wildflowers.

Retail High Street multiple: "We are at the discretionary end of the market."

Shopping malls: spend, spend, spend!

Not visiting is a wallet protector

For farmers, advantages of losing farming subsidies included not being beholden to any bureaucrat and farming what they liked.

Emporium's window sign:

> "Meals 25 cents.
> Good square meals 50 cents
> Reg'lar gorge 1 dollar."

Pinch every penny twice.

(British) must take risks. You must swim backwards even if you bang your head ... If (UK) fail to take risks ...
   "China will have our lunch and India will have our dinner."..."
(*Digby Jones* 2005)

Poverty level is 60% of median wage; for a married couple about £180 a week (2005).

Money is what prevents people saying, "Hey you!"

The garage owner had not taken credit cards for a year; card companies charged 2.5% commission. But business was very quiet.

Winning Words

Sloth is a rebellion against the pistons of commerce, the ringing of phones and the post-it notes.

The American taxi driver said, "If I need major healthcare I must file for bankruptcy."

Ostrich eggs were £22 each.

The fire started. The superstore owner, fearing that, in the confusion, people would steal many goods, locked the fire doors. Many people died.

In a traditional Western marriage, romantic and sexual love is disparate to a financial contract. Divorce settlements demonstrate that brutally.

After a 16 hour day, he could no longer smile and eyes were red and sore. With bare feet, he could only bear to stand on a carpet.

Youngster used too many paper handkerchiefs for the family to afford. Father stormed into son's bedroom and, using scissors, hacked the box of man-sized tissues into two.

She (film star) has the economic clout of a mid-sized South American state.

Getting your invoices paid by (company) was harder than extracting blood from the desiccated corpse of a moth furred with fungus.

"What is the most powerful force in the world?"
      "Compound interest."
(Albert Einstein)

"I don't believe you. You're not really going to pull the plug on the hospital telephones!" the accountant told the electricity company.
      They had a point, not having been paid for months.

The point for his cumulative monthly income was off the graph paper. What a pain! He'd have to draw some extra lines. But

Money

tucked behind was a spare sheet of blank graph paper placed there in 1995. Such forward planning.

But only a pale reflection of the carpenter who built the great hall in a *Cambridge* college. He knew the oak beams would wear out centuries later so planted a forest.

Superstores, that eliminate rows of shops and their local community, are feudal retailing.

The float full of little girls with pink dresses and fishing nets to collect the pennies moistened the eyes.

In *Prague*, under communism, pensions were better.

For £4 million, owners expected a return of 18%. 10% would not cut the mustard.

Notice on the inside of the staff WC door:
"Use this time to think of ideas to help ... (company) and then tell us! Every little helps!"

It took five years to learn the sharp intake of breath that made your wallet shrivel.

An internal market exploits other people's troubles.

Many clapboard houses because region was all forest: wood was the cheapest material.

"Our necessary friend money spoils things."

Advice on marriage, from father to son born in 1908: "Remember that a four penny pie is now eight penny!"

"It's a big commercial decision. Do you grow maple trees for syrup or wood? Syrup gives yearly income. But, if you tap the syrup, you disfigure the wood. The polished wood, when sold as capital once only, is worth more than the syrup."

The rich always have had the nicest things: castles, women ...

Many roofs sported reed by the reed-bed; there, reed was cheap.

Houses had wires sticking from concrete roofs. That meant they were unfinished, so paying no tax.

The standard cheque (from company) had a column for hundreds of millions of pounds. His fee was substantially less.

Quantitative risk assessment may help decide whether it is logical to invest in accident prevention. *British Rail* valued one life at £0.5 million. So if prevention costs less than £0.5 million, invest. If £0.5 to 2.0 million, use judgement. If more than £2 million, do not invest. (1992)

The matured endowment policy was in an envelope bearing a one penny stamp, to the address in his home town, with his dead father's writing. He thought of all the good and bad events of the last 25 years. He would treasure that empty envelope. Would he write a life insurance envelope that his daughter would see?

"When I see someone driving a brand new *Rolls*, I think, what have you had to *do* to buy that, mate?"

"People are too greedy today. Always, want, want ...."

Money is like dung. If you spread it around it does a lot of good but if you keep it to yourself in a big heap in the middle of the field, it doesn't half smell.

"When I found my granddaughter, aged 17, at ... insurance, was earning £ ... a week, and I, after a lifetime of experience on the land *producing* something, was earning £ ... (less), that was the day I decided to retire."

Nothing stimulated the calculators to come out as much as offering a car lease scheme.
"Don't take it. It's cheaper for the government. That's why they are pushing it so hard. It's a no-brainer."

Money

Self-satisfied affluence.

Harrods: "Enter a different world" Green liveried footmen, multi-millionaires disgorged from taxis.

Padded lift.

Private roads tend to present more potholes.

Home swimming pools appear less opulent, and more of a maintenance burden, when bubble wrap insulation covers.

Being a JP is often something to do for leisured affluent women.

"Where is my mother's wedding ring?" Child had sold to buy drugs.

Of black eye:
"Is it bad?"
    "Eye like an egg!"
    "Put some steak on it if you have some," said the doctor.
    "I felt like saying, show me some, so that I can recognise it!"

Gold rings, cut with a bolt cutter, can be melted and reset.

Suddenly her eyes became puffy and she looked as if she was going to cry, "I am paid so little in the NHS that I have to do ... on a Saturday."

Pensioner couple said, "All we've got to live on is £87 a week."

Running your own business is like peering over a precipice. You have all these bills to pay. What if no money comes in? You will starve.

"The king gave each wife a new *BMW* and a house."

Museums

Modern British natural history museums are full of intense lights, sharp graphics and buttons to push so things happen.

The museum of theology, compared with philosophy, was smaller, more restrained. It had chairs.

This was a glorious real museum. It offered the smell of polish and mothballs, dust and stuffed animals in cases. It displayed dimpled glass containing slowly decaying specimens in preserving fluid with nutritious dregs at the bottom and corks on top. One was in a *Quink* (a proprietary name for fountain pen ink) jar. Rows of yellow labels shone in the sunshine. Each had the year of collection (such as 1897). Drawers housed pressed *Umbelliferae* and other plant specimens.

The museum holding thousand year old texts behind dusty glass and mahogany smelt of mothballs.

Small provincial museums pluck at memories. One in Yorkshire offered: a Pharmaceutical Chemist Qualifying Certificate and one for the Worshipful Company of Spectacle Makers, a truncated triangular glass overhead light, like an old police sign but in red instead of blue glass, and labelled with "Surgery" and "D^r." (with the "r" as *super*script). It also delivered a dunce's cap, shipping routes to every part of the empire on a globe, surprisingly detailed charts of the sexual organs of flowers (knowledge valuable for future farm labourers), a test-tube holder, chemical weights and the gloriously satisfying squeeze of a stamp to emboss paper.

Museums

The *Curie* museum, *Paris*, reminded him of laboratories of schooldays: the desiccator, massive precise balances on slabs, condensers, carefully hand-labelled jars, fume cupboard, electroscope, gas taps and evaporating disk. The Geiger counter clicked enthusiastically and rapidly: a page of her laboratory notebook remained radioactive. He peered at the square of four pastel-pink certificates with golden seals and medals. So that was what Nobel prizes looked like! Four in one family! Such talent! Then his sociological sensitivities kicked in. Had they just been in the right place at the right time, as had the entrepreneur billionaires of the early Silicon Valley? But he had sticky eyes. The pilgrim did not want to detach them.

The design museum was dingy and run down. A film of dirt clung to the inside of display cases where impossible to remove without dismantling the cases. But its ideas were brilliantly clear; dust could not corrupt them.

Only *Catherine the Great* and mice saw the beautiful things in her gigantic hermitage. *(St Petersburg)*.

The ornate wooden cabinet contained folios of *Haydn*'s original sores.

You get an immediate feel for the nude count on first entering a gallery. This one was particularly insipid.

Some animal specimens had a hard life. At first, they were preserved in rum or whatever was to hand.

Spiral iron staircase clanked.

"Mrs F, in memory of her late husband, Professor F, had loaned a painting of a dead hare hanging upside down."

Pressing flowers between paper: "We know that the technique works for four hundred years."

Large creatures look fuzzy after preservation in museum jars: the alcohol partially dissolves the fat.

Winning Words

The cases at the toy museum were at exactly the right height for small people to see the animals going into Noah's ark.

Museums accumulate an unholy combination of high-minded connoisseurs and low-minded collectors.

Beetles are best for cleaning flesh from animal bones for they remain joined in the right order.

The new labels could not be defaced; they were inked, on spirit-resistant labels, *inside* the specimen preserving jars.

Carpet beetles can reduce a butterfly display to dust in two weeks.

There sat many ground-glass stoppered and Kilner jars, some enormous. Just for that floor, emptying out the methylated spirits and topping up was a full time job. Hic!

Music

Musician privately practising: Every day you get to say "Hello" to your instrument. You need to warm up your fingers. You have to practise. It's part of the paid performance

16th century rumble pot (grating boom).

Music can plug us into a *zeitgeist* moment.

During a classical symphony we are always waiting for the best bits.

The deep voice, honey-voiced sisters with the harp, the wind player whose contorted face blew out his soul.

Foghorns from two lighthouses boomed balefully, slightly out of synchronisation, making a kind of rhythm.

Quiet soothing music has smooth sine waves; a rousing or joyous trumpet boasts a jagged array of harmonics.

Concert in O2 arena, London:
"I realise that by attending, some of you have been geographically and financially inconvenienced."
(Leonard Cohen)

Nothing had such an effect on *Sibelius* as the calls and appearance of swans, cranes and bean geese.

She pointed with her 16th century recorder.
    "A shrew lives here," she said.
    It was scampering along the skirting board.

Winning Words

The guitar riff drove heavy metal music onwards, supplied its energy.

How do you portray "The Red Arrows" (the aerobatics display team of the Royal Air Force) in a musical? Men weave about the stage wearing red boiler suits and white gloves against a blue sky with flying-machine music.

Music is human values. That is why, after centuries, it still talks to us. People loved, hated, were generous.

Music's physical records such as vinyl and CDs are a reminder of what you were and are too powerful to cast aside.

At an Open University graduation ceremony: the trumpet "Fanfare for the Common Man" by *Aaron Copland* proclaimed what had been achieved. He helped to moisten many graduands' eyes.

Music to uplift; music to inspire.

The dragon boat rowers stroked their oars to the heartbeat of a central drum, "BANG, bang, BANG ..."

After the music of jailhouse rock, we realised that our palette had a new colour that we had not realised was there.

If you have any rhythm at all in your bones, you will jiggle your toes to this.

A voice so crystal clean, soaring so high, that she could lift you to places that were so soaring that they were ethereal, with doors that you could go through.

When you listen to music that you love, such as *Beethoven's* ninth, you are an addict. You want it to go on and on and you turn up the volume.

The village church acoustics were superb. A *Steiner* grand piano, positioned in just the right spot in the nave, sounded so sweet. Immensely talented youngsters played.

Music

Slow as a heart beat, the insistent bong of stick on stretched skin; at each blow the skin instantly fought back.

Benjamin Britten's memorial: "The Scallop" is an architectural metal shell on a Suffolk (*UK*) beach with words cut out, "I hear those voices that will not be drowned."

A rock vocalist pounds vocal chords for two hours at full volume. Such singers must be healthy and strong. It is a very physical performance to move all that air. Drinking plenty of replenishing water is crucial; ale, less prudent.

Musical composers have agile abstract minds.

A flute of the cruellest sweetness.

It bewitched his very entrails.

Nationalities

African
In many African countries, only the men discussed the world in the village square while the women carried on with the washing.

African ladies, during the graduation of their children, wear much gold.

American
The American looked pale, paunchy and flabby.

An American defending a lumbering pick-up truck, "Why do I need a car that goes round corners well? I don't have corners but travel for one hundred miles in a straight line. I just want something comfortable."

American: "Car with no muffler in the emergency lane: scared the moral shit out of me."

Americans: in-your-face, with wide vocal chords.

Whatever Americans do, they do with effort and well. If you are a waitress, you are a *good* waitress and say, "How are you today?" and mean it.

American and Australian
"We just lined up our natives and shot them," said the American.
    "We did that too," said the Australian.
    "But you were cleverer. You gave them handouts so that they became lazy and faded away."

Nationalities

Americans and Germans
"Americans are like peaches and Germans are like coconuts." (Germans are aloof outside and seldom smile in the street but, once you have "broken through", are soft and you have a friend for life. Americans are soft on the outside, but inside is a big stone that may break your teeth.)

Arab
The Arab women, wearing their headscarves, left the biggest black *Mercedes* that he had ever seen and filed into *Harrods*; their bodyguards looked around.

The two Arabs stood and shouted at each other. They swore and spat so their faces, necks and shoulders were covered with spittle.

The Arabic money exchanger presided over an ice-cream trolley bulging with the notes of many currencies. He would not have lasted five minutes in London.

Arabs and Scandinavians
During childbirth Arab women scream; Scandinavian women are quiet and worry in case they make too much noise.

Australian and New Zealander
They joke about each other, but, whenever there is trouble in any bar in the world, Aussie and Kiwi will stand side to side.

British
A Briton seldom clutches hand on heart while hearing his/her national anthem.

Class consciousness, apathy and under-achievement mire the British.

British: pinched and reserved.

Winning Words

"Charm is the great English blight. It does not exist outside these damp islands. It spots and kills anything it touches. It kills love; it kills art ..."
(Evelyn Waugh)

Scots may use the word "outwith" for "outside."

British and Americans
About "Brits" as military allies, an American said, "We know we are bigger than you are, but don't rub your noses in it."

"Are you a royalist?" the American asked the Briton. "Have you met the Queen?"

American: "I think it is so odd the way that you (British) say 'Schedule'; you say 'Sheduuuuule'."

British, Continentals, Maltese and Bulgarians
The British drive on the left, the continentals on the right, Maltese in the shade, Bulgarians on the smooth bits.

British and Germans
He was the "island ape" ("Englisher") who arrived almost too late, ran through customs, was the only passenger on the airport bus to the plane and held up its departure. While struggling to his seat and offering profuse apologises to a plane full of Germans, he received many stares. He could not blame them.

Bulgarian
Bulgarian (2005) said, "We have not yet shaken off the echoes of the soviet era: you do not have to work particularly hard because the state will provide."

Chinese
"My parents are desperate to have a grandchild because in our culture, grandparents look after grandchildren, take them to school ..."

To the Chinese, the surname, which comes first, is everything.

Nationalities
To the Chinese, Europeans are "long noses."

The Chinese, after buying a precious painting, rap it up and never look at it. Eyes looking at it will stain it.

Dutch
The Dutchman had, on his wall, three ducks, crafted by clog-makers.
    "I like ducks. They are my favourite animal."

The Dutch do not like people who drive large expensive cars.

European and USA
European, compared with USA, culture, cares more about the underprivileged and taxes more.

French
France is a good place to be but not to do.
(High quality of living; less favourable for entrepreneurs.)

"The 'Sil vous plait et mercies' never tip so they are never served well."

"We will chop off your two bow fingers," said the French to the English archers.
    But the English bowmen got the French first; hence the two-fingered gesture.

German
Teutonic rational fittings of a butler's sink.

He watched the Berlin wall fall and national boundaries dissolve and reform like the crystals in a kaleidoscope.

A car is important to a German. They have the wife's little car and the big family car. They clean and polish it. When they have a *Mercedes* they think they have arrived.

Greek
To Greeks, it matters not what great things you achieve in your life, if you die badly.

Winning Words

Greeks and Britons
Briton to Cretan: "Heroic? Yes, we have that word but it is not one we use that much."

Indian
Indians only recognise butter and not margarine.

Nehru collar: spot-on shorthand for Indian identity.

Italian
National stereotypes may change quickly e.g. Italian couples having many bambinos to only 1.2 (2012).

Italians are adept at gestures: hands, arms and feet, facial expressions and mime.

Japanese
In Japan, a reporting meeting is always held in a board room. This meeting was no different except that, curiously, they all sat on one side of a long table. The auditor gathered his breath to speak. Suddenly one wall opened. They were on a stage. Below were 500 staff, all staring at him.

After World War Two, that the Japanese lost because of the atomic bomb, their emperor said, we lost because we did not take technology seriously enough. So do. They did.

Nationality ...
"Our country is rich but corrupt. It will change. It will take 20 to 50 years. But people will get fed up with the corruption and get rid of it."

Russian
Russian about Kremlin: "The 18 year old male soldiers will give you a little light massage as they frisk you."

Don't expect logic from a Russian. Remember the Russian soul.

"Our newspapers told us that in Britain, at − 5°C, schools closed and people died. Here it is normally - 37°C. This year at -

41°C was a little colder than usual; we had no problems. How we laughed!"

Scandinavians and Australians
"It is often said the Scandinavians find the achievement of plenty linked with mediocrity ... so dull that many of them either take to drink or commit suicide. Australians are more likely to commit smugness."
(Elspeth Huxley)

South African
"I will be touching all my thumbs for you."

South Koreans
Kingston-Upon-Thames boasts the biggest population of South Koreans outside their country.

Spanish
How can a nation, civilised enough to offer hot milky chocolate with bounteous brandy, cage a gibbon? It looked upwards at him.

Swiss
"We, the Swiss, want only the best. We have the fall-out shelters although presently we use them only for wine cellars. We want the newest medicines with trade names even if they cost more, the best health care."

USSR
Eighty years of history flushed away like a used condom.

Thai
Thai girls are compliant rather then mouthy.

Turkish
"To chaperone her, I go out with my sister. If they hold hands, I knock them away, get angry."

Western and Eastern
Western kids have a problem. They slouch when they go to school and think, "Should I bother today?"

In the East, they are so keen and proud; they march and study so hard.

They deserve to succeed.

Yugoslavian
"My country (Yugoslavia) is no more."

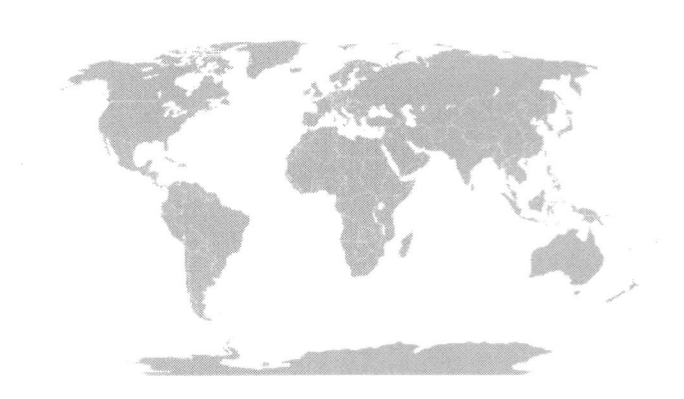

New beginnings

"Four years ago my wife and I gave up our jobs, sold our house and bought a camper van. This is what I do now."

At the back of the church was a poster with a photograph of each new-born baby.

For those who dare to dream ...

"Every man in an architect of his own future."
(German proverb)

"As you slide down the banister of life, may the splinters never point in the wrong direction."
(Irish blessing)

Retiring pharmacist: "I did not know how I would feel on the last day of work. As I got into the car afterwards, it was a feeling of great relief, as if a weight had been lifted from my shoulders."

Can we moult? Can we re-invent ourselves as something else?

Don't delay change. Live your life for you and not someone else because you are a long time dead.

Technological change had influenced his behaviour. At last, after decades of sunscreens that left his sensitive skin burned, he found P_{20} (*active ingredient* is para-aminobenzoic acid; that binds with skin keratin). His pink skin could go brown, at last, instead of red to blistered to peeling.

New Zealand census form: "We are going to grow so we need to know. I'm a bee-keeper. Headmaster. Surveyor. Barrister."

On retirement:
"What is your next project?"
    "Gardening."
    "That is a cop out."

Sunset at *Uluru* was special; this was worth celebrating with nibbles and chilled champagne. For a moment, everyone fell silent, taking in the majesty of the scene and then the moment was lost, the chattering started up again.

Arcadia visions: the simple, pleasurable fulfilling life in contact with nature – but with the bittersweet awareness that the outside world may destroy arcadia.

New horizons

"Can you see anything?"
 "Yes, wonderful things."
(Howard Carter)

The glory of jotting some idea down on a piece of paper and watching the bones of an article emerge. It is a kind of riches to combine a notion from a desiccated academic text and a casual remark from a new acquaintance.

"*Sgt. Pepper's Lonely Hearts Club Band,*" was a response of the *Beatles* to their experiments with LSD.

The remains of the day.
"The evening's the best part of the day. You've done your day's work. Now you can put your feet up and enjoy it."
(Kazuo Ishiguro)

"The best jobs were in joint venture companies because then you have one foot in the East and one in the West."

"The ... group's gone," said the chemistry post-graduate research student.
 "Can't have," said his supervisor.
 "Has. Look."
 "Do it again."
 "Why?"
 "Just do it."
 Repeated: same result.
 "Do you realise that you have done in three hours what ... (company), working for two years, have failed to synthesise?"

He saw current ideas as stale and rotten. He liked to open doors and hatches where others dare not venture. Within might be fresher air.

Winning Words

Who will be the first explorer to witness the colours of the dawn from ground three times higher than Everest: from Olympus Mons, *Mars*?

Occupations

Accountant
The accountant could add up columns of figures in his/her head.

Some mistakes in accounts are inevitable. But, if accounts are not being "fiddled", there should be a similar number within the "in" and "out" sides.

Accounting is the art of the aggressive recognition of profits.

Acquisition managers
"get their rocks off opening and closing branches/companies."

Actor/actress
"I am a blank canvas. Anything can be painted on me."

Administrator
After one of countless NHS re-organisations: "My job had changed from 'lubricator', helping professionals to do their jobs, to telling them they couldn't have the money."

Adviser
"I think it must be rather nice
To live by giving good advice."

Anaesthetist
"I'm a gas man."

"You spend your life putting people to sleep and hoping that they wake up."

Anthropologist
"Your field work is expected to hurt you. It is painful while you are there and painful when you return because you have changed into something else."

Winning Words

Antique dealer
You could tell the antique dealers at the funeral. They had a bluff humour: "... was at the pearly gates and looked up. 'Nice pearls', he said. 'Will you accept a post dated cheque?'"

Archaeologist
Guide livery: pith helmet, leather gourd water bottle and chunky wooden stick.

Artist
painting in unspoilt countryside said, "Sometimes I think I will overdose (on the view) and die of happiness."

BEDE LE VENERABLE

Astronomer
"If we find little green men, who do we tell first? The press, the pope or the prime minister?"

Auctioneer
The agricultural auctioneer would sell the squeal of a pig if he could.

Author
Bede was author, notary and scribe.

Baker
"Have you got a burn? You're not a proper member of the bakery staff unless you have."

Bank manager
The bank manager, who had written down confidential details, after the consultation, theatrically tore them up.

Banker
Ex banker: "Never trust a banker."

Occupations
Being one demands no great talent. They add nothing to society. Rip-off merchants.

Bar person
She'd had to open 76 bottles of champagne on Ladies Day at the races. Her wrist had repetitive strain injury. She was on minimum wage but had received one tip of £20.

Barista
Busy.

Barman
simultaneously flipped a bottle from the fridge, turned the bottle like a pancake, added ice with one hand, topped up with *Coke* using the other, opened the water bottle with his teeth, and energetically agitated his cocktail shaker in a figure of eight. Showman.

Bicyclist
One woman to another on hired bicycles; they had never ridden before, "It isn't as easy as I thought!"

Bouncer
in club: red shirt, black bow tie, solid.

"I am not employed for my fists but for my eloquence and good-hearted nature."

Builder
Surveying the leak, said, "It's a busy roof."
The junction of tiles, felt and polycarbonate was complex.

There's builders' time and everybody else's time.

Business person
The successful business(wo)man works outside the normal boundaries (i.e. some are "crooks").

Butchers
Boater hats.

Cat
The brewery cat was an important worker. He killed twenty mice a day. On his death, a grateful workforce had him stuffed.

Caterer
"I am finished with catering. I have to work so hard that I will kill myself."

Chef
"Always, someone's grandfather/mother makes the best *Apfelstrudel*."

"You should see what a chef does if a waiter comes in and says that a customer is being unpleasant."

Chemist
"Are you a chemist too?"
"I am a pharmacist; not a real chemist."

All chemists bear a mark where broken glass stabbed.

Something for nothing? At the outrage, his chemist's viscera contorted.

Chimney sweep
"I used a 9 inch, then a 7 inch and then a 5 inch (brush) before it got through. You can feel the resistance. If you burn wet wood, sometimes there's a soot ring. You will not break it, but with regular dry fires, it dries out, breaks up and falls down. "

Chiropodist
Elderly husband and wife hobbled and looked pained during bi-monthly outing to chiropodist.

Circus staff
Nostalgia of the circus. Animal trainers. Fire eater with sooty marks, feel heat on face.

Occupations

City wiz kids
Obscene icon: the slick braces of city wiz kids who had made billions over the floating of the pound.

Cleaner
Curved birch branches unsurpassable for sweeping cigarette buts into a pile.

Soft rainwater washes cars without leaving white marks. It seems to clean hands easily too.

To clean a doorstep properly you need a scrubbing brush, rough cloth (preferably micro-fibre), hot water, hard soap and large towel. Get down on your knees and scrub with the whole weight of your body. Finally rub off with the dry towel.

Composer
The deaf composer heard the music perfectly, in the resonant chamber of his imagination.

Conference organiser
"I'm organising a conference this year in Iceland and will need a couple of visits."

Conviviality hosts
The newspaper offered an extended section on "Conviviality Services". Bounteous buttocks illustrated.

Cordwainer
Where have all the cordwainers (makers of soft leather footwear) – and gas mantle repairers, drysalters and hog gelders gone?

Creatives
Many philosophers, artists and other creatives are tortured souls.

Cross-examiner
Cross cross-examination is bad cross-examination.

Winning Words

Curator
The museum curator is the creator, censor, restorer, preserver and story teller.

Dental nurse
knows about the whole patient; the dentist only the specific dental work.

Dentist
As the dentist pricked and scratched, his stomach was so near to the patient's head that he could hear stomach rumblings.

Diplomat
What is important for a diplomat is the quality and importance of his/her connections.

Diva
Before a photograph, trembles slightly all over like a greyhound. She arches her back and thrusts her magnificent breasts towards the camera, to maximise their impact. Her voice is gleaming with spun-gold high notes.

Pop divas project instant emotion.

DIY novice
His complete DIY tool kit contained: locking pliers, light oil aerosol canister and builders' adhesive tape.

Doctor
"I suppose one has a greater sense of intellectual degradation after an interview with a doctor than from any human experience."

(Alice James)

Was there a doctor on board the car ferry? A father had confused bottles of ear drops and *Superglue* and inserted the latter. There was a consultant radiotherapist but he had not a clue what to do. Really, they needed a carpenter.

Occupations

Doctors see every day what others see only once in a lifetime and so become hardened.

Dog (sniffer)
The little beagle sniffer dog sat patiently by the offending haversack.

Driver
To drive in India you need three things: good brakes, good horn and good luck.

Dyer
Black flag: Danish dyers flew because black was the most difficult colour to dye.

Economist
Economics is extremely important as a form of employment for economists.

Editor
The editor lived on his nerves, snarling, eating late, drinking: a veritable tinderbox.

Electrician
wearing metal suit cleaning live high voltage overhead power lines, "I am a Nordic god. I can throw thunderbolts."

"I am a sparks."

The emergency electrical repair man liked climbing up poles. He was licensed to go anywhere off-road without permission. He had his big umbrella to keep rain off the cables, a current identifying detector, safety glasses, leather *Teflon®* gloves, blast proof boiler suit – and a spade.
"I've found DC cables, laid by ... corporation, dated 1897, still being used," he said, "As good as new. I'm lucky. Been everywhere. Met such a range of people."

Embalmer
By appointment.

Winning Words

Emergency workers
Before the flood, the first decision they made, after the chief constable with the scrambled egg on his uniform arrived, was to keep the canteen open all day.

Who will lead communication: ambulance, fire or police?

Emperor
The emperor's death should be heroic: he dies in a battle or a woman poisons him. The emperor lived to be a *Methuselah* (78, when most men died at 45) and died in bed. So they fabricated a fable. He had died of constipation after eating watermelon (an exotic fruit that only the wealthy could afford).

Engineer
The (civil) engineer who built a bridge in *Zambia* in the early 20th century committed suicide after finding that it would not join; it was 18 inches too long. Then they tried in the cool of the morning at about the temperature in England. The bridge fitted.

"To one person that glass is half full. To another it is half empty. To an engineer it is over engineered."

Entertainer
An enjoyable mental occupation.

Escort
The escort agency section was the longest, most illustrated, part of the *Yellow Pages* telephone directory.

Expert
 "An expert is a (wo)man who has made all the mistakes which can be made, in a narrow field."
(Niels Bohr)

"I like arguing with barristers. You can do that if you are 'the expert.' They ask you a question, yes or no and you say it cannot be answered but the question they should ask is ..."

Occupations

Explosive manufacturer
She worked hard in the *Lyddite* (picric acid used as an explosive) factory and it turned her as yellow as a canary. It killed her. Before that, when she was not working, she had all the time in the world.

Farm labourer
"When we were threshing (corn) it was so dusty that you could not see to the other side of the road. No masks in those days!"

A group of men waited to be selected. Those working on one farm were called "hands"; those on two or more, "hinds."

Farmer
could do a year's work, harvest a crop and plant a new one in fifteen weeks.

"I run a small beef-animal enterprise."

Wore a green peaked cap emblazoned "*Fisons.*"

Harvesting the ripe fruit was urgent or they would rot.

He was a good farmer. The animals in the farmyard wanted to do something for him. They set up a committee.
    "Let's give him eggs and bacon," said the hen.
    The pig looked concerned. The hen *participated* but the pig was *involved*.

Tired earth must be turned before it can work again.

To make the field grow, farmers demanded ditches dug as deep as graves and enough stones removed to build a house.

When your Wellingtons are rooted in six inches of unctuous mud, the stream trickles by, boughs curve overhead, brambles snag your hair and you feel blood on your wrist, you feel connected, mingled, part of the Earth. The feeling of belonging, of the farmer inheriting the family farm with wide acres of wheat fields, is overwhelmingly powerful. If the farm is lost, the feeling of failure is corrosive.

Winning Words

Fire-making
The house husband/wife had "*Cinderella* duties": cleaning and remaking open fire.

Firework manufacturers
"The world's best pyrotechnicians, veritable artists of the big boom."
(Patricia Schultz)

Fisherperson
"You give the rod with a viscous conger eel hooked on the end to the most experienced fisherman in the boat. His job is to beat it unconscious with his "policeman" (stout stick/truncheon)."

Fish filleter's knife was half ground away. He honed it on marble every ten minutes.

It is crucial when fishing for halibut that your boat is bigger than your halibut.

Fitness instructor
The fitness instructor, long blonde hair bobbing, boxed and did karate chops to loud pop music.

The gym instructor was young and taut; members were lardy.

Forager for free food
Mr .... , *Brylcreemed* black hair, braces, tie and sack, worked along the hedgerow. He collected food for his rabbits.

Forensic entomologist
understood environment and was expert at identifying the time and date of death from maggots in a corpse. Only interested in truth. People lie; maggots do not.

Gardener
"I've taken off the leaves or the potato blight would go down into the tubers."

Occupations
The gardener gave a master class in bonfire nurture: feeding it little-by-little, fluffing it up and drizzling in morsels.

General practitioner
They liked their GP.
"Why not go and stamp and scream on the beach," she said. "It's what I do."

French General Practitioners (GPs) (2007) are like British GPs of the 1950s. their consulting rooms are in their houses and you park in the streets outside.

Gentleman
The 19th century "gentleman" did not work. He had independent means; *Darwin* is one famous example. Less famous is *Espin*. He used *papier-mâché* extensively, and dabbled in astronomy, radiology, microscopy, newts and composing music. He was also a vicar.

Gondolier
had lost his hat and continuously chatted on his mobile.

Hairdresser
"Mobiles should not be allowed in barbers. Of course, when they ring, they have such important messages. But then they jerk and throw their arms around. I have sharp scissors. I could cut them."

"Look how the lino is worn around the chair. I never wear expensive trousers. It's the little hairs. They're as sharp as needles and grate and wear away."

The retiring hairdresser had started at the age of thirteen. His boss had worn a black hat, mirror-polished shoes, and white shirt and dickey bow. He and his boss had walked along the main street. His boss had stopped to talk to a road sweeper.
"Listen," the boss said. "No man's job is more important than any other man's. And his 1/6 is just as good as yours. That's an important lesson." *(1/6 was one [shilling] and six pence pre-decimal currency worth 8p)*

Winning Words

Harbour master
He went from being an air-traffic controller of RAF planes at 1,000 mph to a harbour master of ships at 8 mph.
    "Slow down," said the ships' captains.

Hay maker
Wet, compared with dry, grass, was much harder to collect. "Make hay while the sun shines." His overheated, hot body now understood that proverb.

Headmaster
A retired headmaster sited somewhere on the confidence/pomposity spectrum.

Historian
"Every historian has his or her lifetime, a private perch from which to survey the world."
(Eric Hobsbawm)

Dissected with the historians' scalpel.

Househusband
logical because wife could earn more: "I am a kept man." (Commonplace in Britain in 2014.)

Impaler
Vlad the ....

Interpreter
"A teacher said to me, when I left school, 'You have a talent for language. What you must do is to read all you can. It does not matter what it is, or what language.'"

Journalist
The correct relationship between a journalist and a politician is as between a dog and a lamppost.

Most of what journalists do, and most of what scientists do, are antithetical to each other.

Occupations
Labourer
"You were, for eight hours, back-filling heavy clay into a trench and it stuck to your spade and you had to scrape it off and dip

the spade in water. It nearly pulled your arms from their sockets. You were ready to drop into bed by the time that you get home, or, rather, to your digs. You hadn't got a home."

It is the manual labourers – those who do – who make a difference. It is the man wearing big muddy boots who fixes a tarpaulin over your leaking roof to stop rainwater pouring off your light bulb. It's the man who pumps out your septic tank so that your faeces do not drown you. The scribblers and chatterers don't do a lot.

Lawyer
"I'm a jumped-up office boy," said the international lawyer.

"Young commercial lawyers in the top five law firms may be expected to sometimes only have four hours sleep a night. Huge sums are involved, say £1 billion. Just the interest charges are phenomenal. That justifies their £500,000 a year salary."

Lecturer
"What have you got in there?" said the lecturer, hitting the student over the head with a book. "A brain, or a dumpling of fat?"

Lumberjack/jill
"Is that a women's land army uniform?"
    Looked irritated.
    "No. I was a lumberjill. It was the women's timber corps."

Maestro
An alchemy exists between maestro and musicians. I lay down the chemicals at rehearsals but bring the match to the performance.

Manager
"How can you be a department head without a Swiss army knife? Who opens the parcels and wires plugs?"

Winning Words

Before becoming an administrator (manager) in the NHS, you need an A-level in cynicism.

"There is no point is beating about the bush. Your job is redundant."

Marine biologist
"There are no sharks that will harm you. Trust me: I am a marine biologist."

Marketer
His psychological profile marked him as marketing man.

Marketers, entertainers and other show-offs.

Self-description: "We are the mental gadflies that glide across many multi-coloured pools."

Mathematician
An extrovert mathematician: someone who looks at the other person's shoes.

Marauder
State-sponsored: *Francis Drake* (16th century).

Media trainer
"Watch out for the googly and be ready to bounce it back."

Metal detector enthusiast
The wheat crop had gone. The ground was bare. The metal detecting enthusiast unearthed, on the footpath to the village church, a little bronze bell containing an iron clapper caked in soil. He washed them clean under the tap.

He shook the bell; it rang, tinny but clear. We gasped. The last time it had been heard was nearly a millennium before. It had adorned a child - or sheep. The bell around the neck of a *wether* (castrated ram) was a *bellwether*.

Meteorologist
Between consenting meteorologists, opinion is that predicting one week ahead is fantasy.

Occupations

Midwife
One of her sisterhood lugged me, squealing, into life.

"She's got to keep her hand in." (unfortunate expression)

Military
"Every young male must do military service. It widens their employment prospects, helps them defend themselves and teaches them discipline."

Miner
All the redundant miner did was to potter around his greenhouse and go to pigeon races every fortnight: a 73 year old man in a 53 year old body.

Monk
To encourage monastic humility, he did physical labour and milked a beast.

Monks were forbidden candles in the library for fear of setting fire to irreplaceable books.

Mother
"I have given suck and know how sweet it is to nurse the babe that milks me."
(William Shakespeare)

He was 9 lbs 3 oz. It was the ounces that were the hard work.

Hot curry induces labour.

"When you have a baby, when you are not feeding them, changing their nappies, or talking to them, you are just looking at them, so smooth, soft, and warm. That's where your time goes."

Mover
White van man.

"Man and Van."

Musician
To no longer be a violinist, would it feel like sawing off your arm?

Myth maker
Icelandic sagas.

Nurse
At 11 pm on Christmas Eve (after the show), the nurse in charge of ... ward at ... hospital, wore a pink body stocking and grass tutu skirt.

"Was he really the person to hand the controlled drug (diamorphine: *"Heroin"*) to?" wondered the out-of-hours pharmacist.

Nurses are "people pleasers/patient advocates."

Opera singer
"Some people are just born with a *Stradivarius* inside their head."

Optometrist
"You have maturity vision."

"You are entering a stable period,"
    "How long will they last?"

Overseer of weaving
in his glass-sided cabin, had a precision balance in a glass case and a textbook on steam boilers; saucy seaside postcards partially obstructed his window.

Painter (decorator)
said, "If you can piss you can paint."

Personnel officer
Personnel: "the glam. department".

Occupations

Officer gave interviews about redundancy in a glass-sided office like a goldfish bowl. "Haven't you had training? Where is your private room so nobody can see? Where is your equipment: the box of paper handkerchiefs?"

Pest exterminator
The pest exterminator looked concerned.
"I've lost my ferret," he said. "Sometimes a big rat will take a small ferret. But if you see her, call to her. She will come to you. Lift her up and put her in a box."

Pharmacist
"Pharmacist? Gee, you must have a lot of free drugs!" *(American)*

The addict threw the empty methadone container at him, catching his leg. On removing his trousers that evening he was disturbed to see a long scratch.

Photographer
The photographer tried to bribe a Salvation Army man for his uniform so that he could get into the hospital, to take photographs that would be splashed around the world.

To youngster (in photograph), "Don't stick anything out" (meaning tongue) "Always a good photographic principle."

Pig
Backyards bustled with prickly pear. Pears fed the family pig. In November, it fed the family.

Pilot
The pilot came out to have a pee. She had lots of stripes and a nice pony tail. The flight was flawless.

Plasterer
Plastering is a good trade in *Venice*; salt and moisture wear everything out quickly.

Winning Words

Policeperson
Had to go back to basic coppering skill: "What's going on here, then?"

The policeman in the North territory (*Australia*) had a gun big enough to split a tree trunk.

Pony
Little pit ponies were more useful than big shire horses for they could work in smaller tunnels.

Presenter
"We've all been on a presentation course. Don't put your hands in your pocket."

Priests
are a kind of "parasite" (like gut bacteria) that help us make life digestible.

He only just got through the floods to the service at the funeral. His socks and trouser bottoms were soaked. The sky through stained glass was dark, except for the lightning flashes.
　　　　Between thunderclaps, the priest said, "God bless all those whose health ... has served."
　　　　Two grandsons read "Hail Marys."

Prison staff
Quieten down the prisoner, by injecting with paraldehyde. Bind in straitjacket before awake.

Production line operative
"It is so boring, doing this all the time, stuck in this hell-hole."

"I *hated* ... (company). A bright summer day and stuck inside. All I could see was a patch of sky through a skylight."

Prostitute
When the theatre was not full, the prostitutes used the boxes for business.

Occupations

"They're on the game", said his wife.
"How do you tell?"
"Their dress. And the eye contact."

Commercial street workers.

He sat on a hygienically shiny pink chair in the waiting room of the genito-urinary clinic in the company of several professional (the oldest) ladies.

Older prostitutes tend to have lower fees; their profession is the only one where you pay less for more experience.

The professional ladies were in ones, twos, and threes and lined the country road. Other wares were also for sale such as potatoes, beans and toilet paper. By the evening, the girls had covered their legs but exposed their midriffs.

There are always ladies of the night.

Psychiatrist
to a patient, "Don't worry. You are not deluded. You only think you are."

How many psychiatrists does it take to change a light bulb? One, but the light bulb must want to change.

Psychoanalysts
Many doctors of psychoanalysis had hung up their brass plates. *(Austria)*

Reporter
"Wouldn't you like to be a reporter?"
"Oh no," said the reporters' secretary. "It's a terrible job. After a child has died they have to go around and ask the family how they *feel*."

Representative
A crowd of representatives of an international pharmaceutical company on a jolly: handsome effervescent clones, badges dangling.

Retired General Practitioner (doctor)
"My accountant phoned me to confirm that I had done no work for the last year as he had to certify that fact. I told him that, not only could I certify that I had done no work but also that, if I had, I should be certified."

Road mender
A strong young man said, "Road menders do not have long enough tea breaks. A pneumatic drill weighs as much as a man and every time it goes down, you have to lift it up. My muscles were not used to it and my back ached."

Roasted chestnut seller
"Clank," vibrated the shovel on the brim of the charcoal brassier selling roasted chestnuts: the voice of advertising.

Sailor
Cross-channel ferry crews are more floating *McDonald* landlubbers than sailors.

Scientist
Every top manager at that company was a scientist; each had the marketing ability of a sponge/slime mound.

Not only anointed people wearing white coats can do science but also anyone else. Pigeon fanciers, for example, can repeat *Darwin*'s observations on pigeons.

Secretaries
inhabit a pink-coloured ghetto.

"There's no contact now – no chance to use my shorthand – just two hour tapes from 'Robo ...' and piled in and out trays."

Security guard
At 1 am, that part of the airport was in darkness, the guard, in a chair, asleep.

Occupations

Self-employed
after about three years, become unemployable. They have become too used to doing things "their way."

Servant
As domestic servants became harder to find, labour-saving gadgets were useful as "servant pacifiers."

Sheep shearer
Advice from sheep sheerer, "only use the white bits." Darker wool suggests faeces.

The roughest and wildest characters, the sheep shearers on the farms, possessed the softest hands. They had been immersed in the Merino's wool. It contains the closest oil (fat: lanolin) to that which humans' secrete.

Shoelace retailer
"Now, don't you go committing suicide with them!"

Sociologist
"What do you get if you cross as member of the mafia with a sociologist?"
    "An offer you don't understand."

Soldier
The custom of the changing of the guard, with such young soldiers, jerks tears.

Sole trader
That month the sole trader had a negative cash flow.

Solicitor
All boasted mirror-polished black shoes and spoke of their "costs" (fees).

Stock market traders
The stock market traders inventing fiendishly incomprehensible derivatives had good MBAs. They looked down on their "quant nerds" with physics degrees and they

looked down on the sales people who flogged the products. Senior management only popped in once weekly.

Teacher
"The school had no outstanding teachers, not even one."

Her teacher was like "a stalk with beady swivelling eyes that saw everything."

Why is there a shortage of good physics teachers? Psychological tests show that, generally, people who study physics do not like children.

Teachers get feedback - thirty years later.

Temporary staff
"Oh ... you are a temp. That means you don't get to know anyone."

Thief
All cities have thieves; this one has more than most. Do not take out your wallet on the street.

Tour leader
The best tour leaders are laid back and do not flap, visibly.

Translator
On starting work from home, the best career advice I was given by the number one Russian translator was, "Keep the day job."

Tunneller
Tunnelling engineer: "A tunnel is a hole in the ground with a geologist on one end and a lawyer on the other."

Instructions to a new waiter/waitress: make sure you have a watch, lighter and the waiter's friend: a corkscrew.

The formal glory of the waitresses in their black and white directed by the *maître d'* in pin-stripped trousers and black jacket.

Occupations

Waiter (head)
Observing head waiter receiving tip on *first* day of stay in a hotel: "You obviously get kisses for money."

One waiter pored over a computer printout, looking worried. He must be the manager.

Weatherperson (TV)
The public want a clown with a physics degree.

Welder
"Moles? I'll fix them!" said the welder.
    He inserted his torch, unlit in a hole and turned on his oxyacetylene mixture. He turned it off and threw a match into a hole.
    "Cor, mum, the whole garden blew up," said the lad.

Welder's goggles left a gap around his nostrils. The stray light, after just thirty seconds, resulted in puffy eyes, discharge and possible permanent blindness.

Wholesaler
of "fine healthy leeches."

Physics

Dinner cools quickly on gold or platinum plates.

Motes of dust in a beam of sunlight illustrate the universe's continuous flux.

The Greeks found that some substances, when rubbed, attracted or repelled each other. Examples are ebony rod or the fur of a dead cat. Traffic cones, too, have their electrostatic signature.

"When you can measure what you are speaking about, and express it in numbers, you know something about it ..."
(William Thomson)

When the molten granite of The Giant's Causeway was cooling and so loosing energy, it "tried" to find the minimum circumference: a circle. It could not because of conflict with the neighbouring slabs; each, also, attempted to become circular. So they had to "compromise". Results were usually six sides but occasionally five or four.

Binoculars, the wrong way around, offer excellent optics for concentrating the sun's ray to start a fire.

To measure the depth of a well shaft, drop a stone. Count the seconds to hearing it hit the bottom. The stone will fall at 10 metres per second, per second: after the first second, 10 metres, during second second, 20 metres, and so on. So, for example, if stone takes 2 seconds, total depth is 10 + 20 = 30 metres.

"A good many times I have been present at gatherings of people who, by the standards of the traditional culture, are thought highly educated and who have with considerable gusto been

Physics

expressing their incredulity at the illiteracy of scientists. Once or twice I have been provoked and have asked the company how many of them could describe the *Second Law of Thermodynamics*. The response was cold: it was also negative. Yet I was asking something which is the scientific equivalent of: *Have you read a work of Shakespeare's?"*
(C.P. Snow 1959)

Whip tip cracks because travelling supersonically.

"Anyone who is not shocked by quantum theory has not understood it."
(Niels Bohr)

We use "degrees" (°) to measure temperature because some accurate early thermometers in *Florence* had several spirals (circles) through which spirits of wine (alcohol) could expand, so had angles.

Carob seeds (*Ceratonia siliqua*) were once thought to be of uniform weight (mass): the origin of the "carat" (200 mg) still used to measure gold and diamonds.

When you break a polystyrene (plastic padding) block, the static electricity produced is so enormous the little polystyrene chunks stick to your hands and are virtually impossible to shake off.

Every other century hailstones the size of oranges fell.

The scientific pilgrim travelled to where *Galileo* timed the swing of a pendulum using his pulse. There, within the cathedral church on the cake-icing setting of the Plain of Dreams in *Pisa*, hung, on its long rope, the actual incense burner.

We are scientists so generally, in the long term, we are wrong. (Challenging hypotheses until disproven is deeply engrained in the scientific method.)

Shot through as effortlessly as a neutrino.

Individuals of tidy minds.

Winning Words

Before gunpowder, to crack and extract lead ore, miners lit a fire by it and then threw water upon the wall.

The tornado's long rope undulated like a belly dancer.

The water might have been carbonated and left to go flat. He did not want carbonated water because it would make him burp. He boiled it in a kettle.

Before a skin had formed on his *Horlicks*.

Awesome, heart-stopping glory of a double rainbow, sky between darker, spanning dark storm clouds, above the hill-top church.

As fly swat, a rolled-up newspaper is inefficient. It has too much inertia and air resistance slows. The fly escapes. But a well-designed fly swat works. Its springiness and air holes allow air to whistle through but not all of a fly. A quick smack and the fly is a goner.

Measurement maniacs.

The new and beautiful language of fractals.

Archimedes said, "Give me a place to stand, and I shall move the Earth with it," when he uncovered the physical principles behind the lever.

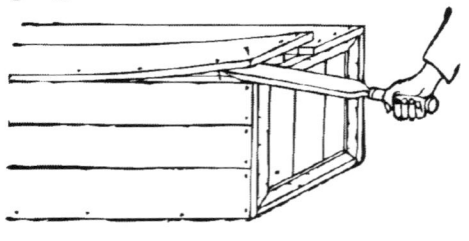

About *Newton*: every generation produces its great leaders and warriors. But a true genius is only produced once in a thousand years.

Early in the day, the channel was full. Hours later it was mud. By living on the waterfront, you could feel the rhythm of nature (lunar gravity).

Politics

Parliament is where you parley, not fight.

The document was for public consumption, therefore coded.

The expensive glossy brochure for the golf course, that would mutilate a forest, was persuasive and creative in the worst sense of the words. Planners were nervous.

The country's boundary was porous.

News is what somebody else does not want you to know. All else is advertising.

"Not sudden change like in ... . That way lies hatred and violence. It will not work."

"Democracy is the worst form of government, except for all those other forms that have been tried from time to time."
(Winston Churchill)

"If a politician found he had cannibals among his constituents, he would promise them missionaries for dinner."
(H.L. Mencken)

"... strong in rhetoric, could think on their feet, knew the system and appeared almost always awake ... all formally attired to enhance their respectability and impression of competence."

Following climate change some countries near the equator may become uninhabitable. Their citizens are expected to wish to move nearer to the poles. *New Zealand* already has steps in place to deter that.

Winning Words

Politicians describe each other with Anglo-Saxon pithiness, occasionally.

All political systems offer liberty, equality and fraternity but may place a different aspect upon a pedestal.

The riot is the voice of those who have no voice.

"An alliance is the union of two thieves who have their hands so deeply inserted into each other's pockets that they cannot separately plunder a third."
(Ambrose Bierce)

After a long peace it is normal to be cynical about politicians. That cynicism is a luxury that ceases during war. Credible government becomes too important.

The government tried to disinfect the situation with information.

Politicians may enter the ... (political forum that you elect) as ordinary and honest (wo)men but all leave as millionaires. Why?

Politics has the ability to focus attention upon an issue and continue until the associated person is fried.

John Arthur Maundy Gregory was the procurer of peerages (handed out after receiving money) for Prime Minister *Lloyd George*.

What makes the better politician: flair and panache or clonking perseverance?

Marinated (in communism).

Politics

A crowd of thousands queued to see a film about an early 20th century pimp in Cuba. It was really a political satire. The director could say things in a film that could not be said on the radio, television or newspapers.

"(Prime minister) had not so much lost a general election as parked his party in the path of a lava flow, there to be burned and asphyxiated and petrified."
(Quentin Letts)

We like our politicians tough and tender.

Minister of aborigines and fisheries.

Human rights are nonsense on stilts.

The council prevented you giving your ticket, on leaving the car park before time, to another motorist who is arriving. You must key in the number on your car registration plate.

Thermo-political deterrent.

Then they let their greatest beasts out of the pen.

Their prime minister was a professor and botanist: respect.

Ministerial backsides and dispatch boxes were on the leather of limousine seats.

Three things you cannot fight: the government, flash floods and fire *(Bedouin)*

Espresso budget: short, sharp, bitter.

When a new war starts, our leader (although seldom a priest) often says, "Bless you." We like that.

The exchange of gifts between leaders at the solstice is a token of friendship that started in Babylon.

Winning Words

(Six millennia ago) "Stranger on the horizon ... rather than raise a spear, men and women agreed to take a risk, to welcome that 'unknown' across their threshold. Might be fatal ... but ... could import new ideas, new skills, new goods, fresh blood. ... guest – host friendship ... sealed with public gift-giving."
(Bettany Hughes)

I'm for the little guy and against the big bullies.

Compared with those drunkards (19th century politicians) he was a mere shandy drinker.

Politician who did not succeed because he never shook hands or kissed babies' heads: Alas, he never conquered but then he never stooped.

The most outrageous ideas (e.g. the world was round) mooted first at travelling fairs where the government could not interfere.

Sound bites of politico-media complex.

"Politicians are good at conning people."

Never criticise the King. The King is always right. Criticise his advisers.

The Aztecs in South America played a ball game. It was a metaphor for life and death and used to settle political disputes. They used a three kilogram India rubber ball. They wore leather thongs around their waists and hit with their hips. The loosing team members were decapitated. Their beating hearts were cut out and placed upon shelves.

The first concern of government always has been defence, the second, law and order and the third, education, health or whatever was fashionable.

"I've worked with politicians for years and, even if they don't say anything, I can look at them and think: you are working out what that development means for *you*."

Politics

The greatest asset a head of state can have is a good night's sleep.

"The (British) NHS is like a bonfire, the staff fired by the value of caring, not profit. They will keep throwing on people like ... (business-focussed new manager). Each is like a hot water bottle full of water. They will burn producing a lot of smelly smoke. Eventually, the fire will go out. The hot water bottles will also change."

If we are not careful this government will know the "price of everything and the value of nothing."
(Oscar Wilde)

Churchill was a good gang leader: he insulted *Hitler*.

His inner Marxist stirred.

The greed creed of the grocery grandma.

The ballot is greater than the bullet.

The Manichaean impulse: the urge to divide the world into blocks of good (us) and evil them).

Power

A carpenter, repairing a lock in a residency, spied a consultant in bed with a nurse. After that, the consultant could not do enough for the carpenter.

Capitalism stimulates wants by advertising, resulting in artificial scarcity.

Even after death, if included, with photograph, in a bound copy of the obituaries of Fellows of the Royal Society (FRS).

Thicket of rules.

All professionals tell heroic tales to each other.
The pharmacist still bristled with outrage.
    "A woman wagged her finger at me in a shop full of people. 'You have tried to poison me,' she said."
    "No. I have not."
    "Yes you have."
    "If I had you would be dead."

Newspapers speak truth to power.

Any satellite launch needs heft. If nearby, you feel it in your ears and gut.

Psychology

Island peoples tend to be introspective.

Untidy desk carried a sign, "A tidy desk is the sign of an untidy mind."

All our lives are collections curated through memory.

Our minds are only wired to integrate about seven things into one gestalt whole. Computers are our superiors; they may handle far more.

The retired dentist had named his star in *Orion* "pink acrylic."

"Does my head in."

A gravel drive has a short-term memory: tyre tracks remain initially visible.

A wide chest and narrow waist give men formidable reproductive advantages, say evolutionary psychologists.
   Or as one gym manager said, "No pecs, no sex."

After sex, one behavioural psychologist turned to the other and said, "That was great for you. How was it for me?"

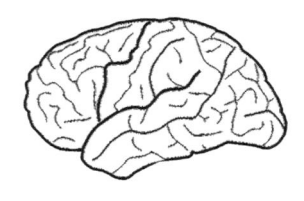

Reading

Furious, he gulped down the article.

It's good for a book to look battered. It means it has been read.

The emotional poise of a bag of garden peas.

He sighed contentedly. The boutique hotel bedroom offered a splendid *smörgåsbord* of upper-crust magazines and broadsheet newspapers.

"I'm newspapered out."

Rich in rhetoric.

Glossy magazine in top Chinese hotel:
"Readers were noble and had hope. They were elite individuals with both the resources and the vision to be trendsetters."

"Historical novels are engrossing. They make you feel that you have learned more about being human. But they are shallow: one-string fiddles. For the full orchestra, read *Olaf Stapledon*'s 'Star Maker' (1937)," argued the science fiction enthusiast.

Relationships

He was as friendless as a virus.

Cuddly as a cactus.

Memories lacerate.

"I will call witnesses – national figures – who will tear his reputation to tatters."

"To put two people back together who have been divorced needs two to three years," said the vicar. "It is like unravelling a skein of wool. Cutting it will destroy it."

Union representative: "He could pick flesh off a fossil."

Miners' picket during strike (UK):
"If a policeman was on fire we would not even pee on him."

The union official said about appeal against redundancy: "Writing a statement was ball-braking."

Whenever more than two people meet in warm friendship, to the tabloids, it's a "romp".

Being jilted, being so scorned, scrambled her internal wiring.

"I have plenty of people to do things with, but nobody to do nothing with," confessed the widow.

He wished they would allow him to grow his own weeds in peace.

Winning Words

The person deferring to others, rather than always dominating, is usually liked better.

He beat his wife using a big stick for one hour.

"Together, we are a force of nature."

The monstrous moggy and the moorhen ignored each other.

About sharing opinion: "There is no air space between us."

"If he is a bad king, the council will give the queen permission to kill him by poison. It occurs in that hut."

Six degrees of separation separate anyone from anybody else on earth.

Mother about young son: "He belongs to me."

... gypsies have an unofficial marriage at the age of twelve and two or three children by the age of twenty.

"He was a friend that few pensioners possess, someone who had stayed in contact and a friend from schooldays."

Sensuousness

Palate-puckering.

His head foamed as if it contained sherbet.

Special taste sense for curry: the trigeminal.

Scones sated.

The shouting of excited Chinese was so loud that it made his ears hurt.

When stretching after exercise, your Achilles tendon feels warmer, suppler.

Tears are just secretions like mucus from the nose or wax from the ear. But tears wash the mind and everything seems clearer.

Licking envelopes until tongue cakes with mucilaginous gum.

Tyres rap and squeak on slippery cobble stones.

Hard thump, thump, thump, of speedboat on waves, aggravates back problems.

Fireworks sear eyes.

Removing *Cellophane* from any packet: extravagant crisp crackle.

The delight of having your body core warmed through.

Are the pleasures of the hearth and the smoky taste of barbequed food throwbacks to a Stone Age fire?

Kneaded putty rubber from Malaysia feels wonderfully soft.

Winning Words

Which gives the greater pleasure? Popping bubble wrap or splintering ice in puddles? What a crackle, the toddler thought.

The rock festival vibrated his chest, stomach, spine and throat. Participants looked content as if quietened by the music or maybe that vegetable smell was dope.

The chestnuts popped off their charred skins on the hot drum top, where the street vendor shuffled them. The soft insides warmed his throat on a freezing night. Ten francs for a small bagful.

On the overgrown railway embankment grew blackberries, bloomed with yeast, ripe, swollen, about to fall off. He bit into one. It splattered his palate with sun-warmed juice. Its taste was so sweet and intense that he closed his eyes and almost staggered.

Tingling tongue.

On cracking open the plane door, the heat hit like an open oven door.

Salty water mixed with toothpaste.

Flexed toes on algae-covered board under full moon.

Strange fungi in damp bog.

The bass of the organ in the ancient church was so low that it warmed her stomach / vibrated his larynx (voice-box).

He did not clean the brace very often so his mouth did whiff a bit.

He sat on the end of the breakwater. He felt the waves shake it through his pants.

Espresso coffee, tortured rasping of steam. He could not wait for the cup. Was that addiction?

Sex

He was just another man, another spiller of seed and cigarette stubs.

He was puffed up with testosterone and not an ounce of sense in his blood.

The girl in the bar wore a tiny black top and had bare arms. She wore trousers instead of a skirt but that wasn't so bad because they hugged her little round bottom real tight.

One waitress, who always had a lovely smile, walked, placing her feet down firmly with black high heels, resulting in a riveting swivel of the hips. One day she wore flat heels: the effect was muted.

Everything was mating; the dragon flies were glued, hovering in pairs. So did the blue butterflies.

... eyed the shoot, about eight inches high, with a knob at the top, in a pot on her desk.
"I wonder if more women than men buy those," he said.
"Everyone who has come in has made a rude comment," she said, looking at the phallus-shaped plant shoot in the flowerpot.

Female tears instantly reduce male testosterone.

He liked that, in moderation.

"women's weapons, water drops"
(William Shakespeare)

Winning Words

"Pneumatic autocutie."
(A.A. Gill)

>such as a curvaceous girl reporting weather who reads from an autocue but is not a meteorologist; the antithesis of, say, a long grey-haired middle-aged female professor. Long hair meant sexually free but grey meant "past it": conflicting messages. Some men are reputed to have insufficient mental processing power to reconcile the appearance of the latter on mass media: their brains boil.

The 19-year old student daughter retuned home to the ...'s farm said, "I couldn't get into my usual parking place because a boy and a girl were fornicating in it and they would not stop."
    Her father replied, "Any chap who takes his trousers down in this weather deserves to squirt his end off!"

St *Thomas Aquinas* thought that prostitution was a necessary evil, like sewers, in big cities.

They paid for a gorilla-gram. He had long hair and a tattoo. She unzipped him. He read a poem. He carried her around the room. Then he guided her hand inside his loincloth.

Generally, when two men discuss cars, there will be an understanding of a shared subscript of car as mechanical aphrodisiac.

The chairman of a meeting of GPs (1970s) said, "Look at us. We are all male and in our 50s. Let me show you the future."
    He guided up a 30 year old girl.

A cabaret of brilliant colours, long-legged dancing show girls with pert nipple shields.

At the age of 35, human female fertility falls off a cliff.

David's plump testicles are a source of international male anxiety. (Renaissance sculpture by *Michelangelo*).

Sex

In Russian, a bus is male, a window is female and the road is neutral.

The men were dying off like flies; the women lasted eight years longer.

From his student days, he had kept in touch with eight men. Half were dead. Of eight women, all still lived. (2007). It was a better reason than most for going to the gym.

She felt ripe.

Chinese woman said, "I have a daughter. I think that is better because we now have so many more men. Perhaps we will have male concubines."

The line of single shoes in the shop window was barren. Each awaited a mate.

"The title 'men' is generic and applications are welcomed from all sexes."

Nothing else being to hand the six-year old boys used a Barbie doll as a battering ram.

"If you sprinkle
While you tinkle
Please be a sweetie
And wipe the pan."

14 year old pregnant girl, asked who the father was, said, "When you have eaten a plate of baked beans, you can't say which one made you fart, ducks."

Black tights sheathed her legs that seemed to go on and on at the "Tramps Ball."

A screen separated the male and female attendees at the seminar. Only the male European lecturer could see them both. Almost all questions came from within the all-enveloping burqas. Better watch out lads, he thought.

Winning Words

Two girls swayed along the pavement ahead, clung to each other. Suddenly, one, wearing a soft long skirt, lifted it up and she was not wearing any pants: an interesting eyeful.

The surest way to benefit from industrial quantities of sex is to become a rock god. But one trade gets the girl far more easily than crooning: daubing.

Signs for WCs in a hotel within an agricultural area: "Bulls" and "Heifers."

19th century doctors suffering repetitive strain injury to their wrists encouraged the development of electric vibrators. Clitoral and g-spot masturbation of "hysterical" women, who had never before experienced orgasm, was popular; repeat business was routine. It was a "cash cow."

He should have a warning tattooed on his testicles.

The little man had always claimed that he loved big breasts. So they bought him a roly-poly kissogram. They got plenty for their money: £40. She was huge and her breasts had varicose veins. They almost sagged to her knees. He was only little and she grabbed him by the collar and squeezed his face between her breasts. He could not escape. His arms and legs waved about. (She had muscles). He has gone off breasts now. A girl, hearing this tale, scowled and pointed her nose in the air.

Female ferrets, without sex, die.

All men want are sex, food and clothes.

Kennedy had a permanent erection (priapism) and was "bonking" at the height of the Cuban missile crisis.

Pornographic prose needs to be processed but pornographic film goes "Zap!" straight into the brain.

Blow job? You get more protein from the average egg yolk.

Sex

Sex is on a spectrum.

A bearded man shows his masculinity all over his face.

Comely, affectionate and accommodating young ladies, who were dressed for a hotter climate, appeared eager to talk to him on early morning TV.

He had never seen so many men in frocks as during the meeting of the pope and archbishop.

Jiggling redhead.

Every diner at the hotel was female, engrossed in their laptops.

"The soft and milky rabble of womankind."
(Alfred Tennyson)

"From one side I'm a woman, from the other side I'm a man," sings the hermaphrodite sea hare. "One side it's a funnel and the other it's a spout."

She's got a baby in her belly and a boy put it there.

Portly confidant, "Food is the old man's sex."

Wives utter 10,000 syllables a day; husbands 4,000.

Boy girls generally have an Adam's apple. The operation to remove it is very expensive.

The girls, all exposed long legs and backs, were clubbing and looked up for it.

Frisky.

Girls take turns and co-operate; boys compete or ignore one another.

The corridors to the library were lined with an altogether more bounteous class of lady; particularly the water nymphs.

Winning Words
"A safe onward journey, gentlemen."
(*All passengers were male*: 2005)

High heels are pedestals that a woman chooses to exert simple, primitive control over the basic limbic root of men's brains. High heels turbo charge her manipulative body language. Click, tap, click, tap, shoulders back, breasts thrust forward, swing of hips and child-bearing pelvis emphasised. They give a few inches of extra stature, too.

Apparently, about 60,000 years ago, when *Homo sapiens* meandered out of Africa, there was some hanky-panky (consensual or otherwise) between them and *Homo neanderthalensis* because, outside Africa, the human population (2013) contains up to 2.5% of Neanderthal DNA.
      Don't knock it. It might save your life during the next bird flu pandemic. It might help you (having unwisely chosen your red jumper and so upset a bull) vault over that five-bar fence. Or even help some future *Newton* combine the baffling complex physics of the very small and the very large into one simple grand theory.

It was fine for him to look at her eyes but not anywhere south.

Silverton (former silver mining camp, Colorado, USA) had 44 bordellos and 117 ladies of easy virtue or fallen angels.

She was simmering for sex like a pan on the hob.

He's passed his "Flirt by" date.

Whisky-flavoured condoms.

Sex is exchange of perspirations.

Soaked with sex.

Female, compared with male, priests have different tones: gentler, cooing, and motherly.

Her black glossy hair tumbled to her bottom.

Sex

For a guide, they chose a girl of outstanding beauty. She wore a long dress, but slit sufficiently to reveal lovely legs, occasionally.

"She (date of birth 1911) painted her nails red and vamped them, the bosses, with her huge brown eyes."

The sounds of *Prague* traffic muted slightly. A crowd of schoolgirls on a holiday trip surrounded him. His pulse quickened at so much pulchritude and adolescent lustings.

"The cock may crow but it's the hen that delivers the goods."
(After Joel Harris)

Sometimes men want to see naked women and that's where they go: the topless bar.

After copulation a man's blood stream is so full of strong chemicals that he has no choice but to sleep.

All the other men had a bigger - and longer - one than him. His amateur compact camera with its three times zoom, fully extended, was tiny compared with the enormous telephotos sticking forward from the crowd of professional photographers in *Dublin*. They were waiting for someone; he joined them.
"Who is it?"
"*Elle McPherson.*"
"Hello fellas," she said.
Every man assumed a silly look of total titanic lust.

"I (a man) was in this entirely female-staffed (retail establishment). You know, they go on about a man in a way that we would not be allowed to go on about a woman. This really handsome man came in and they were all saying what they would do with him. And then his prescription was for a *serious* pelvic infection. I laughed. I may have a bit of a beer belly but I haven't got a serious pelvic infection."

It was "Jeans day" at the superstore. You paid £1 to wear them. Some of he girls fitted them very nicely.

Winning Words

"I am a babe magnet," he giggled, high on *Prozac* and booze, to his wife (before their divorce).

"Sex is just like hunger. If you are hungry, you must eat a meal; then you are satisfied and can go on some more."
(Hindu commenting on erotic carvings of global reputation)

The male was consciousness and the female energy; together like yin and yang, they make one.

80% of pay-as-you-view movies watched in *US* hotels are pornographic.

There was a deafening rustle of nylons a she crossed her legs.

The assistant returned after serving a female customer.
"She wanted ibuprofen and *KY jelly*. If the headache doesn't work, she'll give in."

Three inch heels and bare midriff.

Farmers give the best sex.

On aging, women become pear, men apple, shaped.

He has the hots for ...

When ... matrons over fifty dress in black, they are saying, "I am not available for any more babies."

Girlies stop the car in the car park and immediately use the rear-view mirror to re-apply their make-up. Chaps screech to a juddering halt and immediately leap out.

In the museum, she saw toy soldiers.
"Look, Dad: war heroes," said the boy.

Men are activated to buy diamonds by their guilt gland; it is situated roundabout their testicles.

Sex

When you grow old, girls no longer snag you on the street.

"I want to be rammed full of life as I was at my beginning."

Ravens mate on the wing.

Men tended to be macho to the female executive. To calm men down, she had a pet dog that could do what she could not. The Rhodesian ridgeback would get up, sniff and nudge them in the groin. After that, they behaved like bunny rabbits.

The Romans thought that cucumbers, being cold, cooled sexual ardour.

The biggest turn-on, for women, is male sweat. It contains the same pheromones that make male pigs, intent upon copulation, slobber.

Almost all the delegates were male, middle aged and grey. Repeatedly, they eyed the young female delegate with the short skirt and black tights.

Feel the firmness of the fruit of the cheese plant, old man, and weep.

He could no more keep away than stop himself sneezing.

To a female being shown how to use weights:
"Don't worry. Your body is not programmed to build male muscles. The weights will just make your body taut."

The respectable hotel was once a Victorian flagellation brothel.

Just in case, she put on her new black knickers.

There's a "Who's Who" (British book, first publication 1849) and a "Who's had who"; the latter is bigger.

Natural perfume.

"Here, have some more of this parsley: it gives you an erection."

Winning Words

"If someone important came to the meeting, she would abandon her power dressing with stern suit and gold and wear something more feminine with a short skirt. She would sit in front of him and there would be all this crossing and uncrossing of legs and a vast expanse of thigh."

Far too sultry, sexy and appealing to men.

Some of the green men (Pre-Christian symbols with vegetation growing from mouths) in churches are carved doing naughty things and woodwork has been constructed to hide them.

Until puberty, boys and girls are just young vital beings. Only after puberty do gender expectations limit them.

How did we know that it was a female skeleton? Because, nestled within the bones was a tiny skeleton, of an eight month term baby.

Women's *Probus* is cosy; men's is businesslike.

Rats exhausted by copulation can start all over again if a new female is placed in the cage: "The Coolige Effect." The President and Mrs. Coolidge were being shown, separately, around an experimental government farm. When Mrs. Coolidge came to the chicken yard she noticed that a rooster was mating very frequently.
    She asked the attendant how often that happened and was told, "Dozens of times each day."
    Mrs. Coolidge said, "Tell that to the President when he comes by."
    Upon being told, President asked, "Same hen every time?"
    "Oh, no, Mr. President, a different hen every time."
    President said, "Tell that to Mrs. Coolidge."

Few women choose to split concrete with jack hammers, chase tornadoes or rod-out blocked sewers.

A father with daughters can't be a male chauvinist.

Sex

Roland, the randy ghost, was a roundhead imprisoned for excessive drinking and wenching. Victims hear lecherous laughter and feel a clammy hand up their dresses.

A very very well mannered screw of convenience.

After her accident, she went to parties in her wheelchair and invited young boys back to have sex with her. Would *Depo-Provera* (the proprietary name of a contraceptive, injected intramuscularly, that had a long period of action) be better than condoms – that might not be used?

Men are physically incapable of saying "No", to an attractive woman.

What defines human sexual desire, what separates us from animals, is that we desire not a sensation but a person.

"After intercourse every animal is sad except the rooster and the human female."
(Latin proverb)

He seemed to enjoy plunging around inside her.

We seethed together. Everything about us was heat and itch.

After male and female wolves mate, his member is so engorged that they are stuck together for half an hour. It is a good mechanism to exclude other males and their genes.

My apricots have shrivelled.

"I have so filled her with my eager life fluid that she could have had no response but to conceive."

Images of women: the Madonna, the harlot, the blue stocking.
Of men: the saint, the stud, the scholar.

Most "twitchers" (birdwatchers) and amateur astronomers are men. They are obsessed about the size of their telescopes. Your name does not have to be "Sigmund" to suss out what is going on.

Winning Words

Copulation? It's like having a really good sneeze.

"A million million spermatozoa,
All of them alive:
Out of their cataclysm but one poor Noah
Dare hope to survive.
And among that billion minus one
Might have chanced to be *Shakespeare*, another *Newton*, a new *Donne* –
But the One was Me."
(Aldous Huxley)

"A woman can only become a man's friend in three stages: first, she's an agreeable acquaintance, then a mistress, and only after that a friend."
(Anton Chekhov)

Are males or females better drivers? The answer lies in the wing mirror of the beholder.

Monkeys screw all the time.

The daughter of a catholic mother falls pregnant.
    The stepfather says, "If she has a child, I leave."

A life-sized 3-D hologram, allowing leisured, close-up scrutiny, is pornographic.

On the beach, only the young, toned and beautiful, generally, completely stripped.

Greek view:
"It is fine to have a mistress as long as you don't flaunt her in public or humiliate your wife."

She looked so young, innocent, and helpless between the crisp sheets of the hospital bed. Two years later she was an unmarried mother.

Sex

One lad smirked to another, "Look at that! Have you noticed that *all* the girls with babies have tight or unbuttoned tops?"

He had to retrieve his denture plate from his first wife.

Quills are fabricated from swan feathers. Those of cobs are too stiff but those of the hens are just fine.

The teenage boy floated on his back, wearing sunglasses. On that naturist beach, a selection of nude females sauntered by.

"Sex at age 90 is like trying to shoot pool with a rope."

(George Burns)

The light porn channel by night carried the God-slot on daytime TV.

She liked growing things in abundance. He liked killing them by mowing grass or exterminating weeds.

Eroticism is being tickled by a feather; pornography is being hit with the whole chicken.

Yes, she said with her eyes.

"The one good thing about children is making them."

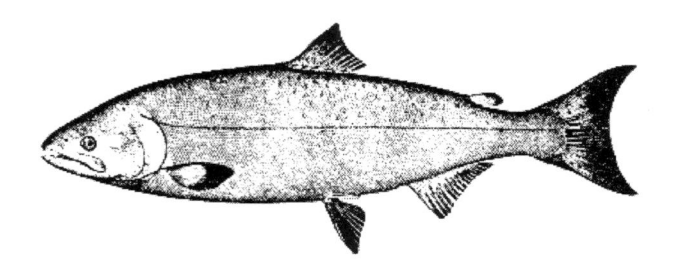

The salmon (attacked on heroic journey to spawning ground; lying there dying) tried to figure out, as he blew his last bubble, why sex was so much trouble.

Smell

Occasionally the breeze blew from a farm housing altogether too many cows. Then their ammoniacal outpourings tainted the restaurant's dishes.

Two hundred parishioners in the village hall produced a smelly meeting.

Transparent strained old perfumed wine smelling of fragrant musk.

Honeysuckle after a storm.

Spring ploughing, ice darkening the stream.

Wild garlic *(Allium ursinum)* flowers on the river bank.

A drowsy flaming June baked the cricket bat willow, freshly dressed with linseed oil and the fresh-moved grass of the village green.

Carbolic soap.

Humans are scent pigmies. One comparison notes that bears can detect honey three miles away.

Taste needs smell and v.v. Each demands contact with actual molecules. *(See Chemistry section for examples)*

The gigantic rubbery tree root, when split, smelt of fresh peas.

Surf: hissing brine.

Smell

"There's a funny smell in the bedroom," said dad.

He felt the plastic light switch. Cold. He could not see any dead animal.

"When did you last wash?"

Son said, "It's my broken stink bomb."

Joss sticks.

16th century, expensive perfume often branded, "*London. Paris. Havana.*"

She sat down to smell the coffee, a pause, a parenthesis, in the headlong rush of life.

Promising odour on opening the church door: bats, books and doctrine.

Thick dark layer of dead flies stinking in carport.

Fermenting, semi-rotten apples on opening the door in his grandmother's house.

The fumes in the air in *Shanghai* smelt chemical and made eyes bloodshot. No wonder they served cough sweets with the in-flight meal.

Swarfega: the nostalgic smell of his father's car maintenance.

Outside the massage parlour wafted the smell of bad eggs.

The air expelled from the tyre delivered a mind-altering essence of rubber, solvent and grass meadow with cow pats. Glorious; he sniffed deeply.

"You've got dog mess on your shoe."

He had. A gargantuan wedge filled the space between heel and sole and oozed out the side, brown, slimy and stinking.

"We thought the smell was a patient but it's wherever you have been. Look at the marks on the floor!"

A palaver with tissues, bleach and deodorant followed.

Winning Words

"It's in the crevices of the heel. I'll get rid of it with a cotton bud."

Meanwhile the queue of patients waiting for their prescriptions, lengthened. They, and his sudden indigestion, grumbled.

A summer thunderstorm with violent rain smells of flower petals, potato-fields, grass (cis-3-hexanol) and the pungent smell of the powerful disinfectant ozone (O_3) after lightning hits atmospheric oxygen (O_2).

Wherever its crust is thin, earth spews fiery bad breath.

She dipped string into molten beeswax fifty times. Between times she left it to dry. The conical candles resulting smelt better then tallow.

Kerosene from central heating chimneys hung in the still frosty air of the housing estate with its similar houses. But a happy, family smell.

Giraffe house: pungent smell of "poo" and "wee".

In *Roturua*, sulphur city, everywhere was the stench of sulphur dioxide and hydrogen sulphide (H_2S: "bad eggs smell"); that is as poisonous as cyanide but easier to detect because of its smell.

The cellar, blasted into the rock, smelt of the angels' share.

The "new car smell" is solvent-based paints, solvents and adhesives. Glorious, but some people get headaches and some markets overseas dislike it, preferring interiors with no smell.

He could smell the worry in the air.

He buried his nose in the raspberries and then the tayberries; the latter smelt heavier, sweeter.

The unctuous beeswax dressing smelt of sun-scorched Mediterranean pines.

Smell

Thick smell of teak oil preserving the rustic individual beams of the *gite*.

It was not flattering to expose such plumpish midriffs. The smell of heavy-duty perfume was near the pungency requiring a civil emergency reaction to an industrial gas leakage.

In an open top car you have all the smells such as fish from the lorry ahead.

A three shirt (and underpants) trip. So he would smell fresh even if he did not feel it.

If his de-odorant is woody oriental, body spray aromatic *fougère* (fern-like) and fine fragrance ozone aldehyde, the olfactory prescription resulting is disastrous.

Amongst working looms: hot glorious grease.

Beautiful lilies covered the still pond; underneath, a stagnant stench.

England is too cold for medlars *(Mespilus germanica)*, a Tudor favourite, to ripen. If stored, they smelled sweet as they rotted.

So many aromatic plants in the parched gorge: juniper, eucalyptus, thyme, marjoram.

At the prestigious symposium, the male toilet was smelly. Urine there did not used to smell like that.

On the morning air hung the sour smell of a dragon. Maybe myths resonate with us.

Uncontrolled diabetes has a fruity odour. A failing liver smells fishy. Failing kidneys smell ammoniacal.

Sickening stench from fish-meal factory: "We call it the smell of money." *(Iceland)*

Stair well of museum: blend of stagnant air and wax polish. Dark displays and faded municipal pride.

Winning Words

After three days, fish and houseguests must go.

Many scented candles flickered.

Chips in newspaper and iodine-sharp tang of seaweed squelching underfoot: a nose brothel.

He gingerly smelled the bottle top. Big mistake. Organophosphorus! He recoiled, washed his face, rinsed out his nose and mouth, brushed his teeth, gargled and went for a walk in the open air. He gulped it in.

The lily smelt of lavender and pepper when he thrust his nose within its bloom. The stamens powdered his nose with red spots. He washed them off. He sneezed furiously.
"Dad, you've got a yellow nose."

Pots of jasmine were exclamation marks on the patio.

He said incredulously, "You stuck your whole head in the septic tank?"
"No choice. Poverty. Can't afford ... 's (drain unblockers) extortionate rates. Had to find the blocked exit to rod it. Worked. Not my favourite job."

Streptomyces (bacteria producing a volatile metabolite: geosmin) cause the pleasant smell of freshly dug earth.

When we enter a room we discover what is going on by looking; a dog smells - with sensitivity around 100,000 times more acute.

His house had that institutional smell of lavatories and cats' fish.

The smell of filmy ferns in the greenhouse, more fragrant in the summer heat, should be bottled.

Putrefying wax? No. Unwashed trainers.

Nowadays, youngsters are not allowed to smell chemicals such as phosphorus, cyanide or benzene: their loss.

Smell

Ex-smokers are addicted to bonfires. They lean on their forks downwind of the smoke.

Sheep suffering from toxaemia of pregnancy smell like pear drops.

Hot bulb (1909) *paraffin* (gloriously smelly) engine, laboured: "GLUG-glug," when the load of a traction engine was applied.

Heady: suntan oil, chips and petrol.

Urinating on gorse and aniseed bushes stimulated a burst of their scent.

Harrods' food hall. Sausage; hams of assorted shapes; fish with gaping mouths.

Stench of pungent putrefying giblets in the WC of the "rust bucket" ship in tropical heat.

Aromatic herb liquor. Bundle of sticks sealed within its bottle.

Sociology

Being a native speaker of English is like possessing a reserve currency. Although numerically not insignificant, English is self-sustaining for more sociological reasons: Britain's empire, the financial dominance of the *USA* (that speaks English) and English being the language of elites. But brushing up your Mandarin might be prudent.

It is so hard to break the habit of putting toilet paper in the WC and placing it in the little bin with other fouled paper instead.

You are what you seem to be so be very careful about what you seem to be.

Sociologists' quip: "There will always be death, taxes and *Max Weber.*" (a founding father sociologist).

When people settled down they could specialise.

"My spear? It is part of me," said the tribesman. "It protects me from wild animals."

During the open garden day in a neighbouring village, he felt he belonged: "at home." The soil, pine needles to remove, road banks, drainage ditches, gravel crunching underfoot on drives – and the folk – were the same.

Sociology

The *Brontë* sisters were shrewd sociologists, although they did not realise it.

Bardot was the spark that lit the fuse that started the sexual revolution.

Clitoris of culture.

Even if you win the rat race, you are still a rat.

Polish prejudices.

Family photographs are propaganda tools. People always smile. But body language and discarded photographs tell the truth.

Economic "law": zero cost = infinite demand.

In the "ghetto" where the architect, barrister, consultant surgeon and professor lived, each expected to be number one and was not. Each suffered status anxiety, poor things.

In the South of England (2012) graduates outnumber those with no academic qualifications.

The procession included The Lord Mayor, with raised naked sword: a display of *power*.

The first rite of passage is down the birth canal. Other rites include marriage, professional registration, becoming a parent, retirement, a lousy review and death.

"Really old dads" struggle and wheeze during the 30 yard dash fathers' race. They embarrass their children.

Every idea has to wait for its time.

We all love institutions; they are our most powerful societal group.

Hinge point.

Winning Words

Sociologists and humbler observers of the human scene.

Old scientists contaminate the young with their ideas.

History is not what was but how we are told, and so think, it was: the propaganda of the victors.

Living history is the recollections of the survivors.

"Education" is not a neutral word. It is the imposition of one set of values upon another.

You may be unaware of being part of a particular group. For example to belong to the 4,500 residents who receive a water supply from a particular water storage tower with its particular content of say, chorine, lead and *Escherichia coli*.

An algorithm crunching big data may ladle you out as receptive to a particular marketing campaign such as giving to a particular charity.

Superstore (...) purchased small independent pharmacy; staff sad. Moving day saw medicines transferred by exchanging crates. In one crate, expected to be empty, a potato rolled about. Colonisation by grocers had begun.

Gossip is the cement that holds organisations together.

The native Indian culture did not value the accumulation of wealth.

Turn a vicious into virtuous circle.

Mantelpieces, even without fires, are an important comforting manifestation of the past.

Human experience (culture) has more layers than the dictates of neuroscience or genetics proclaim.

Giving blood (*UK*, no charge) might be viewed as a symbolic transfusion of altruism.

Sociology

Where bureaucracy disappointed, favouritism appointed.

Ground the data so much that his molars hurt.

Traditions may seem to have existed for ever but many are only a generation or two old.

Any attempt to classify social phenomena does violence to their complexity.

A sociologist can "contrive" any result to a questionnaire: a source of pride.

The biggest cultural change, arguably, in our history resulted from an artefact made in *Venice*: the magnifying glass. It exposed the worlds of the very small and the very big, forcing us to realise how limited are our senses and how insignificant is (wo)man.

Europeans are disappearing because of their low birth rate.

Anthropologists consider certain material objects to have "itness" or "thingyness", as if they possess their own intelligence. Illustrations include fetishes. A modern example is a pessary package containing its information leaflet. The very structure carries its own kind of intelligence without human intervention.

I shop therefore I am.

Things were changing so quickly that no-one knew what was expected of him/her. A founding father sociologist, *Emile Durkheim*, called this *"anomie."*

When the train is late the conversation is predictable; it bonds.

"Ooh! It's from a feminist perspective!"
    "Now, now, lads." (1999)

History turns.

They were written out of history.

Winning Words

All societies have creation myths. Ours is better than yours.

City: gigantic machine for exchanging ideas.

Sociology seldom has smoking guns.

It is the balance that matters. The milking stool has three legs. If one is too strong or removed, the milkmaid falls off and the milk is spilt. Pillars of British society, arguably, are: monarchy, parliament and law.

Many races and cultures meld together.

People in authority have the "power of naming." For example, a medical practitioner may name a disease; the patient may instantly feel joy or despondency.

Hinge of history and legend.

Palimpsest of history.

History rhymes, sometimes.

Women are generally guardians of the family archives of memories.

Digital memories wiped, "without" trace, by accident or design.

They tried to use millennia-old morals but they were a poor fit.

Technology

Rusty red rooster (railway).

Belt, braces and string.

Stones spat from tyres.

Controlled rage of jet engine.

"Any sufficiently advanced technology is indistinguishable from magic."
(*Arthur C. Clarke's*) Third "law."

Winning Words

" ... little wood burning stove in my boat gives four kW."

Moore's "Law": computer chips double in power every two years.

Fax machine patented in 1843.

Do you feel scared that the internet will leave you behind?

Venetian gondolas fabricated precisely lopsided so that, on punting, they travel in a straight line.

In the 14th century hotel, the door squeaked, dry and rasping. He dripped on shaving oil ("Enjoy", said the label). Liquid engineering resulted in silence.

Lashed to the (ship's) tender wall, the axe blade and handle were painted red and not just to be pretty.

A 1940 Battle-of-Britain searchlight used 10,000 watts; an equivalent (2010) used 125 watts.

"Flint hand axe 700,000 BC."

The computer worked slower than continental drift.

"and soon the noble steamer strode out at full steam upon the waters ..."
(Jules Verne)

Using his wriggly plumbers' serpent, he unblocked the moss-filled downpipe, eventually. Stagnant water gushed out. It soaked and delighted him because it meant success.

He peered upwards. So *that* was how the fairground horses went up and down: a crankshaft. But, instead of linear reciprocating to rotating as in his motor-bike engine, the reverse.

Technology spanning two centuries: incandescent tungsten, halogen, compact fluorescent lights (CFLs), light emitting diodes (LEDs) and, from the street outside, sodium lamps, illuminated her room in the upstairs, downstairs terraced hotel.

Technology

To waterproof bricks, fire three times. They look a tad charred and are expensive.

Changing gear was like stirring a pudding; the steering wheel offered an alarming amount of slack. But it smelt pleasant because of "new car" air freshener.

The sweetness of the first virginal spin of the new washing machine: tight, melodic, well-mannered, and restrained. Contrast with the aged thundering thumper punctuated by the ugly screeching when it hesitated to turn - at all.

Vacuum plumbing of ship's WC pulled in offerings with explosive suck.

When a cathode ray television was switched off, the picture changed to a fading dot. Its memory fades too, as sales of flat screens increase (2007).

Seismic instruments measuring a range of parameters, including: temperature, bending of the ground, chemicals including (radioactive) radon gas plus measurements from satellites, attempted to predict the next eruption.

An *espresso* coffee maker may cease to suck water for its tank if a mucilaginous slime coating obstructs. Cut through it with a litre of 1.5% citric acid solution.
    Rinse through copiously or, "It tastes bitter! Are you trying to poison me?"

"You will have to nurse the old engine," advised the mechanic. "Plenty of oil."
    Despite that it blew up (*Rover* 216).

"CHUG ... chug," the succulent sound of a 1918 diesel tractor pulling two trailers up the hill; a cowboy hat protected the driver's eyes from the sun.

Winning Words

Early flights from the United Kingdom to Australia took 12 days including 42 refuelling stops. Sometimes the *Bedouin* took pot shots.

The magnetic levitation train travelling at 268 mph, the boys' toy, brought tears.

That lawnmower is a brute.

Every vintage car had a sheet of cardboard underneath its engine, to prevent oil spills contaminating lawns.

Medieval artisans, crafting stained glass windows, were early, but unaware, nanotechnologists. Red and yellow colours resulted after light reflected from gold and silver particles in the range of 25 to 100 nanometre (nm). 1 nm is one billionth of a metre. 1 nm is about as big as some molecules or a $100/000^{th}$ of the width of a human hair.

The railway wash basin, where you pushed *up* on the plunger, required trial and error. Instructions used an unfamiliar alphabet. Thank you, diagram.

The main blocker of sludge filters is human hair.

In the airport cloakroom sat a big box full of strips of condoms. Just take a handful. None of your vending machines here.

Even the best Norfolk reed thatch degrades from golden yellow to grey in two weeks. Painters of idyllic cottages on chocolate boxes must have worked quickly.

A tropical fungus has developed (2007) a taste for DVDs, so destroying digital data.

1950s *Kodak* cardboard slide mounts moulder in attics or skips as they slide into legend.

After the bonfire, all that remained of the vacuum cleaner was the spiral steel backbone from the sucking hose: an arthritic *Slinky* (toy invented in the 1940s).

Technology

At rest, the hovercraft's skirt looked crumpled and flimsy, but in motion was round and turgid.

Australian proudly showing off "dongle" plugged into laptop that allowed internet access from flat: "I don't have to go into any dodgy internet cafes. It's dear – £50 a month (2006) – but worth it for me."

New date stamp (2006) made of plastic, not metal, and the rubber was white. He defiled it with black ink for the very first time and stamped his commonplace book entry. In 2014, he unearthed the stamp, unused for years; he discovered that its embossing expired next year. But his ink pad had dried up; a new one, delivered to his door from *Hong Kong*, cost just 99p. Artefacts remind us of a changing world.

They purchased a job jot of door chimes, seconds, cheaply. They worked fine, but when warm, over-delivered: they played tunes, unprompted.

The techies had gone in.
"They had done all the checks, removed ugglies with anti-virus so that the computers were crisp and fresh."

A shower without the water pressure is a dribbling prostatic thing, not an eighteen year old lad peeing after a gallon of lager.

Lard lubricates the ride up the Eifel tower.

The wave-cutting catamaran could cope with waves up to two metres high.

An open cast gold mine is pretty, even painterly, in its own way.

Helicopter: overgrown sand fly.

Hard water encrusted the boiler with dense, crystalline, gritty, dark yellow scale.

Proud stainless steel chimney stuck out of the side of the garage, its flume steamy but cold, its heat ingeniously extracted.

Winning Words

White screen had its own tiny matching white remote control. It slid down the side of the screen: tidy logical mathematical mating.

1950s *Technicolor* is garish, intense,

Elderly hot water tap:
"You have to pull and turn it until you meet the sweet spot."

Microfiche readers once were the cutting edge of indexing.

In that museum, a female figure held up the latest technology of her time: a film camera, light bulb and telephone.

Seaplane engine: angry bumble bee.

"Look what we (Thai) can do with the technology!"
 Naked V8 truck engines astern thundered power into narrow boats tailing long propeller shafts: truly hot rods.

The self-defence system of *Bartitsu* echoes the use of a walking stick.

On the icy hill, the big car, even with its anti-lock brakes, traction control and other bells and whistles, would not go where the wheels urged. It slid down the slope and crunched another car.

Steam train carrying load up gradient puffs out black smoke and white steam.

He swallowed, dry throated, anticipating his hot tea. The travel kettle's light, normally dim red, flared bright orange in protest. It sparked and smoked. Oh dear: he had left its switch on the wrong voltage. The lights in his corridor went out. How embarrassing. But they returned: bless you, hotel circuit breakers.

As vulnerable as a house with shallow foundations next to a hedge of *Cupressus leylandii*.

Even a blunt nail will go in if you hit hard enough.

Technology

Trams ran quietly; sewing machines made more noise.

Five locomotives moved the coal: two at the front, one in the middle and two at the back. They stretched a mile.

Supercar engine design bursts holes in bonnets like *The Incredible Hulk* and his shirt. A family of supercars vomits superlatives.

Tickertape under a glass dome: archaic machine.

To clear the railway track they used black (gun)powder. They would lower a man in a barrel, blast, clear and blast again.

The little car drove like a go-kart.

We all secretly dream of the train that whistles in the night-time.

A bus journey replaced a train between stations; the bus was faulty, inside was a loud continuous buzzing.
    Its driver said, "It's two crossed wires behind the dashboard. When we get to the station I'm going to take it around the back and shoot it."

The electrical storm was directly overhead. He ran to disconnect the wire from the telephone socket to the computer modem. Too late: spitting crackling noises. Fried. Message: "modem undetectable."

The message on the answer phone was lower pitch, wistful, a little sad.

The *Jaguar* would not start. The repair man started it instantly by just pushing the gear lever completely into "park."
    "I feel so silly."
    "Don't be. You are not the first and won't be the last. We get a lot of calls from *BMW* drivers."
    What a nice man.

With his dad, he had built the hi-fi cabinet around a twelve inch speaker, chest height, lined with carpet and ballasted with a hundredweight of sand. *Cilla Black* had belted out 15 watts of

Winning Words

"Anyone Who Had a Heart"; glass shook in their window frames.

The lawnmower had an intermittent fault. It would re-start after a rest.

The cars did not cost a lot to service, unless they had suffered a "coming together."

Generator: rusty leaden hulk covered in cobwebs, home to spiders, disintegrating, heavy to heave up the steps into the gargantuan skip at the council dump.

Honeysuckle? Snip with secateurs. No. Telephone wire. Whoops!

It takes a hundred chickens, continuously defecating, to generate one hundred watts.

The satisfaction of putting on ear protectors, goggles and gauntlets, selecting a fault line in the impertinent stubborn log and inserting the narrow edge of the wedge. He hammered it in "Bang!" with the big lump hammer. No log, however tough and free of cracks could resist that steadily increasing pressure. He then burned it to ash. Humans had triumphed!

The new vacuum cleaner was gloriously powerful. Stubborn dust in chair button holes was a goner.

The blue-dyed poisoned cut grain was positioned under the sink, behind the *Rayburn*, in the clothes cupboard and in the loft.
    "You have no pets?"
    "No"
    "The mice are greedy. They'll eat it all and go away to die. They become dried up and don't smell."

Embedded in the concrete were the corpses of moles.

The squeaking wheel gets the grease.

Awake in the darkness of night: the red blink of that reassuring sentinel, the fire alarm LED.

Technology

Such delight at making a telephone card, inserted in a street phone booth, work between countries.

Manufacturing maple syrup: "This is the part where we evaporate it to syrup. It goes along these five channels, getting thicker all the time. Like my old man said of his wife of fifty years, 'Maybe she's slightly slower and nobblier but she just keeps getting sweeter all the time.'"

One milk float towed another using a thin wire. The lead float attempted to infiltrate the juggernauts on the roundabout. Prudent to give them room.

The elderly fax machine still worked and remembered his name.
    He stroked it. "Thank you, loyal old friend."

Parliament building used latest technology: air-conditioning required tonnes of ice.

Art deco skyline observation car (railway) jade pink, stainless steel and *Perspex* [poly(methyl methacrylate)] water dispenser. Water in cones. Giant toggle switch activated. Wistful " - - o -" horn before each intersection.

Notice on cold water dispenser, "Please phone us, talk about anything. But our main strength is water coolers, definitely."

The fish processing machine (The *Chinton*) with huge iron gears, that topped, tailed and filleted the fish, replaced thirty Chinamen.

A small leak will not sink a great ship.

The seaplane roared up as the waffle went down.

Buying a *Jaguar* and only using it to go to the supermarket is like buying a lion, calling it "Tiddles" and taking it for walkies.

Hot water tank made intestinal noises.

Winning Words

Trams hurtling through the night.

"They were real engineers in those days. They could make anything with a chunk of iron, a tin can and a fag packet."

Happiness would be a household with a toaster that popped out toast which fell back into its slot instead of random landings.

The line was faint, hissing, popping, metallic echoing.
"Speak up," he said.
Who could it be, phoning just after 6 pm? (Radio-telephone from off-shore oil rig).

The train started to burrow through the buildings of the city.

Machine emitted fearsome clunks and roars while sorting and stapling sheets: "the photocopier from hell."

"Oh look," said the trees in the forest as the axe arrived. "Part of it is one of us!"

Warm fire door? Never open it or an explosive flash fire will incinerate you.

In his workshop he cast lead bullets.

Engineering maxim: if it looks right, it is right.

Pleasure of watching needles swinging purposefully around precision-made dials.

Indians bred bald dogs, with abnormally high skin temperatures, as hot water bottles for their beds.

The serious hi-fi aficionado teeters on the edge of obsession.

On unscrewing the top, the polycarbonate lemonade bottle became less taut, less excited,

An access panel was down; it revealed stark intestines.

A breeze that stoked the fires and furnaces of man.

Technology

Purchase giving full weight to the "bathtub curve." Initially equipment needs frequent repair, during midlife seldom and towards the end of its life again needs more repair.

"How did you get the pear into such a small bottle?"
"It grew there from a bud."

One elderly sister to another (1959), "I was watching him (the announcer on the television) while you were taking off your corsets. It's all right. He did not look at you once!"

Open-engine surgery is expensive.

Reinforced concrete crumbles when its iron rusts and so expands.

The 19th century cramming machine for battery chicks forced food into their crops.

Early baby bottle teats were amputated pickled cows' udders.

At the nuclear power station, the pockets of its emergency officer bulged with *three* telephones and a pager.

Corpulent cars are cumbersome cars.

What had blocked the high-pressure gas pipe? A crisp wrapper.

Economists calculated at the start of the 20th century, that, if traffic continued to grow at its present rate, *London* would disappear under mountains of horse manure. It did not because of the motor car. But now we suffer different effluent.

On the motorway emergency lane, tortured steel strips twisted upwards into a ball. The fire and rescue service had ripped open the van roof like a tin can. But one probably too small to accommodate a driver.

Loud enough to boil the marrow from your bones.

The *Shackleton* (an aircraft): "a hundred thousand rivets flying in close formation."

Travel

Travel no longer broadens the mind. Instead of going from A to B, you go from A_1 to A_2 and they are all the same.

All the ... representatives were clones: tanned blonde girls.

"I am a traveller. You are a sightseer. He is a tourist."
(Ryszard Kapuscinski)

"Don't tell me how educated you are, tell me how much you have travelled."
(The Quran)

Is his satellite navigation lady really taking him down this lane with green grass growing down the middle? It is getting wider. Maybe she is right. No she is not, it is someone's drive. In the dark, he cannot turn back or reverse into a muddy field. So onward to a gigantic gravelled square in front of a mansion. Thank goodness there is somewhere to turn around before they set their hounds on him.

Rail travel has a unique cadence and rhythm.

During the next visit, take more co-phenotrope (*Lomotil*).

Legendary café: nice café crème and madeleines; pity about the pneumatic drill.

Travel

He observed native plastic sulphur near the volcano. It stirred dim memories from a school chemistry laboratory. Back in the ship's oak-lined library, he refreshed memory by looking up all the allotropes of sulphur in the *Encyclopaedia Britannica*. He sighed with profound pleasure. The organisers had reached into his brain and hit his pleasure centre. Bliss.

The edges of pavements had cracks, for drivers thought pavements were roads.

Regulars on "the redeye" (early flight such as *Stansted* to *Düsseldorf*).

Plumber who had to travel a long way to work: "If you are marching, you cannot fight."

Spiritual journeys whether ley or song lines.

Health baths steamed in the open amidst the snow.
"Don't go there," she pointed. "It'll scald you."
His nose soon became accustomed to the bad egg smell and filtered it out. Water heated by the volcano was soft on the skin. At the poolside were pumice stones: "cheese graters" to attack corns. Above: dense steam; below: thermophilic microorganisms (extremophiles) producing slime. An otherworldly, relaxing experience. In climbing out into the freezing air, felt cleansed, reborn.

Five men, all grey-bearded, sat in leather Chesterfields in the bar under the engraving of a 19th century cruise ship, and spoke of ambergris, owl pellets and fantastic things.

It is good to be served wine by a Goddess. *Artemis* had long blonde hair, high heels and mascara.

"It makes you feel like a child," she said.
It did. You could not be anything else in proximity to such awesome power and size. The spray at *Victoria Falls* came from all sides, even bouncing upwards from the ground.

Icelandic sagas: to find land, send out ravens. Land is in the direction of the non-returners.

Winning Words

A bone-dropping bearded eagle circled.

Tiramisù ice cream, chunky, granular, melting in the shadow of the leaning tower of *Galileo*'s velocity experiment, having descended against a stampede of goal-oriented Japanese.

The country on the edge of financial melt-down seemed calm.

How fitting to witness through binoculars, in the land of *Galileo*, the four (Galilean) moons of Jupiter flaunting an immaculate straight line.

If we suspect that a snake is in a hut, we burn an old car tyre inside. The snake hates the smell so comes out. Then we kill it.

Seeing so many wild beasts brought tears mixed with the dust.

Memories stirred while he sifted through his business cards; such criss-crossing of the world. So many lovely people who he would never see again.

American: "I've told my daughter that, if she gets her masters, I will buy her a pair of shoes. In *Paris.*"

Forget the big beasts. The little ones terrify. Six tics were clambering up his trousers and two were crawling up his shoes. Tics are more visible on plain shoes rather than trainers. Only one tic needed to get through for the possibility of encephalitis. They liked creases and tunnels. He discovered two tics nestling in his navel.

The footpath was through the field. But the ploughed clods were one foot high. Walking boots became so encased in mud that leaden to lift.

"We call it the tourist tree. It is red and it peels."

A dark chocolate *bombe* travelled poorly in midday heat, but yummy when spooned from its box.

"I am an ice widow. My husband is doing his post-doc. in the *Antarctic.*"

Travel

The "Russian limousine" was an open-backed lorry containing thirty passengers, standing.

Hot water flowed from the tap marked "Cold."

Crabs migrated over the road. They were toxic and caused punctures, especially to bicycles.

"I always dread it when he is the pilot. He always dives down bumpily."

"I've just had the holiday from hell. Moved hotel six times. Wife got blood poisoning in her foot. Had to go to hospital. £500 camera stolen."

During the "white nights" of the short summer, it never really went dark. During the day, residents rested upright against the stonework, eyes shut, to soak in the sun.

He was underwhelmed to observe seagulls floating in the swimming pool leaving their ballast.

They moved house. They packed pieces of their past lives into boxes.

The plane being 2 ½ hours late means that a relaxed audit becomes ultra-pressured.

Amongst the group of tall "long noses" (Westerners) in *China*, the one causing most pointing of the finger and requests to pose in photographs was the blonde.

At airport: "We need to check you for the snivels with a thermometer."
    Checkers entered the plane wearing NBC (nuclear/biological/chemical) protection suits.

"Tombed/noodled out."

The chef carving the duck wore a face mask during a time of avian flu.

Winning Words

"This geezer climbed onto the side of the conveyor to unblock a bag from the admitting chute. He must have been in a hurry. The conveyor stopped completely."

The streets were cool because white-walled and narrow. Moreover, water was poured onto the raised cobbles. As it ran down the hill, the water evaporated, cooling the air.

Sounding like a native is elusive. Avoid duplicate words such as "buttery butter." Do not be curmudgeonly like an old fogey schoolmarm. Avoid inappropriate and comical words. Do not be so correct and literary that sound like idiots. You must not sound like *Eliza Doolittle* in either of her re-incarnations.

"The trail is the thing, not the end of the trail. Travel too fast and you miss all that you are travelling for."
(Louis L'Amour)

The city filled the valley below. It could grow no more, bounded by mountains and sea. It was wonderful to see the size and density but sad to see the smog of pollution. Its filth was like tadpoles trapped within a glass bowl of once-clean pond water, trailing faeces from their rears, so making the water murky.

Travel in early carriages, even for royals, was agony. They had no suspension and no glass, so the snow blew in.

The wonderful logic, seldom felt in the *UK* that only knew flat shapes, of a buttocks-shaped toilet seat.

Fill up your tank with jet fuel, the liquid sunlight captured by prehistoric forests, and fly.

"To awaken in a strange town is one of the most pleasant sensations in the world."
(Freya Stark)

In Iran, everyone drives as if the road is a battlefield.

If you find yourself travelling through hell, keep going.

"The Promised Land" always lies on the other side of the wilderness.

Travel

Look around you. Swivel your head like an owl. You will see no signs of civilisation.

Behind in the plane, some of the girls' hockey team were already pissed. The smell of vomit drifted forwards.

The plane bored down through the layer of pollution where traffic police wore smog masks.
    "It's the tuk-tuks and cooking stoves."

The spirit of the place oozed out in the streets and gutters and its sizzling take-away food.

"We do not sell chewing gum. It costs too much to remove it."

"First you launder your clothes. Then wash with soap. Then with water. Then you wear them inside out."

People seldom stayed in the red centre for more than 12 to 18 months; it was too isolated.

Saffron-robed monks wandered in. Bare feet were essential; the earth must ground them.

Maybe the cathedral bells at *Christchurch* ring out so sharply because they were only cast two centuries ago.

The crocodile had lost its way and was on the 16th fairway.
    "They gape their mouths like that to cool down, not to eat you, usually."

Bungee jumping was free for those over 70 and nude.

He could only measure the passage of time by his chin stubble. His brain had no idea.

The helicopter smelt of diesel, strained and roared, became lighter, went forward slowly. It felt agricultural like a tractor. The hostess was mature, hair unkempt, sturdier, and more heavyweight than the stunning day-time models. The flight lasted only five minutes but she crammed in the safety briefing.

Winning Words

The pool was Olympic size. He imagined the *USSR* elite training their champion weightlifters by the poolside.

"What does ABC mean?"
"<u>A</u>nother <u>b</u>loody <u>c</u>hurch."

When the chillies are laid out to dry in the sun and you pass through in an open rickshaw you sneeze all the time.

The smaller the country, the bigger the relic: they had a whole leg.

He climbed up one mile. Temperature fell from 22°C to 8°C. His beard collected mist as water. He smoothed it out. In that global heritage site were Jurassic ferns, laurels, date palms, some Germans, but no dinosaurs.

Flying for ten hours in an aluminium tube, feeling your veins clogging up, just to get a tan.

Just as an institutionalised animal, if released, will return to the cage of its confinement, so does the hotel guest. There is shelter, food and water, all conveniently, compactly located.

Notice: "If there is a vomiting or faecal accident, report to the lifeguard."

He could hardly see the terminal in the dark and blizzard. A nozzle on a ramp sprayed the aircraft wings with antifreeze.
He hoped the wings did not freeze into giant lollipops with the aerodynamics of a tea tray.
"If the final passenger does not arrive in the next minute, we will go. Otherwise we will be grounded."

They offered *Jack Daniels* or champagne on the return flight. Few drank: all were driving.

Plaster casts were common; many citizens sported broken limbs.

Exotic jungle, decadent, rich with strange perfumes and tastes, peopled with eccentrics and chauvinists of the deepest hue.

Travel

Viewed from above, the Christmas market was a grid. People, many red-coated, moved slowly in channels of light, bobbing like blood cells in capillaries.

In *Prague*, the 15th century astronomical clock had the moon slightly wrong. Moreover, "Greed", "Death", "Vanity" and "a Turk" were not too politically correct .

On the cruise ship, the pool was unheated at 16ºC. He only stayed in for ten minutes, splashed around five times and caught a cold.

Tourists are a herd for milking: mobile cash dispensing machines on the hoof.

Do not feed the chipmunks: they have rabies.

After trains delayed by two hours, response to upset commuters:
    "I've nothing to do with it. Ask the station staff. I just work in my little shop."

Train cancelled. What squalor, sitting on his case amidst crowds and pigeons, eating the second heap of junk chips.

After nine hours scrunched up in a plane seat and three in a taxi you suffer belly ache. Warm milk soothes.

"I've visited *England* and *Scotland* and *Wales*. Isn't your country *tiny!*" *(American)*

Notorious bar served by girls with black fishnet tights and black feathers.

No brush or palette, no lens or prism can convey the grandeur of ... .

Screen saver photographs appearing randomly, reminded him of ... .

Each lad looked so young but was wedded to his automatic machine gun; losing it meant seven years in prison.

Winning Words

Sandalwood powder sold for funeral pyres. Mound of ash afterwards brushed into the river.

"The governor and the Commonwealth and the future of the State of Massachusetts welcome you."

The British had been to *Gozo*, judging by the "VR" (Victoria Regina) on the cobbles.

Stone lions without tongues cannot speak so cannot divulge secrets.

Travel is the midwife of thought.

Shanty town of corrugated iron and cardboard. Little fires flickered above stinking pools of sewage and blue chemical waste where toddlers and sacred cows splashed. Ladders to first storey of cardboard boxes. A *Hieronymus Bosch*. He felt ashamed of the unfairness of international wealth distribution.

Unexpected

He hated computers. For his access code, he chose the year of the *Luddite* rebellion.

A gingerbread cottage with a mushroom on the top. (*Gaudi*)

In a small sterile room where antibiotic powders were ground, the flywheel worked off a hammer mill. That wheel fell off, spun off the floor and ricocheted many times all over the room.
     Two staff present jumped, as one, onto a table, instinctively. They scattered its dozens of Kilner jars. They clung to each other, swinging to maintain balance, terrified.

Mercury-containing cream, packed in non-lacquered aluminium tubes will react, releasing hydrogen. Tubes explode. Splat!

Paintings of farm labourers show string tying trousers; the string is not just there to appear rustical. String tied around each leg prevents a rat running up trousers and biting delicate regions.

Car parked with hazard light flashing. Roebuck deer lay alongside, head raised. Girl driver looked stunned, straight ahead.

Shed full of toxic materials that nobody had wanted to destroy. Now no label legible.

Defective medicines reaching the market are extremely rare. However, many medicines are used. Recall of faulty batches of medicine, from the marketplace, is a routine and pedestrian event. Journalists seldom notice.

Bread used flour contaminated with ergot (*Claviceps purpurea*). Saint Anthony's fire resulted. Consumers died.

Winning Words

Cliff top cemetery. On erosion, bones exposed, tumbling into the sea.

Intravenous fluids were hazy because contaminated. Witnessed. Sterilisation by autoclaving (like pressure cooking) was inadequate. Patients died. (The *Devenport* Incident, UK)

Curare (muscle relaxant) given to patient on operating table without anaesthetic; unable to communicate that, during surgery, in pain.

Barbiturate mislabelled as "xylose" (a sugar) for a test. Patient might fall asleep at the wheel on way home from outpatient department.

During a full moon in a clear sky, over "the smoke that thunders" (Victoria Falls, *Zambia*) was a moon bow (lunar rainbow).

From behind the burqa came cut-glass English.

Was that red lump boiling in water a severed head? No, a big beetroot.

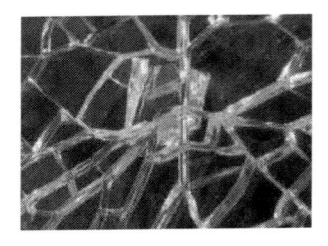

Crack! The strimmer hurled a stone onto French windows. The toughened double glazed glass, installed only the previous day, fractured again. Lines spread over the pane in two seconds; it was still crackling one hour later: expensive.

Drenched by water, above was a perfect semi-circular rainbow.

The aircraft passenger seat boasted a seat belt, but disconnected from its anchorage. The seat back would not stay upright. The entertainment controls were sealed up. But the flight itself seemed perfect.

To receive water at the correct temperature from the mixer tap required knowledge of algebra, perseverance and luck.

Unexpected

The tidal surge meant eight severe local flood warnings. They were cut off on two sides.

The woman with the wings of an angel sat on the great cock (hen).

Surreal sight: train at *Haddiscoe*, Norfolk Broads, UK, inching forward in flood water, its carriage lights reflected in water. Had the ballast supporting the line been washed away?

He stared at the many different shades of cooking oil in partially filled bottles, for sale.

The 18th century eruption lasted for six years. They thought it the work of the Devil.

Was it the usual chocolate by the bedside? Yes, crunchy but unusually hard. But it did not dissolve: it was not chocolate. It was not anything he had ever experienced - and unpleasant. He had better spit it out, rinse his mouth and brush his teeth. It was Chinese tea for infusion with boiling water.

When walking along a footpath, remember to swerve to avoid the razor-sharp unsheathed machete sticking outwards at right angles to the bicycle saddle.

"I had never been so frightened, trapped between the river and the sea. We took all our electrical things upstairs. We even took some sandwiches and a thermos. We could not leave because of the cats."

Extreme weather, the storm expected once every thirty years, flushes away bridges. New channels are carved into beaches, exposing pipes and cables, shallowly buried. Slick of brown flotsam flows along current, rolling sluggishly in waves. It rolls them onto the shoreline and grades by size: large branches, bamboo twigs, prickly pear fruits, avocadoes, straw bales, polystyrene packing and plastic bottles.
    People die.

Winning Words

Lump stuck in his throat. Bread, pretzel and a hot drink would not dislodge lump. However, on lying down, suddenly swallowed it. Body can fail, abruptly.

The *BMW*'s throttle stuck at 136 mph; its brakes soon burnt out.

During the flood, a canoe paddled down the High Street.

Printer cartridge dripped black ink onto brand-new white carpet.

"Now that this man is in my life, my plans have gone. I do not know where I am."

The Navaho native Indian climbed into his *A C Cobra* V8 muscle car.

Old age is the most unexpected thing to happen to a (wo)man.

The little owl flew down the chimney, perched on a picture, fluffing off soot, and looked at her.

The only other traffic on the motorway was a bicycle, horse and donkey-drawn cart.

Slimy seeds of the tree tomato *(Solanum betaceum)*.

He chewed sideways like a giraffe.

Signs on public houses: "The Dog's Bollocks", "The Loaded Hog."

Maggots glowed on the ceiling of the cave. They clustered into large specks; some were smaller, brighter and blue. Some winked. Insects flying along the subterranean river thought their lights were a way out. Sticky mucilaginous threads entangled them. Insects reeled in like on fishing lines.

What was that desperate but routine sighing? The lift.

Unexpected

Out of the darkness on the footpath appeared an elephant. It was only a small one, but it was an elephant, seldom seen in *Suffolk*.

The magnesium carbonate was heavy (density 1.8). It was odd: thixotropic, a solid cake until shaken. It then morphed into a liquid gel.

A background buzz started. A swarm of bees filled the garden. They retired inside and closed the door and windows. Considering the threat, it seemed prudent.

It looked like a traditional mercury clinical thermometer but said, "Gallium inside." His mind flashed back to a chemist jokester giving him what had seemed an ordinary spoon to stir his tea. He had stared in disbelief: the tea-spoon end had disappeared; the gallium metal (melting point 30°C) had melted to a pool on the bottom.

What littered the side of the swimming pool? An artificial leg.

As incongruous as a gold tooth on a rat.

After head stuck out of window of a coal-fired steam train, a red-hot live cinder smacked into his eye: blinded.

Speedboat wake overturns lumbering houseboat.

The door to the railway toilet, carelessly latched, swung open while he was brushing his teeth. Two blondes stared at him. At least he was not squatting on the WC.

Sister lost aged five: "I looked for a four-leaf clover. I found one so I knew she would be alright."

Keep a year's food. Just in case.

All the 20,000 women, and even some girls as young as ten, at the conference seemed cloned. Each wore immaculate clothes, new shoes, long dresses, not a trouser in sight, and back–combed hair.

Winning Words

On smoothing the gravel drive with a spring tine rake, he caught a tiny field mouse, pierced through its tummy. It must have been dead, dying or silly; otherwise it would have scampered away.
    He gave it a shallow grave, "Sleep well, little fellow."

Gloriously granular goat's cheese: moist; appeared creamed with gas.

Getting rid of 200 kegs of gherkins in brine is difficult.

Tactic to deter cold (telephone) callers:
"Let them go on a bit and then say, 'Will you be my friend?'
    Then keep on saying things in the same vein. They soon hang up."

The biscuit pot, when opened, said, "Stop! Move away from the cookie jar!"

The family cat jumped through the open window and landed on the bed.

"How will we know it is closing time?" said the shop staff over the road.
    Since the repair we no longer had to bang the door shut with a hammer.

In the drawer of the antique were a lock of baby hair and a milk tooth. Who from? Their DNA would tell.

The rubber ventilator bladder had holes in the base so the anaesthetic could not be given accurately. The "scene of crime" photograph showed clearly.

Unexpected

Why was the swimmer, ever and again, ducking down into the water? Something important and pink was at the bottom.
"Shall I have a go?" asked another swimmer.
He dived and returned, offering a set of false teeth.

Ploughing along in the pool was dreamlike: he had, while turning underwater, two girls as outriders. One wore a teeny-weeny blue bikini and the other a teeny-weeny red bikini.

The chest waders, as he unfolded them, gushed a strong smell of rubber that made his head swim, like an old anaesthetic mask. The waders were so long. He expected them to be trousers but they came to his chest. When hanging up empty they looked fit for a giant. On wading in, they were buoyant: contained air made his legs want to float up. But in deeper water to his waist, they clamped him. They squeezed his testicles.

Car, accelerating up a cobbled hill, sounds like wringing a sheet, and so popping, many "bubbles" of bubble wrap.

Company staff had not expected to pay for the expensive extra service demanded. It was legally required. They looked like children, smacked, who did not know why.

For horse riders to activate the (traffic) lights, hit the rod.

He learned forward and inhaled deeply, "I love wood smoke," he said, coughing.

The infusion that he made from the raspberry tea bag tasted so odd that it was undrinkable. The urn, presumed to contain boiling water, held hot coffee. Once explained, his raspberry coffee switched from poison to drinkable.

Crop of *blue* flowers (cornflowers).

Outrageous fortune.

If an anaconda snake seizes you, do not try to fight it. You will not win. As it fastens its coils around you, ensure that you can reach its neck with your hands. Then bring its head to your mouth and bite it on its - very sensitive - nose. It will uncoil and go away
(Briefing by *French Foreign Legion*).

The *Pinocchio* Effect: when you lie, your nose engorges with blood, gets bigger and may itch, so you scratch it.

Was this pouring rain, and squalls, buffets of wind that abruptly bent plant stems to the ground, the faint breath of hurricane *Lili*?

The statue had three breasts: two for milk and one for wine.

A vegetarian keeping a butcher's shop.

The glass-domed plinth in the museum appeared to contain a wrinkled relic. It was *Galileo*'s member. It looked like an uncooked fish finger.
    It was *Galileo*'s finger, the very finger that pointed when he said, "It moves."

The pain under his arm was puzzling. Only then did he see the jellyfish.

Where did that plume, that dark column of smoke drifting lazily skywards, originate? It was the county library, next to the fire station. A tragedy: all those books, irreplaceable local archives, newspapers, destroyed. He felt glum.

Unexpected

Burning body on the desolate shore:
"All of Shelley was consumed, except his heart, which would not take the flame, and is now preserved in spirits of wine."
(*George Byron*)

Even if a monkey makes nasty grimaces at you, do not shoot it. It has fifty friends and they will kill you.

He was bivouacking out, looked around and saw stars. But why was it so *warm*? While he had slept, a flock of sheep had crowded around him.

A blackbird flew into the kitchen, ate the trifle, got drunk and spent the afternoon sleeping it off.

Lamb: one minute you are skipping up a hill in the sunshine, and then your bum is swimming in mint sauce on a plate.

The lightning struck and the foliage parted. There was a stream of flashes around his legs. It was like being hit between the shoulder blades but it cured the bursitis in his shoulder blades for three days.

Three-inch nail inside tyre. Could that have caused the car to be uncontrollable?

In the torchlight, through the goggles of his gas-mask, embellishing the back of the cave wall, marks like hieroglyphs seemed etched. They were bio-vermiculations ("bioverms"): slime that lived. They looked like the tracks of slugs.

Wholesaler of sterile maggots to clean wounds.

Winning Words

Viewpoint

One man looks through bars and sees only mud; another man looks through and sees the stars.
(After Frederick Langbridge)

"Women?" said the man.
   "They can push our buttons. Sometimes they can make us so happy and then they make us so sad. They control us."

There is no noisier or lonelier place than a light aircraft, fifty feet above the ground, flying solo for the first time.

The lotus flower is a (Hindu) symbol of beauty growing from a muddy unpromising river.

"What I hated was that I knew what I would be doing this day, week, year. The only thing that was different, exciting, was the holiday."

The job of ... really was playing in the traffic.

He had the gift of tongues.

"good kitchen ... is the great laboratory of the household."
(Isabella Beeton)

In business, striving for perfection is uneconomic. 95% is good enough; the last 5% requires huge effort and returns little. But exceptions include amputating legs, dispensing medicines and packing parachutes.

"My (mosaic) career is like *paella*," said the Spaniard.

After serious error found by inspector, "We're stuffed."

Viewpoint

His wife had to accept that he worked in a girlie-colonised environment.

Whisper from one seasoned professional to another after hearing newly registered professional speak, "She was good but too bumptious. She has not made her big mistake yet."

CPD (continuing professional development can be a tonic: a gadfly to a sluggish horse.

Every discipline has its automatic explanations for the inexplicable, such as "It's a virus" (medical practitioners), "It's of religious significance" (anthropologists) or "It's a magnetic effect (astronomers)."

If you were meant to be in one place, you would have roots.

Lifelines can harden into shackles.

"the Froth of Folly, the Scum of Pride"
(John Strype)

The (occupation) was over-octane.

"... don't do any work. They are all fur and feathers."

Economics: the dismal science.

Scientist: "There is a hierarchy of explanation with mathematics on the top, then, physics, chemistry, biology, biochemistry, psychology and sociology. Surely you have met that?"
    Artist: "*No*. Who says that? Scientists, I suspect!"

One third of the thoughts of those over the age of 65 are related to death.

Categorised by counting cells, we are only 10% mammalian (human). The other 90% are bacteria, fungi and other microscopical cells.

Winning Words

Civilisation's artefacts are often shiny such as gold, jewellery, polished stone, guns, and glass but humans' natural state (their skin), when not sweating, is matt.

Look at yourself in the mirror. You have two eyes *at the front of your head.* They are not at the side of your head, like the flounder or rabbit: nearly 360° vision, always looking around because you are prey; you fear being eaten. You lack such vision. You are *the predator*: it is you who eat. You are dangerous.

Both serial killers and captains of industry are ruthless and treat people as commodities.

Over the long view, we are all dead.

Doctor said, "Homeopathy? Don't believe in it. It's as effective as fertilising a field with a fart."

Honeyed days.

"Salad days"
(William Shakespeare)

Some "goods" are "bads" (such as tobacco).

During the British invasion of *Tibet* in the early 20th century, the soldiers/explorers thought that clapping was a sign of welcome. However, it was to scare away devils.

"We do not see things as they are. We see them as we are."
(The Talmud)

Beware buying the used vehicle with a "look at me" high-level exhaust pipe exit. How long has it spent in deep water?

Maybe it was not the most prudent admission to the banker in the dark suit because she suddenly looked a little concerned.

Theatre or cinema: mere second-hand emotion.

Tweaked memories.

Viewpoint

"The world is an entirely different place to the man of five foot seven from what it is to the man of six foot two."
(W. Somerset Maugham)

He is all gong, no dinner.

"It's as much use as shearing a piglet. You get a lot of squealing and no wool."
(After Vladimir Putin)

"There is no bad without a good."
(Russian proverb)

A country childhood always sits within you, always filling you with a sense of wellbeing.

"A day without laughter is a day wasted."
(Italian proverb)

Cubicised letterheads/pastel art deco railway posters looked dated.

From the octagon room at *Greenwich* Observatory, history oozed.

In part playful, in part divine.

Happiness is, "Stand upright in a cool place."
(from bottle of "Domestos")

Water photographed using long exposure looks like mist: ethereal.

Such profuse thanks from members of the public made his frozen feet worthwhile.

After so many travels, the accents, the houses, the ambience *(spiritus loci)* were so familiar from his youth. He just wanted to absorb its comfort through his skin.

Advertising can look like whimsy: a gorilla here, a meerkat, there.

Winning Words

"I cannot recommend science as a career," said the sheik. "Mathematics or engineering, yes."

"What a charming/interesting ... (e.g. picture)."
       He could not think of anything else to say; it was worthless.

There was great interest in early X-rays. They were obscene because the viewer could see through clothing.

"Our (Cuban) newspaper is four pages: all good news. I get my news from *Google*."

He squirmed with embarrassment. His ears turned red.

It is more difficult than talking and chewing gum simultaneously.

"Why is it 'a pair of socks' (two objects) and yet 'a pair of trousers' (one object)?"

Doubt is a slug. It eats away at you in the night.

We are like *The Roadrunner*. He avoids being squashed or eaten and runs along smoothly. But then he runs over the edge of a cliff. That is OK because he can run fast and his legs still pound away. But suddenly he realises that, underneath, there is no ground. His belief gone, instantly, he falls.

"If you are snagged in another's dream, you are lost."
(Gilles Deleuze)

Jade's colour combines the sky (heavens) with the solidarity of earth.

In the East, the greatest honour is to create or receive a job from a family member; in the West that is "nepotism" and, generally, condemned; only employment based on merit is applauded.

His enthusiasm was so fierce that I feared that, were I too near to him, I would burn.

Viewpoint

- 4ºC, with a heavy hoar frost in the mist, feels quite pleasant.

"With a new job, the first year is interesting, in the second year you learn a lot but in the third you think, is this all there is?"

Window displays containing dust and dead flies will not attract customers.

On a Monday morning, does your heart sing?

The wail of a gifted four year old who later committed suicide. He witnessed the toppling of a great beech tree: "Even when I die I will never be so beautiful."

Which ... will stick on the *Velcro* of memory longest?

"He would not get a job in any other ... This place is steeped in nepotism."

"My husband is just an ordinary bloke but he is one in a million."

I share, you sample, they steal.

"Big Brother" thrusts at the cutting edge of the kingdom of shame.

"I am as free as a bird."

The man had a clock with no insides: a metaphor for a man with no thoughts, a zombie, or a psychopath.

"You only have one wedding ring? I have three: the engagement ring, the wedding ring and the suffering."

The toxic friend may sound friendly but is really putting you down.

A masochist designed the flip-flop. On knobbly stones, the pain, normally distributed across the sole, is concentrated between the big and next toe.

Winning Words

"There is something of the night about him."
(Ann Widdecombe)

"We have time. Our clocks have no hands. Only space."
(Aborigine)

Briton: "Aboriginal dancing has more emotional impact than *Madame Butterfly* at the opera."
Australian: "There you go then."

Television is about novelty and fashion.

The farmer suffered the sort of patrician received accent that, after ten seconds, made most other English speakers despise him.

Less welcome than *Escherichia coli* at the meat counter.

"What is the most important thing? People, people, people."
(Maori proverb)

If someone is giving you a really hard time, imagine them wearing something silly such as a chicken costume.

Academics, administrators (managers) and practitioners (doers) seldom see eye-to-eye.

Research scientists are insecure because ever fearful of the next peer review. They are also preening megalomaniacs because they want to be the first with a discovery. Being second does not cut the mustard – just as flying the second fastest jet fighter means that you are dead.

"You might look askance at disposable plates, knives and so on from a conservation viewpoint, but here, the critical resource is water; there is no washing up."

Caldron moment.

Any party is a celebration that we have survived.

Viewpoint

A diamond's fire is like looking through a small hole at an incandescent furnace.

Mad as a bag of hammers carried by a jogger.

Welled up from the deepest reptilian parts of his brain.

The strikingly marked police car hid down a side road. The dark-uniformed policeman left the shadows, stepped onto the verge and stared at his radar gun that pointed at the driver.

Bright as tarmac.

A voice more sandpaper than silk.

He suddenly felt he had a worth.

With insight you can see the whole universe in a nutshell.

The real man likes dark chocolate and a whole stilton cheese (until cholesterol blocks arteries).

"My default setting always has been envy," she said.

After inspection: "We've had a kick up the backside."

The young men were always interested in the same paintings that the young ladies studied and the eyes of those ladies were always wandering off towards the glossy haired smart young men from college.

Completely submerged in the hot bathwater, he heard his stomach growling.

The insurance salesman makes £100 commission on each sale. He only sells one in ten.
    So every time he is rejected, he thinks, "That's £10!" and smiles.

If we did not have honey, dates would taste sweeter.

Winning Words

Second World War: *UK* 1939–1945 *v.s. USA* 1943–1945.

Halloween cherubs or imps: money with menaces.

Grimy railway window *vs.* invisible coach window; surely the latter had recently been cleaned with paste, carefully polished off. Respect!

Alliance of the disappointed and never appointed.

He sees himself as a great man with history in his eyes and does not concern himself with the small detail.

A tinderbox of emotions.

Evolutionists (Christian), before *Darwin*, not only thought there was a continuous stream of creation from crawling things to fish, birds, monkeys and man – but also that evolution continued upwards to angels, archangels, cherubim, seraphim and God.

Everything was so good that he feared that it would not last.

Viewpoint

"I did not like him from the start."

The lamb was cold. The roll was stale. The young waitress did not know how to open a bottle of wine.
> "I've paid £20 for it. Don't you think you should be able to open it?"
> She stood there and giggled, "I've never done it before."

The floor-scrapings of history.

"Why should the moon care if the dog barks at it?"
(Polish proverb)

Staff had reversed the sign of the direction of lane swimming. Anti-clockwise had become clockwise. His mind and body were used to backstroke in one direction. In the reverse direction he was clumsy: he banged his arm.

He looked at the mobile phone as if it were a wild animal.

Traditional names suggest traditional virtues. The Romans said: name is destiny.

He hated mean pinched multi-storey car parks designed for machines and not people. Corners were tight and steel pillars girded. Thud. Please let the graze not show. But the dent did. Faeces smearing the pedestrian corridor increased loathing.

Celtic calf converted into "The Book of Kells": "They took my life. They scraped my skin. They inked me. Some holes were started."

The heart of the garden is the shed.

Sound muffled by snow outside or olive oil within the ear?

We try to make sense of our lives as best we can.
> "We are all just 'winging it'"
(Richard Linklater; film "Boyhood")

War

For defending castles, molten lead is more environmentally friendly than boiling oil: collect lead and recycle.

Air force: we have long been on the tip of the blade.

Hell hath no fury like a non-combatant scorned.

Military principle: concentrate force.

The rhetoric became reality.

Venom.

During the German occupation of France, curfew posters were underlined, twice, in black: "ON PAIN OF DEATH"

"There is no point in crying like a woman when you did not fight like a man."

"We will take you down," said the hackers wearing paper bags (to website). "We are legion."
They did. (1011)

Sunk in the axe up to the shaft.

Civilians caught in desolate war zones suffer stunted lives.

Cromwell's troops "slighted" the castle by pulling down a wall. The castle could no longer be tenanted.

Singapore had assumed that "a great imperial power" (*Britain*) would defend it during World War 2. Britain failed to do so and surrendered Singapore to the Japanese after only seven days.

War

Phalanx of soldiers, matching.

The British inverted the concentration camp (Boer War).

Stainless steel was a spin-off of World War 1 gun manufacture.

"The nation had the lion's heart. I had the luck to give the roar."
(Winston Churchill).

"We have a shortage of men. Wars have killed them off."

Tins allowed food preservation in the winter so armies could also fight then. Troops had to open with bayonets; tin openers arrived later.

Eternal flame:
"Your name is unknown,
Your deed is immortal."

One reason that the Iraqis "lost" is that bombs were so loud that their noise perforated ear drums. Troops could not hear orders.

All nations have their blood lusting periods.

This most bellicose of governments.

"Oil is the Devil's excrement."
(Pérez Alfonzo)

One hundred warriors fitted inside the last great (25 metre hull) *Maori* war canoe, hand carved from a single tōtara tree.

Small soldier; big helmet and submachine gun.

Spewing hatred.

"Stuff happens."
(Donald Rumsfeld)

Winning Words

The Cheyenne Mountain was beautiful but it contained *NORAD*. It could launch a nuclear retaliatory strike.
    The American said, "Kind of scary but reassuring to know it is here."

He chased (in trench) a rat to kill it but the stick broke when he swung it.

Bilious hatred.

Out of that kitchen window he imagined the nuclear mushrooms growing tall. Crouching in the cupboard under the stairs piled with sandbags would be safest.

... that spite can contrive.

"Have a good plan, execute it violently, do it today."
(Douglas MacArthur) a general.

Ricin (W) bomb developed around the time of the Second World War.

Cash is a sinew of war as it is of everything else.

During his war-time work, the brilliant mathematician constructed a formula for the optimum size and spacing of bombs to achieve maximum damage.

After jingoistic comments about World War 2:
    "Yes, I was there. It was awful (zipping gesture to mouth). But it's time we forget as people die, eventually. I mean, we do not go on about the Napoleonic wars, do we?"

The book of photographs of the 20th century was nearly cuboid. The main impression, from start to finish, was of wars. Starkest photograph: three bodies lined up in mud and, in a corresponding line, three heads.

In HMS *Victory*, the reliable marines were stationed between the officers and the, possibly rebellious, crew.

War

A wooden mallet tapped the white chunk of explosive into the blunderbuss. The gun exploded with a deafening bang.

Might's right.

He had absorbed countless TV images of Red Square with intercontinental ballistic missiles trundling before fur-hatted great-coated generals. Just one could bury his country. Today he enjoyed his *café latte*, ate a tasty sandwich and visited a toilet boasting up-lighters set into a marble floor. Disorientation about how the world had changed overwhelmed him.

After the third Punic War, Romans, to curse *Carthage*, poured salt over it.

He used his scimitar (ten kilos) to cut the man straight down the middle – and his horse.

"Slot them."

During World War 2, the Dutch starved. Their skin turned orange. They only ate tulips.

Napoleon wanted to have lucky generals.

Trendies, toffs, students and men with impressive beards united to save *Saddam*.

War is harrowing. Yet it is the harrow that pierces the ground and produces the great smiling fields of corn.

Fed up of being pushed around like a pea on a plate.

Spectrum: assertiveness, aggression and bullying.

"The attacks of the wild beast cannot be averted with only bare hands."
(African proverb)

Winning Words

Modern weapons contain so much fissile material that the battlefield has no bodies. They burn so completely that nothing remains: not even bones.

To those skilled in leech craft, they offered a rich fee of unweighed gold that they might heal the heroes of their wounds gotten in battle.

Sinews sprang asunder - the tendons burst.
(Beowulf: Anonymous Anglo-Saxon poet)

Generally, generals who fancy a good strut are well advised to stay in their barracks.

During a dinner the night before the battle of Waterloo, a politician said to a general, "Will we win tomorrow?"
　　　The general grabbed an ordinary soldier, "It all depends on this scruffy article."

The spires of the twin cathedrals rose from the fog of war. Were their ideas still intact?

The civil defence feeding bowls, stored since the Korean War, were brittle, like the polythene sheet on the chicken shed.

One bad general is better than two good ones. (Any decision trumps conflicting direction.)

The stench of panic was in the city.

Weasel words that sanitise horror: "Neutralising enemy", "Negativised", "Loss of assets."

You can do anything with a sword except sit on it.

The inner demons, quiescent for so long, have started to breed again.

War

Nuclear weapons: "It is wise to keep your head down or be somewhere else when they are throwing around buckets of sun."
(Civil Defence Adviser)

Kuwait bears the same relation to *Iraq* as a man to his hand; a man is loathe to be parted from his hand.

Could the girl at the self-defence class really place her thumbs over her attacker's eyeballs and SQUELCH?

Tyrants and their tanks.

He could run even with his feet blown off; only stumps remained.

He hated the sight of those little (nutritious) cheese balls: they meant he was going over the top.

Jersey girls, who, during the German occupation (1940–45), fraternised with German boys, were called "Jersey bags."

Names on gravestones of Royal Navy staff:
"knooman, paymaster, ordinary seaman, artificer, assistant apothecary, stoker."
    Most had the patina of green copper with black and red lettering; some were tarnished (cheaper metal presumed).

Lice (human, collected), heated up on a tin lid crackle. Fat pool results.

The political imperative is to put an international force into the field, quickly, and get one from each country killed, as soon as possible.

"Technoporn" of *Harrier* jump jet: small but solid with many bombs and rockets a-dangling.

Bile oozed from every pore.

"Heat not a furnace for your foe so hot
That it do singe yourself."
(William Shakespeare)

Winning Words

In World War 1, chemists knew sin (poison gas).
In World War 2, physicists (atomic bombs).
In World War 3, perhaps it will be the biologists' turn; genetic bio-engineering would do for starters.

Fear is when you want to lick the gummed paper for your self-roll cigarettes and you have no lick.

Damsel of death.

The proud native island inhabitants had statues but were extinct. First exterminate, then celebrate.

Babbling militants of exclusive cultures:
 ... "mangy little curs a-yap above their minute hoarding of shrivelled bones."
(James Leslie Mitchell)

A keen razor wounds with a touch that is scarcely felt or seen.

No relative, who had gone to fight in the Second World War, would talk of it. Presumably, it was so horrible that they just wanted to forget.

Anger is one of the sinews of the soul.

Of fallen comrade: "You never forget the face and it (h)urts."

Beware the fury of a patient man.

She bore the fruit of her violation. (post-rape pregnancy)

Faces pinched with hatred.

Roman emperors, at times of bad foreign wars, doubled the bread ration and opened the circus.

"Oh, hush the noise, ye men of strife."
(Edmund H. Sears)

War

A general wearing, on his chest, sufficient medals to make you sneeze. (Bright light can cause sneezing in a significant minority of the population.)

If the trumpet is of uncertain sound, who, then, shall prepare for battle?

The early Islamic world had the best mathematicians. What was this Christian nonsense about the trinity: 3 = 1; it could not be. So started the first war waged against Christianity.

Why were windows so near the pavement? Fallout shelters, legally required.

Anyone could visit the bunker under the county hall. It was not secret. Blast doors were capable of withstanding a nuclear explosion, maps with plastic overlays to map wind-blown fallout plumes, twin microphones enabling simultaneous talk to both local radio stations (one might still survive to broadcast), air filters against radioactive dust and a 5,000 gallon water tank.

Fizzing with fury.

The large painting was of British general field officers of World War One. They all sported brown riding boots. Many "Sirs" and "Lords" featured: an aristocratic bunch. Generally from a safe distance, they had led their lower classes to slaughter.

"Gulleting."

"wars, terrible wars, and the Tiber foaming with much blood." *(Virgil)*

The deterrent "MAD" (<u>m</u>utual <u>a</u>ssured <u>d</u>estruction) is a phallic symbol. It convinces them that they are men.

The gallant officer could not return to claim his dance: his leg must be amputated.

Writing

Imagine your writer's commonplace book, nearly full, lost. It is irreplaceable. Retain it on your person or in cabin luggage, if travelling. Inscribe with your name, address and telephone number; an honest person may return it.

There are three golden apples: one for me because I told the story, one for you because you heard it and one that I throw over my shoulder for the person who told me.

Cherished myths.

Greatest hits of ...

"Do you really have a manual typewriter? Can I see it? Wow!"

The interviewer was but a husk of the poet.

"Words are sacred. They deserve respect. If you get the right ones, in the right order, you can nudge the world a little."
(Tom Stoppard)

"The palest ink is clearer than the freshest memory"
(Chinese proverb)

"What kind of writing pays best?"
"Ransom notes."
(Dorothy Parker)

"Advertising is the rattling of a stick inside a swill bucket."
(George Orwell)

Writing

"KISS": "keep it simple, stupid" from Occam's razor: "entities are not to be created without due reason."
(William of Occam)

"Snottites", a succulent word, flourish in dark caves, metabolising hydrogen sulphide (H_2S) and dripping off dangerously corrosive sulphuric ("battery") acid (H_2SO_4).

Something about the wide open skies of *East Anglia* helps a writer think.

Getting an award as a writer is like haemorrhoids. Everyone will get one if they wait long enough.

Butler of great house kept "(Butler's) pantry book": notes that might be useful to anyone following him.

She wrote like an angel.

About foreign office mandarin:
The problems were so well put that you felt that they had been solved merely by being so elegantly summarised.

Runes are straight because, compared with curves, easier to cut into stone or wood.

Jane Austen's delicious romantic rituals make her stern moral philosophy more readable.

Bliss: he found his proper smelly rubber, his special real India rubber that did not smudge his 2B pencil. The treasure lay on the grass like an item of litter.

Comment to fellow consultant:
"Someone's shown you how to put in all the mealy words."

Winning Words

"Words are ... the most powerful drug used by mankind."
(*Rudyard Kipling*) Audience: surgeons.

The filigree work of the incredible detail of compiling the "Oxford English Dictionary." The scriptorium was a corrugated iron shack where the public's thousands of definitions arrived.

The suffix "off" intensifies (e.g. die off).

"A man would do nothing, if he waited until he could do it so well that no-one could find fault with what he had done."
(*John Henry Newman*)

"It sharpened his eyes and made him see through the large words that puff out the bosoms of mankind."
(*Thomas Mann*)

Pruning rose bushes helps you think of weasel words, written, if necessary, in your blood.

A swear word must be short like a punch.

Correcting errors in a manuscript is like heaving stones from soil: both are obsessive behaviour.

Language is the very stuff and marrow of our innermost selves.

Was his name "Don" short for "Donald" – or "Adonis"?

Over time, words often acquire opposite meanings e.g. "terrific" once meant "inspiring terror"; modern "youth speak" is "wicked."

About e-mail: "He will tell that you are tetchy."

"Yolo," is teenage lingo for, "You only live once," especially if drinking or not drinking alcohol.

"Redonk," (abbreviation of "redonkulous") is teenage lingo for ridiculous or unfair.

Writing

His mind seethed like long-boiled syrup. He longed to ejaculate some onto cold marble so others could judge whether his caramel was toothsome.

"There's no money in poetry, but then there's no poetry in money, either."
(*Robert Graves*)

"The job of the newspaper is to comfort the afflicted and afflict the comfortable."
(*Finley Peter Dunne*)

Loom of language.

All words can do is to, temporarily, lasso ideas.

He spoke about the dead English of *Chaucer*: "It is quite a shock to someone brought up on the revised edition of the Bible. You do not realise what is gone."

He became excited, threw his arms about and generally behaved as if drunk.

The bookshop in ... was in a semi, crammed with second-hand books, sagging shelving, yellowed cardboard labels and narrow aisles. It teamed with treasure hunters.

"Look daddy, I've got these!" (armful of ten books)

A playwright is considered a vandal and, ten years later, a fossil.

It's the human interest stories that really spike the ratings.

Sensitive introspection as if a blue tit had written a book about what it was like to be a blue tit.

Winning Words

Name of a staff newspaper for a factory that had many pipes: "Voice from the bowels."

The "organised" always have three working writing implements.

"I never saw a pen scrape and scratch its way through another man's verbs and adjectives so relentlessly."
(Mark Twain)

I only write when I feel spiteful.

Words matter.
The King James Bible states, "In the beginning was the word."

A sentence can lift spirits or cause despondency.

Origin of "mince words": butcher put tough meat through a mincer (minced) to make tough meat more digestible.

Write things down and they may ossify and eventually become a sacred revered text.

Synopsis of Western beauty: males are tall, dark and muscular; females are slim, long hair and tanned skin.

"Resistance was obviously useless against a family *(Manutius)* that could invent italics."
(Lynne Truss)

As frustrated as a writer using a ball pen on greasy paper.

"Avoid too many writers. Writers are like fleas. They are not designed to obtain nourishment from each other."
(John Braine)

The public are getting bored. It is difficult to make the story sing.

Livingstone's early letters were on his prestigious home letterhead, then on plain sheets. Finally, to conserve space, he used cramped tiny handwriting.

Writing

Ernest Hemingway had the same hotel room for several years, four wives and several mistresses: one per book. He wrote twenty-nine.

"Would you like to use the library for a talk and a book signing?"

Tell these things cold to scientists and they will rail, rebel.
But tell it as a story and they will listen and think about it.

The bookshop oozed respect for culture. Dark wood, green carpets and a lecture area where authors signed books underneath.

"I do sweet and tender and very, very steamy in turn. Steamy pays better. Bodice ripper is new kitchen."

Ireland, that little island on the edge of Europe, peripheral to America, by some quirk of socio-historical chemistry, had produced three Nobel Laureates in literature.

Poet: my most creative time is lying in bed at 5 am when the thoughts of the night mix with the thoughts of the day.

The words are uplifting; they sing.

Fierce books of instructions.

Which is the "*kiki*" and which the "*booba*"? Most people answer that the "*booba*" is the rounded; the "*kiki*" the more spiky. On speaking, the shape of your very flesh: your mouth, probably dictates your preference, regardless of native tongue.

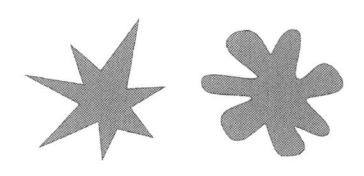

X-ray any odd or flabby word to find the bones of its meaning.

Winning Words

"Did you write with a fountain pen at school, grandpa?"
"Always. Nothing else was allowed."

To hammer in a three inch stake with a lump hammer you need anger: spite. After nine, your writing is shaky.

Words whirl away down the drain (of history).

If you introduce a gun at the beginning of the play, you had better use it by the end.

Poetry is that which is lost in translation.

His language clotted and curdled. People sniggered at his words and thought them dangerous.

Which is fact and which is fiction? The unbelievable is probably the fact.

Rulers use elaborate Latinate words (e.g. ambulate, urinate, defaecate, oocyte cryopreservation); the serfs, pithy Anglo-Saxon.

Chew every book to get out its juice.

Her fork skittered across the plate as she shovelled food into her mouth, "Advance of £14,000 for a novel! That's what we all need!"

Further Reading

- Absolutely *anything*.

That forms part of your apprenticeship and continuing professional development.

It is difficult to over-emphasise this.

Non-fiction and fiction writing

Magazines, generalist e.g. *National Geographic, The Week, Intelligent Life.*

Newspaper, national e.g. *The Guardian/Observer, Huffington Post.*

Newspaper: your locality.

Periodical of your hobby, occupation or profession. For example, for pharmacists, the *Pharmaceutical Journal* (published since 1841).

Specialist self-help book for *your* writing area e.g. novel.

Wikipedia.

Writing Magazine.

Winning Words

Creativity

Weber R.J. *Forks, Phonographs, Hot Air Balloons: A Field Guide to Inventive Thinking*. New York: Oxford University Press. 1992.

StumbleUpon
web based "discovery engine": www.stumbleupon.com

Grammar (UK) and Spelling

Use the British Council's Learn English website:
http://learnenglish.britishcouncil.org
Go to subsection on writing.

Dictionary www.oxforddictionaries.com

Senses (especially non-visual)

Ackerman D. *A Natural History of the Senses*. London: Vintage Books 1992.

Viewpoints

Van Maanen J. *Tales of the Field On Writing Ethnography*. Chicago: Chicago University Press 2011.

Word-processing

Work through all of a "Teach Yourself" book for your particular software. Your time investment will repay.

Index

A

abstract 93, 250, 273, 331
acceptance 93
acolyte 321
Adam's apple . 385
Ade, George ... 125
adrenaline 138, 160, 168
advertising 437, 452
Aesop 79
aficionado 414
Africa 139, 286, 386
airport 146, 176, 278, 334, 362, 408, 419
alcohol 24, 138, 170, 218, 219, 220, 224, 226, 233, 269, 319, 327, 367, 454
Alexander 249
Alfonzo, Pérez 445
algebra 426
algorithm 402
Ali, Muhammed 148
alien 309
alphabet 20, 181, 408
amateur society 90
American West 188
anaesthetic 269, 314, 426, 430, 431
ancestors 252
Anderson, Sherwood .. 281
angel 255, 302, 427, 453
anomie 403
anonymity ... ix, 95, 98
anonymous 100, 101
Antarctic 418
anthropologist 343
Antony 224
aphrodisiac 197, 382
Aphrodite 174, 296
Apollo 287
Aquinas 382
Aquinas, Thomas 382
Arabian Nights 214
archaic 180, 311, 411
Archbishop 187, 253
Archimedes 368
armchair 57
artefacts 61, 92, 259, 409, 436
Artemis 417
arthropod 306
artist 34, 59, 94, 132, 177, 347, 352
asbestos 276
Athill, Diana ... 207
author .. iv, ix, x, xi, 2, 5, 8, 12, 14, 38, 43, 47, 48, 49, 60, 62, 64, 67, 71, 140, 271, 344

B

babe magnet ... 388
Babylon 371
Bacon, Francis 138
bacteria 61, 156, 265, 297, 360, 398, 435
  Escherichia coli 402, 440
balance 10, 243, 358, 404, 425
banknotes 317
Barbie doll 383
barbiturate 426
Bardot, Brigitte 401
barista 34
Barnes, Julian 247
barrier reef 284
batch .. 34, 112, 305
Bates, H.E. 82
bats .. 103, 162, 395
Beatles 224, 341
Bede 344
Beethoven 330
beetles 163, 166, 252, 328
Beeton, Isabella 434
bellicose 445
bells 193, 271, 280, 410, 421
Benenson, Peter 148
Bennett, Alan ... 13
Beowulf 448

Winning Words

Berne Convention 5
Berra, Yogi 149
best seller 106, 314
Bible, The ... 21, 47, 183, 247, 455, 456
big data . 6, 97, 402
biological clock 38, 138
black gold 318
Black, Cilla 411
blade 406, 444
blizzard 422
block
  Freudian 31
  writers' .... xi, 20, 28, 105
blonde 118, 121, 352, 416, 417, 419, 429
blood. 62, 118, 149, 151, 167, 176, 236, 251, 260, 263, 267, 279, 283, 299, 302, 322, 351, 372, 381, 387, 402, 419, 432, 451, 454
  cells 423
  cochineal 164
  Dactylopius coccus 169
  lusting 445
  pressure 310
  thickens 312
Bohr, Niels 350, 367
Bond, James ... 186
bonfire 159, 216, 237, 254, 273, 283, 292, 301, 353, 373, 408
bookshop 258, 455, 457
Boolean function 97
Bosch, Hieronymus 424
Boswell, James 203
bottom feeder 202
Bradbury, Ray 29
Bradley, Anna 190
brain 15, 19, 20, 21, 23, 27, 34, 56, 130, 138, 203, 211, 243, 263, 266, 279, 301, 305, 307, 355, 384, 417, 421, 441
  basic limbic root 386
  compost 22
  jackdaw mind 86
Braine, John .. 456
breaks .28, 39, 210, 362
Brewer, Ebenezer 92
bridge 70
Bristol, Lee 319
Britten, Benjamin 331
Brontë sisters .. 22, 57, 401
brothel 304, 389, 398
Browning, Elizabeth Barrett 22
bubble wrap .. 145, 201, 325, 380, 431
Buchan, James 318
bud ...296, 396, 415
Bulgaria 282
Burns, George 393
Burns, Robert .. 80
Busby, James. 273
Bush, George H.W. 184
Buson, Yosa 80
Byron, George 433

C

cabin 206, 282, 285, 358
cabinet of curiosities xii, 5, 100, 177
cabinet of curiousities Barnum's Freak show 92
cadaver 284, 307
cadaverine 303
cage . 149, 261, 337, 390, 422
calligraphy 78, 131
Campbell-Johnston, Rachel 214
cancer 25, 266, 310, 312
cantharidin 312
canyon 287
capitalism 374
carat 182, 367
Carter, Hodding 245
Carter, Howard 341
Carville, James 320
cat 13, 120, 168, 178, 209, 213, 279, 303, 346, 366, 430
cathedral 133, 187, 249, 255, 281, 291, 367, 421
Catherine the Great 327
champagne 199, 223, 225, 340, 345, 422
chaperone 337
charm 274

462

Index

Chaucer, Geoffrey 304, 455
chauvinist 390
cheating 105
check-ups 26
chef 346
Chekhov, Anton 392
Chesterton, G.K. 167
chicken....155, 159, 224, 304, 309, 390, 393, 440, 448
chipmunk 423
Churchill, Winston.....190, 225, 268, 369, 373, 445
Cicero 22
Cinderella........ 352
circus................ 346
Civil Defence College........ 284
Clarke, Arthur C. .32, 89, 256, 405
Claude glass ... 130
Cleopatra 224
clone................. 429
coal..136, 170, 283, 411, 429
cobbles.....420, 424
coffee.....21, 25, 28, 34, 40, 119, 150, 218, 229, 233, 234, 315, 318, 380, 395, 407, 431
Cohen, Leonard 141, 329
Coleridge, Samuel 77, 220
comfort zone 29
complication 59
computer ..8, 9, 10, 27, 87, 89, 95, 104, 259, 365, 406, 411
cloud 9

flash drive 9
spelling checker...... 9
concrete.............. 12
concrete (opposite abstract).........7
Congreve, William 142
conservatory .. 162, 195, 266, 279, 282, 311
Constable, John 186
continuing professional development 435, 459
continuous process 34
Coolige Effect .390
Cope, Wendy 80
Copernicus, Nicolaus....... 84
Copland, Aaron 330
copyright..............5
course
   BA 7
   commercial.... 7
   MA................3, 7
   MBA 112
   MFA................7
   MOOC 7
   seminar 383
   supervisor. 185, 341
cow.. 132, 163, 224, 232, 305, 384, 395
Cox, Brian...........5
crabs 419
Craptonite 122
Crick, Francis.290
crocodile... 92, 124, 421
Cromwell, Oliver 178, 248, 444
cruise ships 277

crystal..... 187, 265, 330
culture.. 12, 19, 31, 42, 96, 101, 110, 247, 283, 334, 335, 366, 401, 402, 457
garden........ 239
Cupid............... 298
curare 426
curfew 444
Curie................ 259
Curie museum 259, 327
cutting-edge ... 109
cyanide... 170, 238, 313, 396, 398

D

daffodils............ 76
Darwin, Charles . 27, 28, 84, 159, 163, 185, 260, 321, 353, 362, 442
data..................... 98
bank 99, 100, 106
big........... 92, 97
bio 315
destruction 408
National statistics 186
primary .. 87, 88, 92, 95
secondary 88
tertiary........... 88
Davidson, Robyn 46
Dawkins, Richard 154, 253
De Quincey, Thomas...... 220
Dear Reader ... *See* "godlike view"
deer. 173, 260, 293, 425
dentist..... 269, 348

Winning Words

deterrent. 371, 451
Devil 254, 308, 427
diamorphine.. 311, 358
Dickens, Charles 57, 284
Dickinson, Emily 80
Dictionary
  Oxford, on line 460
  Phrase and Fable 11
  scriptorium 454
  tertiary data. 88
dinosaurs 136, 240, 422
dispensary 279
divorce............ 322
DNA.. 61, 154, 290, 301, 386, 430
doctors ... 112, 190, 348, 361, 384
dodo. 155, 167, 216
dog.. 124, 145, 151, 152, 153, 154, 164, 167, 186, 193, 241, 247, 254, 280, 295, 304, 315, 349, 354, 389, 395, 398, 443
Donald Rumsfeld 445
Donne, John ... 392
Doolittle, Eliza 420
Downtown Abbey 186
Dowson, Ernest 215
Dracula 131
dragons 289
Drake, Francis 356
drug dealers.... 219
Dryden, John ... 81
duck. 158, 335, 383
Dunne, Finley Peter 455

E

eagle 165, 418
earthquake.... 143, 315
editor............... 349
education..98, 108, 109, 110, 372
effluent............ 415
egg ... 164, 187, 201, 204, 234, 288, 292, 307, 325, 350, 384, 417
Einstein, Albert 84, 121, 210, 255, 322
elephant....38, 126, 166, 190, 302, 305, 313, 429
Eliot, T.S. 80
emergency 138, 153, 332, 349, 397, 415
engineer 350
England 21, 93, 171, 249, 319, 350, 397, 401, 423
English, native speaker 400
entrepreneur. 112, 327
envy.......... 298, 441
erectile dysfunction 307
ergot 218, 425
eroticism......... 393
errors 15, 17, 18, 454
erythropoietin 312
Espin, Thomas 353
ethereal...290, 330, 437
ethics............... 100
ethnographers.. 93
exercise.22, 23, 37, 40, 68, 128, 147, 379

expert.... 21, 29, 43, 86, 91, 129, 350, 352

F

faeces 231, 234, 268, 269, 305, 355, 363, 420, 422, 443
false teeth 121, 431
farmer..... 187, 200, 230, 290, 317, 351, 440
father
  adviser........ 323
  biological.... 383
  dead... 210, 324, 395
  family 176
  incompetent 348
  older .. 149, 240, 244, 401
  relation........ 145
  religious 253
  resigned 242
  son student 297
  status. 186, 299, 322, 346
  wealthy........ 196
  with baby ... 241
  with daughters 390
Fermi, Enrico. 137
  paradox 137
ferret 118, 384
fertile for thinking 33
Fibonacci sequence 85
fiction ....xi, 4, 7, 8, 13, 32, 41, 46, 56, 57, 58, 59, 63, 64, 68, 96, 98, 99, 101, 256, 376, 458, 459
filler articles 42

Index

financial meltdown 418
fishnet tights .. 423
Fitzgerald, F. Scott 112
flats .. 169, 276, 280
flood 208, 288, 303, 350, 427, 428
flu 386, 419
flunitrazepam (*Rohypnol*) 311
flux 209, 366
fly swat 160, 368
Fong, Kevin 146
football 140, 372
Football 273
Foucault, Michel 31
fountain pen ... 150, 326, 458
fractals 368
Francis Bacon 93, 138, 297
fresh air 27, 236, 286
Freud, Sigmund 31, 130, 248, 296, 391
Frost, Robert . 297
functional magnetic resonance imaging 74
funeral 120, 139, 143, 286, 312, 344, 360, 424
fungus 154, 163, 239, 290, 303, 310, 322, 380, 408, 435

G

Gagarin, Yuri 194
Gainsborough, Thomas 29, 132
Galileo 136, 367, 418, 432
gallium 429

Gaudi 132, 425
geezer 420
genre 59, 65, 67
gentleman 29, 148, 185, 195, 353
gestalt 21, 106, 375
ghetto 177, 236, 362, 401
Gill, A.A. 382
glycophosphate 236, 237
Goffman, Erving 79
gold 6, 87, 112, 125, 127, 153, 169, 170, 172, 173, 182, 189, 195, 210, 282, 318, 325, 332, 348, 366, 367, 390, 409, 429, 436, 448
Goldilocks 136, 234
Goldsmith, Oliver 215
Google . xi, 5, 6, 90, 92, 97, 438
goose 122, 204, 305
grammar 9, 10
  adjective 8
  British Council 460
  passive 13
  verb 8
grave 215, 304, 430
Graves, Robert 455
green men 390
Greene, Graham 174
grief 213
gulleting 262
gun .. 360, 441, 445, 447, 458
gunpowder 368
Gutenberg. 91, 181
  Project 67
gynocracy 177

H

hairdresser 353
Haldane, J.B.S. 252
Haley, Alex 53
hammer . 138, 169, 210, 412, 425, 430, 458
handouts 332
Hanrahan, Brian 11
Harris, Joel 387
Harrods. 195, 196, 200, 325, 333, 399
Harvard 93
Hawthorne, Nathaniel .. 125
Haydn, Joseph 327
Haynes, Andrew 147
heart
  ache 297, 299
  Anyone who had 412
  attacks. 10, 223, 266, 311
  beat 25
  civilisation .. 298
  cockles (valves) 233
  feel with 130
  flutter 65
  garden 443
  inability to pump 312
  lion's 445
  of beloved ... 192
  pain in 264
  rate 23
  rusted to dust 213
  sank 200
  shrivelled 211
  stopping glory 368
  symbol 296
  weighed 249
  worms 269

heft..............374
Heidi Thomas. 174
hell.. 180, 304, 360, 414, 419, 420
Hemingway, Ernest 457
Heraclitus of Ephesus 210
hermaphrodite 385
hierarchy of explanation 435
historian...........354
history.............458
  artefact.......403
  commonplace books.......93
  flushed away 337
  folk 89, 257, 404
  how told 402
  natural 240, 326
  natural of senses....460
  observatory 437
  pre-.......57, 158
  turns...........403
  written out. 403
Hitchhiker's Guide to the Galaxy........249
Hitler, Adolf ...373
Hobsbawm, Eric 354
hockey.............421
hogan...............278
Homer...............81
Homo neanderthalensis................386
Homo sapiens 386
honour.... 102, 134, 438
Hood, Thomas . 77
Hooke, Robert 111
Horace 81
hospital .. 132, 153, 179, 193, 198, 200, 218, 256, 261, 267, 274,

Winning Words

280, 284, 286, 315, 322, 358, 359, 392, 419
hostess 421
Hubble, Edwin 134
Hughes, Bettany 372
humour 27, 58, 344
husk..................452
Hussein, Saddam 152
Huxley, Aldous 392
hydration 25
hydrogen ..31, 295, 396, 425, 453
hydrogen bomb 295
hydrogen sulphide... 396, 45

I

ibuprofen.174, 388
icon...248, 251, 347
idea
  dust could not corrupt . 327
  linear headings 8
  novel perspective 91
  scattergram... 8
  skeleton 8
  spidergram.... 8
  illumination 26
illustrations 15, 45
imp 442
index 50
India 188, 277, 293, 321, 336, 349
india rubber 8
ineffable............21
inheritance powder.......170
internet 88, 208
interview....43, 348
intravenous fluids 426

Ireland.............457
Ischia 302
Isle de Paris 299

J

jailhouse rock .330
James, Alice....348
James, William 100, 101
jargon 11, 270
jazz....................271
jellyfish....232, 432
Johnson, Boris 317
Johnson, Samuel 203
Jonah complex 273
Jones, Digby ...321
Jonson, Ben 81
journalist..........354
journals 29, 95
JP 185, 198, 201, 325
Julian of Norwich 250
jumbling together 63
Jurassic 422

K

Kant, Immanuel 126
Kapuscinski, Ryszard......416
Keats, John 83
Kemp, Harry ..255
Kermit the Frog 302
KGB 223
kiki-booba.......457
kinetics 219
King 211, 241, 250, 372, 456
Kipling, Rudyard 44, 246, 454
kiss...................297
Knackers' Yard 306

466

Index

knickers .. 209, 218, 304, 389
Knight, India . 177
Kuhn, Thomas . 84

L

laboratory 251, 327
L'Amour, Louis 420
Langbridge, Frederick ... 434
Langland, William 79
language 20
Laurence, T.E. 273
Lawrence, D.H. 299
Laws of Thermodynamics 367
Lawson, Nigella 177
layout 43
  sidebar 43
  strap line 43
leader 364, 371, 373
Lennon, John. 208
Leonardo 132
letters to editor 42
Letts, Quintin. 371
library . 15, 91, 168, 177, 190, 280, 313, 357, 385, 417, 432, 457
  dusty sources 91
lice 449
lighter fuel 219
Linklater, Richard 443
lion 62, 160, 161, 189, 202, 307, 413, 424, 445
little green men 344
Livingston, David 456

Lloyd George, David 370
lobster 223, 305
lollards 21
lollipop 422
London ... 110, 111, 141, 157, 160, 181, 187, 193, 198, 218, 274, 277, 278, 282, 286, 289, 292, 329, 333, 395, 415, 460
long noses 335, 419
Longworth, Alice Roosevelt ... 129
lover . 294, 299, 300
Lowell, Percival 134
Lua 161
luddite 425

M

MacArthur, Douglas 446
Mach, Ernst 85
machete 427
Macmillan, Harold .... *See*
mafia 363
Mammon 254
manager . 145, 195, 276, 280, 344, 356, 362, 365, 373, 375
manipulate ... 8, 33, 58
Mann, Thomas 298, 454
Mantel, Hilary ... 5
mantelpiece 402
manual typewriter 452
mānuka 313
market
  amateur societies .. 90

for work 2, 3, 7, 14, 30, 47, 49, 65, 75
magazines.... 42
mass 46
match expectation 43, 50
non-fiction topic 41
physical........ 90
readability expectations 14
marsh 239, 281, 284, 285
Martel, Yann .. 251
Martindale 47
Marx, Karl 110
masochist........ 439
mastery 86
materia medica 313
Matheson, Chris 149
Maugham, W. Somerset 93, 437
maxim 96, 414
maxims ... xi, 6, 92, 96
McPherson, Elle 387
megalomaniac 440
memories 178, 208, 258, 326, 404, 417, 436
Mencken, H.L. 369
Mendeleev, Dmitri .. 84, 169
Mesopotamia ... 57
metaphor . 76, 111, 253, 372, 439
methadone..... 267, 359
Methuselah 350
metonym........... 76
mice 315, 327, 346, 412

Michelangelo.. 382
microorganism 417
microscope 177
Middleton, C.H
.... 238
midwife 357
Milne, A.A. 145
Milton, John 93
Mitchel, James Leslie 450
mithridate 313
Möbius strip ... 309
mole 301
moles 412
monkey .. 160, 183, 253, 433
Moore, Gordon
.... 406
Moore, Henry .. 34
Moore, Patrick 136
morphine 311
mothballs 326
mother 224, 357, 378
 of all mothers
 .... *See* Lua

N

Name characters
 63
names
 famous 99
Napoleon, Bonaparte 170, 447
National Trust
 .... 191, 196, 208
necropolis 258
Nehru collar 336
nepotism . 438, 439
neutrino 367
Newman, John Henry 454
Newton, Isaac 320, 368, 386, 392
NHS 142, 153, 193, 263, 264, 265,

Winning Words
 280, 325, 343, 356, 373
Nietzche, Friedrich ... 255
Nightingale, Florence 38
Noah's ark 328
Nobel prize 327
non-fiction ..4, 7, 8, 41, 42, 45, 58, 96, 101, 105, 459
Norwich, Bishop of 195
nostalgia ..172, 346
novel 68
 length 58
 modern 57
nuclear 135
 power ..267, 415
 protection suit
 419
 stars 135
 war 100, 166, 446, 449, 451
 waste 135
nude .327, 393, 421
nuggets 4, 45
nurse 197, 268, 348, 357, 358, 374, 407

O

Olaf, King of Norway 250
Olivier, Laurence
 198
Olympus Mons 342
open fire ...57, 197, 275, 352
opinionated 43
optometrist 358
organophosphorus 398
orgasm 317, 384
Orwell, George
 452
ossuary 302

ostrich 322
owl .. 165, 176, 193, 417, 421
Oxbridge.. 111, 177
 Cambridge . 112
 Oxford 111, 460
oxyacetylene ... 365
oxygen .. 19, 27, 28, 260, 263, 396
oxymoron 227
ozone 285, 396, 397

P

pain 10, 39, 62, 113, 128, 158, 161, 258, 264, 266, 322, 426, 432, 439
painterly .. 130, 409
Paracelsus 173
paracetamol ... 310, 311
paraldehyde 360
parameters 407
Paris 150, 327, 395, 418
Parker, Dorothy
 452
Parsons, Tony ..32
patrician .. 196, 440
pattern .. 43, 77, 83, 263
payment 96
peers 40, 192
penis 212
pension 323
person
 first 62
 third 62, 69
perspective 31
 feminist 403
 Foucault 31
 Freud 31
 Goffman 79
 helicopter ... 114
 writer's 44
pets 412

468

Index

pharmacist .22, 99, 145, 200, 259, 312, 339, 346, 358, 359, 374, 459
philosophy 110, 172, 183, 249, 326, 453
phosphorus 173, 305, 398
Picasso 132
pigeon 302, 362
Pinocchio 432
plagiarism .. 14, 96, 112
plan
  alarm clock .. 40
  habit 40
  linear 8
  manageable tasks 38
  milestone 40
  motivation ... 35
  plot 59
  SWOT analysis 35, 36
platinum 366
Plato 109
Poe, Edgar Allan 82
poem 58, 382
poet 12
poetry 152, 458
police 126, 140, 159, 198, 200, 241, 326, 350, 421
polish 207, 261, 326, 335, 397
politically correct 423
pollution .. 420, 421
  smog 420
Polti, Georges .. 61
pope 251, 385
Pope
  Pius XII 310
Pope, Alexander 129

porn 179, 187, 218, 393
Postman, Neil. 240
predator 436
President 182, 184, 263, 390
  Vice 263
  WI 141
Presley, Elvis .. 224
prey 166, 436
priest 360
prism 423
prisms 94
privilege 91
Probus 390
professional 90, 102, 198, 281, 343, 374
professional bodies 90
profit 218, 317, 319, 373
proofread 14, 17
propaganda 89, 401, 402
prostitute 361
protagonist 69, 151
provocation .. ix, xi, xii, 92
psychoactive 24, 25
psychoanalyst ... 361
Putin, Vladimir 437
putresine 303

Q

Queen 121, 178, 186, 200, 309, 334
Quiller-Couch, Arthur 12
Quran, The 416

R

rail 324, 416
rainbow ... 368, 426

Raphael, Frederic 204
rat 159, 162, 254, 301, 359, 401, 425, 429, 446
readability 14
  score 14
reading room .. 281
redundancy ... 359, 377
references 96
rejection 24, 26
relic.. 163, 422, 432
Rembrandt 118
repair 264, 293, 349, 411, 415, 430
research . 6, 32, 38, 86, 87, 98, 113, 162, 341
retirement 99, 148, 258, 280, 340, 401
rhyme 76, 77
rhythm . 11, 76, 77, 111, 329, 330, 368, 416
Rice-Davies, Mandy 100
ricochet 425
riot 370
rite of passage 401
ritual 203
rituals 34, 453
Ritz 271
rock god 384
Roget, Peter 94
Rolls-Royce ... 181, 283, 324
rose water 312
Royal Institution 274
Rudner, Rita .. 261
runes 453
Russell, Bertrand 309

469

Winning Words

S

sagas 57, 61, 87, 358, 417
sailor 362
salmon 165, 298, 393
sauna 276
Sayers, Dorothy 215
scale 230
scales for modern writing 61
scholarship 14
scientific method 367
scientist 362, 435
Scotland . 287, 319, 423
seagull 419
search engines .. 90
Sears, Edmund H. 450
secret weapon, see commonplace book 3, 4, 45
sedentary 23
selling .. i, 4, 34, 41, 47, 59, 67, 362
sentinel 412
serendipity. 22, 30, 87
Shakespeare, William ... 5, 57, 79, 82, 212, 260, 281, 357, 381, 392, 436, 449
shanty town 424
Shaw, George Bernard 145
shed 171, 281, 443, 448
Shelley, Mary ... 85
Shelley, Percy. 214
Show. Do not tell 62
showroom 278, 290
Sibelius, Jean. 329

signpost 45
simile 76
Simon, Paul 58
simulator 57
sin 302, 318, 450
siren .126, 188, 299
sleep .. 38, 138, 142, 146, 183, 218, 229, 343, 355, 387
asset head of state 373
biological clock 38
value to writer 26
slimy. 135, 288, 395
slug ... 281, 304, 438
Smith, E.E 66
smörgåsbord 5, 376
snake 418, 432
Snow C.P. 367
soap. 120, 151, 170, 173, 287, 347, 394, 421
socioeconomic classifications 102
sociologist 363
solicitor 363
Solomon, Ed... 149
solution .. 35, 59, 60, 161, 407
song ... 58, 111, 134, 251, 296, 417
spectrum ultraviolet .. 159
splinters ... 105, 339
Stapledon, Olaf 376
stardust 135
Stark, Freya ... 420
sticky eyes 327
stilboestrol 313
Stoppard, Tom 452

storm 168, 237, 288, 368, 394, 411, 427
Straus, Levi 33
strip club 292
structure 11, 49, 251, 403
Strype, John ... 435
studio 277, 281
stumpery 239
style 8, 11
Styron, William 125
suicide 206, 313, 320, 337, 350, 363, 439
sulphur dioxide 396
suspend disbelief 59
sweet spot 410
Swift, Jonathan 7, 81

T

tabloids 377
tactics .... xi, 14
talisman 93
Talmud, The ... 436
Taylor, Elizabeth 116
tea 187, 410
teachers ... 281, 364
teeny-weeny 431
telescope. 134, 135, 136, 168, 177
Tennyson, Alfred 385
testicles ... 296, 304, 382, 384, 388, 431
testosterone ... 171, 381
Thatcher, Margaret 38, 152, 297
theme 59

470

Index

central message.. 52
courage...... 100
pudding..... 225
sombre......... 59
theology.......... 326
thesis............51, 112
thingyness...... 403
thixotropic...... 429
Thomas, Dylan 22, 209
Thomas, Heidi 174
Thomson, William...... 366
Thoreau, Henry 284
thoroughbred. 180
thunderstorm. 279, 283, 396
ticks................. 418
tips .... xi, 28
title 7, 16
Tolkien, J.R.R. 10, 71
tornado 368
toxic. 166, 169, 171, 218, 232, 265, 313, 419, 425, 439
translations 32
Travis, Trysh ... 94
trinity 250, 451
Trollope, Anthony 9
trophy wives... 319
Truss, Lynne.. 456
tulip..........303, 447
Turing, Alan .. 313
Turner, Tina .. 152
Twain, Mark..227, 456
typeface........... 105

U

Ultima Thule.. 288
Uluru..........29, 171
unions keeping out 303
USA. 183, 187, 226, 300, 303, 335, 386, 400, 442

V

verisimilitude ... 64
Verne, Jules 406
virtues...... 250, 443
virus 154, 180, 377, 409, 435
vivid 10, 76, 82, 98, 120

W

waiter/waitress 364
Walcott, Derek, 81
Wales 195, 319, 423
Wales, Prince of 195
Watson, James 290
Waugh, Evelyn 334
WC 28, 150, 199, 218, 272, 278, 282, 323, 399, 400, 407, 429
weasel words .. 448
Weber, Max... 101, 400
frame human behaviour 101
Weber, R.J 31, 460
Webster, John 215
welfare state.... 249
what it is like to be 57, 104
white nights 419
Wikipedia .. 88, 97, 459
Wilde, Oscar.... 81, 291, 373

William of Occam 453
William, Prince 191
Williams, Robin 251
wizard................ xii
woad................ 254
Wodehouse, P.G. 261
Wollaston, William Hyde 19
womb 244, 267
Women's Institute 141, 272
Woolworths.... 276
Wordsworth, William......... 76
workhouse...... 280
writers' circle 7, 97

X

X-ray 438, 457

Y

Yale.................... 93
yeast 263, 380
Yeats, W.B 74
yin and yang ... 388
You Tube..... 88, 90

Z

zeitgeist... xi, 6, 92, 97, 329
Zen..................... 80
Zeno................. 181
zero................. 308
Zhimo, Xu......... 76
Zipf's Law 10
zombie............. 439

Made in the USA
Charleston, SC
29 September 2014